# COMMANDING PETTY DESPOTS

# COMMANDING PETTY DESPOTS

## *The American Navy in the New Republic*

THOMAS SHEPPARD

Naval Institute Press
*Annapolis, Maryland*

Naval Institute Press
291 Wood Road
Annapolis, MD 21402



Library of Congress Cataloging-in-Publication Data
Names: Sheppard, Thomas, 1985– author.
Title: Commanding petty despots : the American Navy in the new republic / by Thomas Sheppard.
Other titles: American Navy in the new republic
Description: Annapolis, Maryland : Naval Institute Press, [2022] | Includes bibliographical references and index.
Identifiers: LCCN 2021045969 (print) | LCCN 2021045970 (ebook) | ISBN 9781682477557 (hardcover) | ISBN 9781682477564 (ebook) | ISBN 9781682477564 (epub)
Subjects: LCSH: United States. Navy—History—18th century. | United States. Navy—History—19th century. | United States—History, Naval—To 1900.
Classification: LCC E182 .S54 2022 (print) | LCC E182 (ebook) | DDC 359.00973/09033--dc23
LC record available at https://lccn.loc.gov/2021045969
LC ebook record available at https://lccn.loc.gov/2021045970

♾ Print editions meet the requirements of ANSI/NISO z39.48-1992 (Permanence of Paper).
Printed in the United States of America.

30 29 28 27 26 25 24 23 22 9 8 7 6 5 4 3 2 1
First printing

*To my family*

# Contents

# Acknowledgments

**MY NAME is the one on the cover,** but completing this book would have been impossible without the generous support of a host of people. Even as I write this, I feel sure I will overlook at least a few whose names deserve to be listed, so apologies in advance to anyone who belongs here. Know that I am immensely grateful for the support I have received from each and every person who offered feedback, research tips, professional guidance, and mental and emotional support over the decade-plus that this project has been in gestation.

Adam Kane has been exceedingly patient with my ever-expanding timetable for completion, and his support for this project has been unwavering. Thanks also to acquisitions editor Glenn Griffin, production editor Caitlin Bean, and copy editor extraordinaire Aden Nichols for seeing it through to publication. Two anonymous reviewers also offered helpful feedback that made for a stronger finished product.

This book began many years ago as an MA thesis under the guidance of Sally Hadden, who was invaluable in getting me started on my academic career. Wayne Lee was an ideal mentor in the doctoral dissertation phase of the project, as was Richard Kohn's keen insight into civil-military relations. Joseph Glatthaar, Kathleen Duval, and Dirk Bonker provided able guidance on my dissertation committee.

Thanks to the generous support of the Smith-Richardson Foundation, I was able to spend a year as a predoctoral fellow at Yale University's International Security Studies Institute, which was an enormous asset not only to my ability to finish writing the dissertation, but also to grow professionally. Many thanks to Paul Kennedy for his mentorship, and to my co-fellows and the staff at ISS for making it such a delightful season of my life.

While writing both the dissertation and book manuscript, I was fortunate to be able to make multiple trips to the David Library of the American Revolution while it was located at its lovely former home in Washington's Crossing,

Pennsylvania. This beautiful setting provided a wonderful getaway for research and writing retreats, and its vast resources were a treasure for expanding my knowledge of the Revolution and early republic. Meg McSweeney and Kathie Ludwig were charming and helpful hosts on every trip there.

The unfailingly friendly service at the Library of Congress and the National Archives and Records Administration made research easier, as did the supportive staffs of the Historical Society of Pennsylvania, the Peabody-Essex Museum of Salem, Massachusetts, the Earl Gregg Swem Library at the College of William and Mary, and the New York Historical Society.

It is impossible to overstate Christopher McKee's contribution to this book. Over the years, he willingly provided from his vast knowledge in research guidance and feedback, first on the dissertation, then on multiple iterations of book chapters. His enthusiasm for the project inspired and motivated me to keep pressing on with it, and saved me from many mistakes. He has my hearty thanks.

My colleagues at Naval History and Heritage Command have been consistently supportive, regularly asking for updates on my writing and sharing their excitement for this book's progress. Moreover, they are simply a delight to work with, and I cannot miss the chance to single out Ryan Peeks, Justin Blanton, Charles Brodine, Christine Hughes, Dennis Conrad, Anna Holloway, and Matt Yokell for their support and friendship.

In the time I have been working on this project I've lived a somewhat migratory existence, pitching my tent in Chapel Hill, North Carolina; New Haven, Connecticut; and the Washington Metro Area. Some stays were longer than others, but every place was home thanks to the wonderful community of faith I found there. My brothers and sisters at Chapel Hill Bible Church, Trinity Baptist Church of New Haven, and McLean Bible Church of Arlington have enriched my life beyond description, while also consistently showing me I was put on this earth for so much more than lines on a vita. To friends and companions too many to list, thank you.

My family has been faithfully in my corner on this project and everything else I've ever attempted. For their love and support over a lifetime, this book is dedicated to them.

# Introduction

**JUNE 1, 1813.** Captain James Lawrence darted up the rigging of the American frigate *Chesapeake* to get a glimpse of the unknown ship over the horizon. He felt a rush of excitement as he peered through his spyglass at the strange sail, for he had good reason to believe it was a British frigate rumored to be in the vicinity, and that the enemy vessel was as eager to find him as he was it. He was not disappointed—the Royal Navy's *Shannon*, almost exactly equal in size and firepower with the *Chesapeake*, was waiting for Lawrence, alone. Once the *Shannon* drew near enough to clearly identify, a ship-to-ship duel was Lawrence's, if only he chose to engage. For the young captain, there was no decision to make. A year into the war, the American navy had already stunned observers on both sides of the Atlantic by winning a series of engagements with the heretofore invincible British navy, and Lawrence burned for the chance to add his name to those of Isaac Hull, Stephen Decatur, and William Bainbridge, his seniors who had humbled the British—and won lasting glory for themselves—in single combat. Rallying his men, Lawrence informed them of the British frigate and fired up their patriotic passions as he prepared for combat. At this point a few began grumbling that they were late getting paid their prize money for earlier captures. Lawrence promptly ordered all accounts with the crew settled; he wanted every man's heart in the coming battle. The moment all American officers dreamed of was finally his.[1]

Meanwhile, British captain Philip Broke was no less eager to engage. Broke felt the humiliation of his country's losses to the Americans as keenly as any officer, and he was confident his experienced crew was up to the task of avenging British honor. In fact, Broke was so determined to engage the *Chesapeake* that he had even sent a letter with an American prisoner into Boston harbor, issuing a challenge to the American frigate and promising to send away any other ships of the British blockading squadron to guarantee a fair fight.[2] The *Chesapeake* had already sailed by the time the letter reached Boston, but it hardly mattered. Lawrence made course straight for the *Shannon*, and the battle began just before six o'clock that evening.

It was over in a matter of minutes. Lawrence and his men had no shortage of courage, but they had only been together a brief time; officers and men had not had the chance to be molded together into a competent fighting force. They proved no match for Broke, who had commanded his ship and crew for seven years and had relentlessly drilled the men in gunnery exercises to prepare for precisely this occasion. Three broadsides wreaked havoc on the *Chesapeake*, shredding the sails and rigging and killing several crewmen. Brutally accurate fire cut through the American officer corps like a scythe, leaving the ship increasingly leaderless. Multiple helmsmen fell, even as attempts to steer became futile thanks to completely shredded sails. The aimless ship drifted into a collision with its British counterpart, making the final boarding action possible. The *Shannon* hardly came through unscathed. Broke suffered a near-fatal head wound during the boarding, and twenty-five others were killed in the battle. The British attrition was less severe than their American counterparts though; more importantly, the American frigate was reduced to an unmanageable wreck by the time the *Shannon*'s boarding party seized control.[3]

Lawrence was not on deck when the British boarders arrived. He was injured in the first broadside, but doggedly remained in command until a bullet from a British sharpshooter struck him in the hip. Mortally wounded, Lawrence shouted "Don't give up the ship" to his men as he was carried below. It was a hopeless order. Second Lieutenant George Budd and Acting Third Lieutenant William Cox were now the senior officers on board, but Cox carried Lawrence below and was caught up in the swarm of retreating men while Budd was already engrossed in events belowdecks, oblivious to the desperate straits of his crew. With no American officer left to surrender, a British tar lowered the American flag, and the *Chesapeake* joined the British fleet.

Lawrence lingered four days, though mostly delirious with pain. He finally passed on June 5, just as the *Chesapeake* sailed into Halifax, Nova Scotia. The British showed the utmost regard for their gallant enemy, wrapping his body in the *Chesapeake's* flag and burying him with full military honors. The United States likewise showered praise on the fallen captain. Although Lawrence was clearly and decisively beaten and the ship entrusted to his care now in enemy hands, his death insured that no censure would be attached to his name for decades.[4] Lawrence became a national hero, a martyr for his country, and was remembered as a man who had lived up to the ideals of his profession by dying with honor.

He had also defied orders. Amid celebration of Lawrence as the heroic ideal of the young navy, most Americans chose to forget that he would have survived if he had obeyed the directives of the president and Secretary of the Navy.[5] The new secretary, William Jones, had been quite explicit that he was initiating a new strategy upon assuming office in 1813, one that called for avoiding the British and preserving America's precious few frigates, rather than seeking the glory of capturing ships the Royal Navy could easily replace.[6] In addition to the clearly stated general orders of the new secretary, Lawrence also had very specific orders to disrupt the enemy's communication and destroy her commerce; Jones had left him no room for adventurism against an equally sized and more experienced enemy vessel.[7]

Yet a stronger imperative than obedience to the chain of command drove Lawrence. He was part of an officer corps that valued civilian control of the military, to a point. Yet it also prized fame, glory, and honor as much as, if not more than, following orders. The recent history of the U.S. Navy and the civil-military relationship that had existed throughout Lawrence's entire career did little to deter him from this mindset. Prior to the War of 1812, the relationship between government officials tasked with overseeing the navy and its officers was an ambiguous one. The idea that the military should be subordinate to the civilian government was universally accepted in the early republic, but officers and civilian officials often had markedly different ideas as to what that subordination should look like. Naval officers verbally acknowledged their duty to obey the government, and there was never the slightest threat of a naval coup or a rogue captain abandoning his country. However, officers also felt that they were entitled to certain prerogatives, and they guarded their turf zealously.

Naval legislation provided little help. In the Revolutionary War, naval administration was chaotic and civil-military relations came under enormous strain. The Continental navy suffered from severe neglect, and governance by committee insured that oversight of the Revolutionary maritime force was a nightmare. With the ratification of the Constitution, management of naval forces became the sole prerogative of the executive branch, but at first this brought only marginal improvement. An overworked secretary of war superintended the entire American military on land and sea, creating chaos at the top that was barely mitigated by the tiny size of the navy. Finally, Congress provided stability and a clear chain of command by creating the Navy Department in 1798. From that point forward, the ostensible head of the navy—under the president, of course—was the Secretary of the Navy. The first five secretaries—Benjamin Stoddert (1798–1800), Robert Smith (1801–9), Paul Hamilton (1809–12), William Jones (1813–14), and Benjamin Crowninshield (1815–18)—guided the navy through its formative years, and shaped the understanding of how a proper civil-military relationship should function. While Congress always asserted (or assumed) the idea of civilian control, it seldom went beyond that, leaving the details of naval officers' relationship to the Navy Department for the parties themselves to work out. The rules about when to defer to an officer's expertise and judgment and what matters should be left for the officer corps to govern itself were unwritten, and those in uniform were frequently working from a different set of unwritten rules than the secretaries.

At the root of these tensions was the fact that men who commanded ships were used to being the ones giving orders. The era's understanding of the captain's role was not conducive to enthusiastic subordination to civilian authority. The sea was a hazardous place, and death was an ever-present possibility. Ships of the Age of Sail were among the most complex and sophisticated machines in the world at the time, and coordinating all the tasks necessary to make them function required strict discipline even in calm seas; when violent storms or naval battles threatened the lives of all on board, the wisdom of the day held that only universal and instant obedience could ensure safe return to land. Maintaining discipline over potentially rowdy crews hinged on the captain's authority being total and unchallenged. In practice, of course, relations between captain and crew were subtly negotiated, and astute captains understood there were limits to what their sailors would accept without resistance or even outright mutiny.[8] Yet this negotiation existed out of sight. The overwhelming reality was that every detail of shipboard life revolved around absolute obedience and graphic displays of punishment for any deviation.

Perhaps the best summary of a captain's power came from David Porter, a man who spent decades in the U.S. Navy, eventually attaining its highest rank. In 1835, while serving as an American diplomat in Constantinople, Porter noted the parallels between the Turkish sultan's total authority over his people and the power of the captain of a naval vessel. "A man of war is a petty kingdom, governed by a petty despot," he observed. In ways, the captain maintained even more unchecked power than the sultan, for since the latter was "the most absolute sovereign on earth," he could "afford to be kind and courteous to those around him." The ruler of a man-of-war, however, could never let his autocratic bearing slip for even a moment; he had to rule over his subordinates on board with tyrannical authority to maintain their constant compliance. Porter allowed himself to recall with more than a hint of bitterness his own experience as a young midshipman on the receiving end of his commander's bullying, but he apparently never had any negative thoughts about his own authoritarian rule during an extended career at the top of the naval hierarchy.[9]

The power of a captain over his seamen was indeed immense, and officers saw themselves as inhabiting a different world than those who took orders from them. To stoop to receiving orders instead of giving them was a source of frustration for most of America's "petty despots." David Porter, the same man who later compared himself to a Turkish sultan, once groused that the South Carolinian Secretary of the Navy, Paul Hamilton, needed to remember that his officers were of an entirely different class and station than the enslaved laborers on Hamilton's plantation that he could command at his pleasure. "It is supposed," Porter said of Hamilton, "that he has been too long in the habit of driving slaves to know how to regard the honorable feelings of gentlemen."[10] While willing to acknowledge the vague principle of civilian authority, officers also valued their own independence and dignity, and resented it when they perceived civilian oversight as too restrictive.

In the same vein as frustration at being on the receiving end of orders, naval officers' zeal for preserving their reputations also often worked against civilian control. Any understanding of civil-military relations in the navy is inextricably tied to the era's understanding of—indeed obsession with—honor. This was an era in which personal reputation, and the quest to maintain it, dominated every aspect of a man's life. For all their concern about honor, officers at the time found it easier to recognize when it was missing than to define it with precision. A late-eighteenth century military manual conceded that honor was "a vague expression, which custom has given different meanings."[11] Yet virtually any understanding of honor recognized it as being tied to good character; a military dictionary published in the United States defined honor as "a consciousness of worth and virtue in the individual, and a lively desire to preserve the reputation of virtue."[12] More certain than the definition was the reality that a man's honor was incredibly fragile. A contemporary major in the British Army mused that many authors "have wrote on [honor], but I find none that have compared it to the eye, which can't suffer the least moat in it, without being blemished. Honor may be called a precious stone, which the least speck makes less valuable! It is a treasure irrecoverable once unfortunately lost!"[13]

Americans carried over their ideas about honor from early modern Europe, prizing martial valor and risk-taking, personal integrity, honesty, the esteem of the community.[14] Central to this conception of honor was "the rejection of the lowly, the alien, and the shamed."[15] Because of the indispensable yet fragile nature of a man's reputation, it was perpetually insecure, and had to be preserved constantly. There were positive aspects to such a conception of honor. One of America's first military handbooks noted that this endless desire to preserve a man's reputation acted as "a barrier . . . against corruption" and "excited [him] to deeds of valor."[16] In the negative, it could lead men to recklessness, and even carelessness with their own lives, as evidenced by the widespread practice of dueling. An honorable officer needed to prove that he had no fear of death; displays of bravery that would seem insane to twenty-first-century viewers were the minimum standard at the end of the eighteenth.[17]

Closely tied to honor was fame, the desire to be celebrated by one's fellow men. It was a yearning to be a "great man," that is, according to Douglas Adair, "one who stands out, who towers above his fellows in some spectacular way." The desire for fame included not only one's fellow countrymen, though they were certainly part of it, but also future generations. At its heart, the "desire for fame is the desire for immortality."[18] It is difficult to overstate how much these ideas drove naval officers in the Revolution and early republic. "Unless this search for fame . . . is recognized as a primary element in the ethical air breathed by naval officers," Christopher McKee contends that "a true understanding of that corps is as impossible as if one lacked basic data of ranks and numbers."[19] Few expressed it as boldly as John Paul Jones, who boasted that "my desire for fame is infinite," but the early navy was dominated by officers who shared Jones' mindset.[20]

For American naval officers, ideas about honor were hardly unique—they meshed perfectly with the existing culture in European militaries, and in particular the British navy on which virtually every aspect of the U.S. Navy was modeled (even if few American officers were willing to say so out loud). In the Royal Navy during the period leading up to the American Revolution, recklessness with one's life in battle contrasted with an unshakeable commitment to one's prerogatives and privileges in dealings with the civilian government. British naval officers were part of the military hierarchy, and as such obliged to follow orders, but they were also gentlemen of status, and throughout the eighteenth century they carefully guarded their standing even above their devotion to the national good. "A gentleman was the only proper judge of what was needful to sustain his honour," writes N. A. M. Rodger, "and an officer's honour might be offended, in his own eyes, by any order which threatened to lower his consequence, to limit his power and influence, to direct his career or operations in some direction less advantageous than he felt he deserved."[21] In this, they were similar to civilians of noble standing in government, who likewise shunned diplomatic assignments they found unworthy of their stature.[22] The first generation of American naval officers shared this mindset, and the prevailing ideology of honor frequently trumped a commitment to civilian control. Thomas Truxtun, one of the most celebrated heroes of the U.S. Navy, put it bluntly, "I owed my life to the service of my country. But I knew of no duty imposing on me the obligation to sacrifice my reputation."[23]

The army in America at this time did not differ substantially from the navy in its willingness to put honor ahead of subordination. The officer corps of the Continental army had George Washington's iron commitment to civilian control as a model and guide, although at least some officers still nearly exploded in mutiny. A cabal plotted at the end of the war to force their will on Congress at the point of a bayonet—or at least they threatened to. The whole story of the Newburgh Conspiracy is forever shrouded in a layer of mystery, and for at least some involved, the possibility of mutiny was merely a bargaining tactic to pressure Congress. Whatever their full intentions, Washington thankfully managed to avert disaster and maintained his commitment to civilian supremacy to the end.[24]

No such dire threats ever came from the army of the Confederation or the early republic, but that did not mean army officers showed a keen devotion to professionalism or civilian control. While America's naval officers were viciously attacking each other, including slaying one another on dueling grounds, their brethren on land were no different. William Skelton argues that "seldom has an army been led by a more refractory and contentious group of men" than that of the early republic, and an officer "whose career was not punctuated by acts of indiscipline and acrimonious controversies" was "a rarity." A deep commitment to their own honor also strained subordination for army officers, who readily defied orders that threatened their reputations among their peers.[25]

Far from trying to quash this mindset, civilian leaders—be they members of the Continental Congress, Hamiltonian Federalists, or Jeffersonian Republicans—deliberately encouraged it. The reality of America's place in the world made officers in the mold of John Paul Jones and Thomas Truxtun indispensable. The great powers of the era looked on the infant United States and its supposedly unstable republican government with contempt, and the warring nations of Britain and France treated the Americans as minor players in their global struggle. Naval officers understood that they performed before an international audience with their country's reputation on the line. The U.S. Navy existed, in part, to earn respect for the upstart republic. Given this reality, the first five Secretaries of the Navy had no patience for officers who displayed timidity, sloth, or cowardice, yet they tolerated blatant insubordination from captains who showed zeal for the honor of their country. Promoting such attitudes was not without cost, however. These same officers often put their own honor and reputation ahead of the good of the service, and their infighting, even to the point of fatal duels, was a source of constant frustration to the Navy Department.

Beyond clashes over honor, the division of responsibility—and accompanying authority—was at times murky. The nature of sea travel and communications at the time contributed to this. Once a ship left port, the captain—or commodore, in the case of a fleet—was largely beyond the government's reach. With cruises lasting for months, even occasionally more than a year, a naval commander had to be able to adapt to changing circumstances, and obviously enjoyed a great deal of autonomy. Wise civilian leaders grasped this reality and left room in their orders for the captain or commodore to respond to the situation on the ground (or on the water, as it were). This autonomy tended to extend to the ship even when it was in port. While a captain following the orders of the president did not, in a literal sense, wield the same power as an Ottoman sultan over his men, in practice the Navy Department tended to stay out of his treatment of subordinate officers and sailors. This was less true during the Revolutionary War than in the early republic; the ideals of the Revolution often clashed with the authority of the officers on Continental navy ships, and the Continental Congress showed greater concern for the liberty of American sailors than the Navy Department created under the Constitution. In part, the latter's attitudes were a reaction against the bedlam of the War for Independence. A greater willingness to allow naval officers to enforce discipline as they saw fit was just one of many ways the navy of the early republic sought stability and order instead of the chaos and bureaucratic disaster that plagued the Continental navy.

The growth of professionalism and effectiveness from the Revolution to the early republic was also very much a product of the officer corps itself; naval officers took their profession very seriously. While they varied in their concern for the well-being of sailors (and the loyalty they incited from their men),[26] those who achieved highest rank all recognized that training up the next generation of officers was among their most important priorities.

In an era prior to any kind of naval academy, building the officer corps fell to the officers themselves, and captains devoted significant attention to this role. Their loyalty to their profession far exceeded devotion or sympathy to any one brother officer, and the corps grew in professionalism as those at the highest ranks unhesitatingly purged anyone unworthy of a commission. Richard Dale, one of the first captains, bluntly asserted that a "man may be a very good seaman, and be qualified to command a Merchant Vessel, but at the same time be very unfit to command in the Navy." In words that resonated with his peers, he went on to say that "it is the duty of every Officer that has the honour to hold a Commission in the Navy," if he should see that someone holding the same commission is unworthy of it, "to do all that lays in his power" to drive the offender out of the service.[27]

The first five secretaries of the navy were happy to let the officer corps play a leading role in policing itself. This included not only removing the unworthy but choosing those deserving of higher rank. The promotion ladder in the early navy was short. After captain was master commandant, a rank that disappeared briefly at the beginning of the Jefferson administration due to sloppy law-writing in Congress and was restored by executive order shortly thereafter. Below masters commandant stood lieutenants, and at the bottom of the promotion chain were midshipmen. Additionally, any officer could claim the courtesy title of commodore if he commanded a squadron, a fact that became a source of contention when lowly lieutenants styled themselves commodores when commanding tiny gunboat squadrons, thereby diminishing one of the few distinctions long-serving officers could claim beyond captain. From the Revolutionary War onward, captains and sympathetic civilians campaigned vigorously for the creation of the rank of admiral, but in vain.

Stoddert looked to those at the highest rank to choose the best of their junior officers for promotion, and while later secretaries took a more active role in selecting candidates for commissions and promotions, they still gave substantial latitude to captains in dealing with their subordinates. Robert Smith, for example, established a formal examination for promotion to lieutenant, rather than simply rubber-stamping captains' recommendations. Yet it was the captains who conducted the examinations, and managing promotion remained primarily the duty of the officer corps itself. Smith and Hamilton also proved generous with leave for young midshipmen and lieutenants to sail on merchant voyages and learn their profession, but whenever a "young gentleman" was on board a naval vessel, he was indisputably under his captain's authority.[28] When young officers complained to the Secretary of the Navy about unjust or excessively harsh treatment from superiors, the secretary almost invariably ignored them or strongly encouraged them to yield to the chain of command. Not infrequently, this state of affairs led offended junior officers to resign, a reality that both the Secretary of the Navy and the established officer corps were usually perfectly content with. It fell to captains to cull the ranks of undesirables, and they enjoyed substantial discretion to drive a troublemaker out of the service or grant a deserving young man a second chance.

When it came to a captain's relationship with the sailors on his ship, the Navy Department preferred not to get involved. Although during the Revolution Congress occasionally scrutinized a captain's treatment of his junior officers and seamen, from Stoddert onward the Navy Department was usually content to trust the authority of a captain over those under him. In short, whatever the vagaries of the relationship between civilian authority and senior officers, the fact of a chain of command in control of more junior officers and seamen remained unambiguous in the period under discussion, and junior officers interacted with the secretary through their superiors.

All that said, those at the top of the officer corps were by no means independent from the Navy Department, and the first five men who served as Secretary of the Navy spent considerable time and energy asserting their own authority and checking ambitious captains' desire for autonomy. In the Revolution, distracted, strained, and highly inconsistent oversight had left naval officers embittered and even more than a little contemptuous toward their civilian superiors. A decade-plus gap separated the Continental navy from the creation of the U.S. Navy, but such experiences inevitably colored the earliest days of the latter force. The first Secretary of the Navy, Benjamin Stoddert, had to tolerate maddening insubordination from many officers for the simple reason that he was creating an officer corps, and it was necessary to put up with vexing behavior from those who were good at officering while he culled incompetents from the ranks. The second reason Stoddert proved long-suffering with certain captains was because he valued the passion for honor and reckless courage that underlay much of their insubordinate behavior. Stoddert's successors had the luxury of a much more experienced and professional corps, but they still had to asserted their authority, often quite forcefully, with officers who felt entitled to negotiate, or ignore, clear directives from the Navy Department.

By the Era of Good Feelings, the relationship between naval officers and the government had evolved considerably. In part, the evolution of this relationship reflected changing attitudes across the Atlantic, where the British navy was likewise changing when it came to the status and responsibilities of naval officers. During the wars of the French Revolution and the Napoleonic Era, British naval officers began to shift from finding their status in advancing their own personal reputation to demonstrating their legitimacy through subordination to something larger than themselves. N. A. M. Rodger finds that "a new underlying ideal" was emerging "in which duty was beginning to infiltrate the concept of honour."[29] In his social history of the British naval officer corps, Evan Wilson concurs, finding that "during the period of 1793 to 1815 . . . one of the most significant shifts was the relative decline of honour and the rise of duty as the energising element in a gentleman's conception of himself."[30] Officers in the Royal Navy now proved themselves through their patriotic devotion to the nation, including not doing anything to undermine the service for selfish reasons. Signs of this changing sensibility were slowly but unmistakably becoming apparent in the American Navy as well.

Likewise, the U.S. Army grew in professionalism—particularly in its increased devotion to civilian control—in the years after the War of 1812, although arguably more slowly and less thoroughly than the Navy. The disasters of the War of 1812 and subsequent mass exodus of officers who lacked a commitment to the military profession opened the door to major reforms in the Army, including an apolitical officer corps and a growth in accountability and subordination to the government.[31]

Naval officers still cared a great deal about their own honor and prerogatives, and they still clashed with their civilian superiors. Yet such conflicts had diminished in intensity, and a strong sense of professionalism prevailed in the officer corps even when it found itself in tension with the Navy Department. Outright defiance of orders decreased, and when it did occur such behavior suffered sharp rebukes from both the government and within the officer corps. Threats of resignation, fatal duels, and public pamphleteering critical of the government became fatal to an officer's career soon after the War of 1812, whereas earlier such actions were ill-advised but often actually benefited an officer who engaged in them.[32] Furthermore, the creation of the Board of Navy Commissioners in 1815 imposed a bureaucratic oversight that constrained officers' autonomy. That board, however, also became a civil-military battleground immediately after its creation, and its first three members made a bold attempt to seize power from the Secretary of the Navy until the president ruled decisively in the latter's favor. Thereafter, the commissioners operated in accordance with civilian control, but also created room for the officer corps to exercise its expertise and carve out a sphere of autonomy for itself. Successive presidents and secretaries of the navy deserve credit for these changes, as early administrations took firm stands for civilian supremacy even with some of the most successful and popular naval officers. Yet it would be a mistake to see naval officers themselves as opposed to the norms that grew at the beginning of the nineteenth century. In the aftermath of the War of 1812, a much deeper commitment to civilian supremacy had been cultivated not only by the early presidents and Secretaries of the Navy, but also by a new generation of naval leaders that prized professionalism, including due regard for civilian control, and trained up young officers in these values.

# –1–

# "To Be Obeyed It Is Necessary to Be Esteemed"

## *The American Revolution at Sea, 1775–1783*

**AUGUST 14, 1778.** It remained the worst naval defeat in American history until Pearl Harbor. The Bagaduce Peninsula, tucked between Penobscot Bay and the Penobscot River in present-day Maine, was the target of a joint expedition consisting of ships from the Continental navy, the Massachusetts and New Hampshire state navies, somewhat less-than-willing privateers pressed into service, and a force of state militia troops. All had been sent with the task of dislodging a British fort and its accompanying Royal Navy support. Command was divided among three men: Captain Dudley Saltonstall (over what became the largest fleet of the war for the United States), Brigadier General Solomon Lovell (over land-based forces), and Lieutenant Colonel Paul Revere (over the artillery). It should have been a rousing American triumph; Saltonstall's fleet easily outnumbered the British forces on the river, and on land the Americans repeatedly demonstrated their bravery and skill in skirmishes with the enemy. Yet the combined force never got the chance to engage the British. Saltonstall demanded Lovell take the fort and remove its guns before he would bring his ships into action, and Lovell was equally insistent that Saltonstall destroy the British fleet before he would risk his men in an assault on the fort. They argued among themselves for nearly three weeks before finally agreeing to a joint assault. Just as they prepared to attack, long-anticipated reinforcements from the Royal Navy arrived and Saltonstall's fleet raced to escape up the river—every ship for itself. It was a hopeless task, and realizing flight was impossible, the American sailors scrambled ashore, some attempting to destroy their vessels to keep them from enemy hands as they fled. Fourteen American ships were blown up or burned by their crews, most of them destroyed without having fired a single shot. Another twenty-eight were taken by the British. More than five hundred Americans were killed or captured over the course of the expedition. And perhaps most devastating of all in a war effort chronically short of funds, in excess of seven million dollars had been poured into an expedition that suffered all these losses and achieved absolutely nothing in return.[1]

All three senior officers emerged from the disaster with their reputations, and careers, badly damaged. Yet the tragedy at Penobscot Bay resulted from more than just individual (or collective) bad judgment. The mission fell victim to the vexing command-and-control problems that haunted the American colonies at sea throughout the Revolution. At Penobscot, there were plenty of officers, but no one in command. Saltonstall, Lovell, and Revere bickered among themselves in seemingly endless councils without ever taking desperately needed action. Dudley Saltonstall came to bear the brunt of public outrage for the disaster, and he was subsequently dismissed from the navy by court-martial.[2]

It is difficult to feel sorry for Saltonstall; he refused to act at a time when he had a sizable superiority over the enemy, but the broken chain of command made failure almost inevitable, regardless of the odds favoring the Americans at the outset. So went most of the Revolution at sea. While the Continental Congress held authority over military affairs, its actual supervision of naval matters was limited, and at times nonexistent, particularly in the most significant events of the war at sea. Privately financed privateers waged war on British commerce, officially with commissions from Congress, though they began operating well before Congress found the will to grant such authorization.[3] States created their own naval forces, that, like privateers, vied with the Continental navy for resources and manpower. Even the Continental navy itself operated with inhibited oversight from Congress. Officers routinely escaped any kind of censure for ignoring or flagrantly violating orders. Meanwhile, American commissioners in France conceived of, financed, and ordered operations, interacting directly with the captains in command. Divided, muddled authority created constant headaches. Despite all this, the Continental navy did enjoy some measure of success. Yet from a civil-military standpoint, the differences in the management of the Continental navy and its successor, created in 1794 under the Constitution, are stark and fundamental—the Revolutionary War experience gave American leaders a grand example of how not to run a navy.

Foreshadowing things to come, the first colonial navy was created in an ad hoc fashion, as a response to the movements of the enemy and without the knowledge or oversight of the Continental Congress. Prior to the opening of hostilities, American sloops harassed and sometimes seized British vessels on their own authority, without bothering to consult with Congress. Indeed, as early as 1772, the mariner community of Rhode Island swarmed a British revenue ship that had become stranded. They vented their fury at Britain's heavy-handed maritime policies on the *Gaspee* and its hated commander, Lieutenant William Dudingston, wounding the latter with a musket shot and burning the former to ash.[4] Armed ships under orders from state governments also struck at vulnerable British vessels. This is how Abraham Whipple first appeared in the war. Whipple had taken part in the burning of the *Gaspee*, and by 1775 he was still well in front of a cautious Congress in opposition to the British. When the Rhode Island legislature assigned him to command an armed sloop, the *Katy*, and authorized him to "expel and resist by Force of Arms . . . and also to kill, Slay and Destroy" any British officials interfering with Rhode Island's commerce, Whipple went about his duties with aplomb, grounding and looting a British vessel after a half-hour engagement.[5] Another raider dispatched by South Carolina seized a hundred barrels of gunpowder from the British, and the angry residents of the port city of Machias, Maine, rallied around thirty-one-year-old firebrand Jeremiah O'Brien and acted on their own authority to seize a British sloop, then used it to capture the schooner *Margaretta* after a bloody battle that claimed the life of the *Margaretta*'s commanding officer.[6]

Likewise, the first organized naval force of the Revolution also came into being apart from the Continental Congress' approval. While fully committed to the ideal of military subordination to the government, newly appointed commander George Washington simply could not wait for Congressional action in the face of mounting difficulties in the siege of Boston during the summer and fall of 1775. Though confined to Boston on land by the Continental army, British forces enjoyed all the supplies they needed thanks to unimpeded shipping into the port city. Meanwhile, Washington arrived in June to find an army desperately short on gunpowder and other supplies. Accordingly, he fitted out the schooner *Hannah* with guns and sent it out under Captain Nicholson Broughton to intercept enemy shipping and divert war material into the Continental army's hands.[7]

In time, the fleet under Washington's command expanded to eight ships and enjoyed modest success, capturing several prizes.[8] Meanwhile, they also vexed their commander in chief with petty squabbling and demands for what they felt was their fair share of prize money from captures. "Our rascally privateersmen," he complained, "go on at the old rate, Mutinying if they cannot do as they please."[9] Of course, the captains in question were not technically privateersmen, as they sailed under the command of Washington, and could properly be considered a naval arm of the Continental army. Washington used the term here as an epithet, condemning them for working only for money, and not working particularly well at that. The whole of his navy caused him "inexpressible . . . plague trouble and vexation" and brought him "[n]othing but mutinous complaints."[10] In the midst of that harangue, he did single out Captain John Manley as the one man meriting praise. This commendation proved short-lived though. Just a few months later, Manley refused to sail again until he received a bigger ship.[11]

Among its other contributions, Washington's force provided a much-needed nudge to Congress to get on with the business of creating an official navy. The idea was a source of contentious debate in the spring and summer of 1775. Opponents continued to insist that such an act was both madness for challenging the seemingly invincible Royal Navy and dangerous for undermining lingering hopes for reconciliation with Britain. Hopelessly outnumbered or not, Washington's tiny fleet had inflicted tangible damage on Britain and proved a real asset. In any case, Washington was commander of the Continental army, appointed by and reporting to Congress, and thus Congress now oversaw a navy whether it wanted one or not—Washington's ships were a Continental navy even if Congress was loath to call them such. The question now was whether to move forward or continue the fiction that the colonies were not outfitting a force at sea.[12]

Congress ultimately did authorize the creation of a navy, but in the process, it did not automatically make detailed plans for how to use it. The Continental navy never developed or followed any kind of overarching strategy. In August 1775, Rhode Island proposed creating "a fleet of sufficient force for the protection of these colonies and . . . as will most effectually annoy our enemies," which many believed was the best America could hope for against the Royal Navy. More importantly, a defensive navy suited a Congress still, at that time, hoping for reconciliation with Britain, as the Rhode Island delegation made clear in their proposal.[13] After independence, Congress grew more aggressive in its plans for the navy, but ambitions always far exceeded resources, not to mention most major operations were poorly planned and directed. The greatest hindrance to American naval success though, was, of course, the might of the Royal Navy. At the time, the British had at their disposal 131 ships of the line, and a host of smaller vessels, already built and manned for combat.[14] While it could purchase merchant vessels, Congress faced the unenviable task of building most of its naval force from scratch while at war.

Once it voted to create a navy, Congress moved forward with building plans. It is somewhat remarkable how quickly the legislature whiplashed from refusing to build a navy to ordering construction of enough ships of the line that the colonies could, theoretically, compete with Britain's largest fleets. In late 1775 Congress voted to build thirteen frigates, with the goal of getting them constructed and put to sea in only three months. The Continental navy never came close to fulfilling its creators' grandiose hopes, however. Almost a year later none of the original thirteen had sailed, yet Congress voted another nine vessels slated for construction, including three 74-gun ships of the line. While the thirteen original frigates were eventually completed, most of the latter building program never came about.[15] It is fair to question whether zeal trumped sound strategy when it came to constructing the Continental navy. Unable to ever mount a serious engagement with the Royal Navy, most of these ships ended up being used for coastal defense, transportation, and commerce-raiding—at least until they were either captured or destroyed by their own crews to keep them from the enemy. One of the foremost recent historians of the Revolution at sea is sharply critical of congressional shipbuilding priorities, arguing that "low-cost, guerrilla-style tactics" could have been far more effective for the American cause if Congress had not been so obsessed with building a fleet to engage the Royal Navy; such a strategy would also have been far more in keeping with American capabilities.[16]

In any case, with a navy under construction, Congress turned its attention toward governing the force. Naval administration during the Revolution suffered from a severe lack of continuity. At first, the seven-man Naval Committee oversaw maritime affairs. This body survived less than a year, however, before evolving into the Marine Committee, consisting of one delegate from each state. In October 1779, this committee dissolved in favor of the smaller, ostensibly more efficient Board of Admiralty. In order to provide greater expertise in naval affairs, the Board of Admiralty was made up of two congressmen and three men from outside Congress. The creation of the Board of Admiralty was a thoroughly sensible decision but arguably came too late. By the time it was birthed, the challenges facing the Continental navy had become such that no one wanted the job of administering it. The board struggled just to do business thanks to its difficulty assembling its three-man quorum at meetings.[17] Indeed, the seeds of the disaster at Penobscot can be found in Congress' reputation for lethargy when it came to naval operations. Both New Hampshire and Massachusetts rushed to send their own forces as soon as they learned the British were building a fort overlooking Penobscot Bay, convinced that the fort would be complete and fully manned before Congress even got around to discussing possible operations in the region.[18] Congress eventually gave up on the Board of Admiralty as well. Finally, at the close of the war, Minister of Finance Robert Morris assumed complete control of American naval forces, and subsequently sold the remainder of the new nation's ships and left the country without a navy of any kind.[19]

Regardless of which body was governing the navy, turnover was endemic. The Marine Committee consisted of thirteen members, but more than sixty different delegates cycled through in only four years, which contributed to the committee's difficulty in getting a quorum.[20] The problems that the navy's various governing bodies struggled with certainly included disinterested or incompetent members, but there were very real difficulties that even the most dedicated administrators could not fully overcome. For one thing, members of the committees tasked with managing the navy were weighed down by responsibilities and empty-handed on funds. Congress was perpetually short of money, a fact that caused constant grief for Washington and his army as well.[21] Members also juggled several committee assignments, and the time they had to devote to naval affairs was usually limited. In addition, Charles Oscar Paullin finds that there was "a painful lack of system about the business methods of the Naval Department of the Revolution," and the absence of any kind of established precedent left naval overseers feeling free to do as they wished.[22] Chaos at the top was reflected throughout the naval administration of the war, with state navies acting on their own interests at sea and using only informal (and not always reliable) understandings among one another for what coordination existed.[23] Harmony between state navies and the Continental navy was likewise limited. States occasionally appealed to Congress for assistance in naval operations, and when Congress sent Continental navy forces to operate in conjunction with state navies, the Continental captain was in overall command—on paper at least. Orders to one captain from the Marine Committee warned him that while he could make use of a Pennsylvania galley in a joint operation, he should do so only by "taking care not to disgust the Captain" of the vessel. Captains dispatched to work with state naval forces enjoyed the backing of Congress, but that backing only carried so much weight at a time when the thirteen colonies were still struggling to become fully united, and any cooperation desired by the Continental Congress was not guaranteed.[24]

The limited oversight from Congress spilled over into the officer corps; the Continental navy never had a Washington to coordinate all its forces and operations in a coherent, unified fashion. Furthermore, America had no shortage of ship captains, but it lacked naval officers. With its long shipbuilding and merchant shipping traditions, there was an abundance of men with experience at sea eager for commissions in the Continental navy. Civilian maritime trade and naval officering were two different things, however (though there was a good bit of overlap), and the Continental navy's officers lacked their British counterparts' extensive military training and experience. Over the course of the conflict, Congress issued roughly 340 officer commissions.[25] The quality of these men varied greatly, in no small part because of the highly politicized selection process. Good credentials mattered, but having a powerful sponsor in Congress seems to have carried more weight than anything else. Keeping the various states satisfied also played a major role, as it was politically necessary for a man from the state in which a ship was built to assume command whenever possible.[26] While these officers proved a mixed-bag in terms of results, they were uniform in their finely honed sense of honor. At least one historian embarking on a psychological study of the officer corps labels some of the most noteworthy among them as narcissists. While this may be true enough in a few cases, the negative connotations of the term ignores the social and cultural attitudes of the time.[27]

Officers were used to being in command. This is the key to understanding relations between America's first captains and the Continental Congress. While merchant shipping was less rigid than the military, and very small commercial vessels tended to be more egalitarian, life at sea was defined by hierarchy, and officers expected instant obedience to orders.[28] This authority came with heavy responsibilities, however. The captain was also the guardian of the well-being of every man under his command. Men—be they subordinate officers or the lowest seaman—obeyed not only because of the captain's power to inflict punishment, but because they trusted his wisdom and care for their provision. In a real sense, a captain's authority could never be questioned, yet it always had to be earned. As a young lieutenant, John Paul Jones gave perhaps the best summary of the Continental Congress' problem in a letter attacking his superior officers. While complaining of the haughty, "rude ungentle treatment" from captains in his fleet, Jones insisted that more respectful treatment, coupled with efforts to earn men's respect, would be far more effective. In order "to be Obeyed, it is necessary to be Esteemed."[29]

The twin problems for the Continental Congress in enforcing its authority over its officer corps were that officers used to giving commands chafed at receiving them, and also they viewed the Congress as deficient in everything that made authority figures worthy of obedience. The government's ineffectiveness at providing its officers with the most basic essentials of a warship—guns, powder, stores, and decent food for the crews—led to an officer corps with a dim view of its government and few qualms about voicing complaints. The men who commanded the naval forces of the American Revolution were not freelancers or pirates—they understood and acknowledged the concept of civilian control. But their interactions with Congress left them with little esteem for that body or trust in its capacity to come up with and implement a good naval strategy. This soured civil-military relations, and Congress' inconsistent enforcement of its authority led many officers to assume a measure of autonomy their counterparts in the Royal Navy would have found unthinkable, and, quite often, they were able to get away with it.[30]

Such attitudes strained civil-military relations, but they could also be of immense value to the cause. Captains who channeled this mindset in the right direction possessed the courage and daring to overcome the frightful odds posed by the Royal Navy and make real contributions to the war effort. To be sure, the only victory at sea that had a major impact on the outcome of the war was fought entirely by the French navy—Admiral Francois De Grasse's defeat of the British fleet at the Battle of the Chesapeake cut off Cornwallis' last hope of escape from the siege at Yorktown.[31] Even if they did not make a decisive impact, victories at sea by the Continental navy (along with their state and privateer counterparts) imposed heavy financial costs on the British Empire, brought terror and outrage to the British home front, diverted Royal Navy vessels from attacks on the American coastline, and provided desperately needed morale boosts to the American public in some of the worst days of the war.

Captains who failed to channel their zeal and low estimate of Congress in a positive direction created a host of problems, however. Manley was not alone in refusing to command a ship that was too small for his liking. In 1778, when the war had already taken its toll on America's fleets and numerous officers were anxiously stranded on shore, a Captain Waters still rejected command of the brig *Resistance* because he believed "he was entitled to a better vessel."[32] Two lieutenants resigned from the navy when they learned the ship they were assigned to was commanded by a Frenchman.[33] Captains also fought with one another, often viciously. "The Revolutionary Navy," observed Samuel Eliot Morison, "was no band of brothers." Their personal conflicts frequently spilled over into operations, such as when Daniel McNeil and John Manley insisted on sailing individually in ships that were to be part of a squadron because they refused to speak to each other.[34] Internecine fighting among officers also extended to relations between a captain and his junior officers. Messy confrontations among officers were not unheard-of in commercial shipping in the Revolutionary era, and such episodes in the Continental navy often came to the Marine Committee or Board of Admiralty's attention, where it was by no means certain the congressional body would side with the senior officer (often with good reason).[35]

The rather loose understanding of subordination on display in the Continental navy extended further down the chain of command as well. Throughout the war, captains struggled to maintain discipline over unruly crews, at times causing serious problems for the war effort. John Paul Jones put down one mutiny as commander of the *Ranger*, and was later forced against his will to allow a party from the ship to steal the Earl of Selkirk's silver; Jones regarded the theft as mere piracy rather than legitimate spoils of war, but he was also painfully aware that his irate crew would likely kill him and ravage Selkirk's manor if he did not grant this concession. In another instance, Jones was in command of a squadron when the men of the sloop *Providence* requested permission to return home. Jones tried appealing to their patriotism, but he was wasting his breath. During a mild storm, the crew convinced their captain to abandon Jones and make for American shores. Jones was furious, and he almost certainly envied his Royal Navy counterparts who could have easily had the offending sailors flogged through the fleet and their spineless commander cashiered or even hanged. In the American navy, however, Jones could only fume.[36] It might have given him some consolation that he was far from alone in being unable to control those allegedly under his command. Gustavus Conyngham found himself forced by his crew to take a ship he believed, correctly, was a Swedish neutral. The incident harmed America's relations with Spain and was a source of embarrassment for American commissioners in France.[37] Other mutineers were even more successful; Captain James Robinson was commander of the *Fly* until he was "dispossessed of that sloop by a majority of the Crew at Sea," and he was put on board another schooner along with the *Fly*'s doctor and pilot.[38]

Given the inconsistent pay from Congress and the fact that they were fighting a war in the name of liberty, it was easy for the men of the Continental navy to resent their officers, especially since those officers could indeed be much more heavy-handed than necessary. Sailors' degree of devotion to the cause of the Revolution varied greatly, and many of them were decidedly unwilling to undergo extreme hardships in the name of American independence the way Continental army's soldiers endured through the horrors of Valley Forge for inconsistent (at times nonexistent) pay.[39] There were certainly sailors who felt intense loyalty to the American nation, such as James Forten, a well-educated Black seaman who willingly chose imprisonment in a British hulk rather than accept an offer to become a tutor in the home of a wealthy British officer.[40] Many others, however, approached the war in much more mercenary fashion. The most widespread mindset of sailors on American naval vessels in the Revolution was to see themselves as nothing more than temporary hands contracted to a ship, and they were quick to retaliate against any officer who broke the unspoken rules of the contract. Harsh treatment and inconsistent pay or inadequate rations were the sort of violations that left sailors with no qualms about deserting or even outright mutiny.[41]

It is also understandable that captains struggled to enforce their authority and occasionally gave in to the demands of their men when one considers the chaotic state of the Continental navy. Courts-martial were hard enough to hold for officers, and trying men for mutiny and making examples of them was an uncertain prospect.[42] Instead, captains often opted for inflicting severe punishments on their own authority, deliberately exceeding limits imposed by Congress' "Rules for the Regulation of the Navies of the United Colonies" on what they could do without a court-martial conviction. Nicholas Biddle put down a mutiny from a group of sailors with ties to England by giving them floggings of unnumbered lashes, only ending their misery when he concluded the watching crew was sufficiently cowed.[43] John Barry nearly flogged a man to death trying to force him to give up the names of his accomplices.[44] Officers could not assume they would get away with such conduct, however. There were captains kicked out of the navy for what Congress deemed excessive cruelty to their men, but the difficulty of holding a court-martial and generally inconsistent management by Congress reveals why men like Biddle and Barry believed—correctly, in their cases—that they could get away with such treatment.[45] In general, the more successful a captain was, the more leniency he enjoyed in his dealings with his crew, and those cashiered for mishandling the men under their command were usually not much value to the cause anyway. Likewise, a great many sailors believed (again, very often correctly) that they could escape punishment for any number of offenses that would likely have gotten them flogged through the fleet or hanged in the British navy. Officers attempting to impose military shipboard discipline on men steeped in the rhetoric of the American Revolution meant that clashes were inevitable, but the inconsistent oversight and management of the navy from Congress made the situation far worse.

All the problems that plagued the Continental navy throughout the war were on display in its first major operation. Eager to get started engaging the Royal Navy, Congress hastily appointed Esek Hopkins as "Commander in Chief of the Fleet of the United Colonies."[46] Exactly what this title meant was not entirely clear. Hopkins obviously considered himself as the equivalent of George Washington, but whether that was actually the intent of Congress is unclear. The only authority Hopkins was explicitly granted was over a single fleet being fitted out, which made up the bulk but not the whole of the Continental navy; other ships being fitted out elsewhere were not mentioned as being subject to his orders.[47] Hopkins was a reasonable choice for the command—at fifty-seven he had spent years at sea in a lucrative merchant career, but he was also old enough to have commanded privateers in the French and Indian War, where he distinguished himself sufficiently to secure an appointment as brigadier general of all of Rhode Island's troops at the start of the Revolution. In what would be nearly always the case where naval appointments were concerned, his resume was not the sole, or even likely the decisive, factor: Hopkins' older brother Stephen served in the Continental Congress and was one of the most prominent figures in the creation and oversight of the colonies' new navy.[48]

The orders for the navy's first fleet cannot be faulted for lack of ambition. Hopkins was to take his ships southward and "search out and attack, take or destroy all the Naval force of our Enemies that you may find" off the coast of Virginia, before moving on and doing likewise off North Carolina and South Carolina. The British naval presence in the Chesapeake and the southern colonies generally was indeed a source of crisis—as southern delegates were quick to point out—but it seems there was some recognition on the part of the Naval Committee that Hopkins was being asked to do the impossible. The committee concluded by saying that if Hopkins found himself, due to storms or "unforeseen accident or disaster," unable to comply with "these particular Orders," he was to "follow such Courses as your best Judgment shall suggest to you as most useful to the American Cause and to distress the Enemy by all means in your power."[49]

Hopkins immediately seized on the broadest possible interpretation of this caveat. Disregarding his orders entirely, Hopkins set out for the Bahamas, where he managed to seize a scantly guarded British fort and load his ships with a substantial haul of cannon, gunpowder, and other warfighting material. The raid showed the promise of what the small American navy could accomplish; even the mighty Royal Navy could not safeguard all of Britain's far-flung possessions, and juicy prizes were available for the taking throughout the Caribbean. But subsequent events tarnished the new navy's first major success. On its return, the fleet encountered the British light frigate *Glasgow* all alone, a matchup of seven against one. Yet rather than signal his ships into a line of battle, Hopkins became a passive observer of the action, in which the well-drilled British crew fended off its American attackers piecemeal and escaped with only minor casualties.[50]

Initial enthusiasm for the successful raid evaporated quickly as the story of the *Glasgow* fight emerged. The fact that a single ship could escape, largely undamaged, against such overwhelming odds was humiliating, and it did not take long for Congress to conclude incompetence was the only possible answer. It was aided in reaching this conclusion by Hopkins' junior officers. It seems the cranky, short-tempered captain never inspired loyalty in anyone serving under him, and every officer involved in the *Glasgow* fiasco was quick to pile the blame onto their commodore. Congress gave Hopkins another chance, but he struggled to enlist enough seamen to get his next fleet to sea, a problem that plagued every Continental navy captain who had to compete with promises of wealth aboard privateers. After another inept performance when a British ship was grounded within easy reach and still managed to escape, Hopkins' officers turned on him completely.[51] They signed a letter alleging a host of offenses, saying that their commander "ridecules religion" and seems to "despise every virtue." He also, by their account, routinely vented his contempt and disdain for the Continental Congress, calling them "a pack of damn'd fools, ignorant fellows, lawyers clerks," and so forth, further alleging that if he and other officers followed all their orders "the country would be undone." They also accused him of treating prisoners of war "in the most inhuman and barbarous manner." Hopkins' nasty temper was well-known, so these accusations were plausible enough, but they went on to add, rather ludicrously, that Hopkins also hinted to British prisoners (apparently when he was not barbarically abusing them) that he would be willing to sell his services to the British.[52]

Congress was well and thoroughly sick of its first commodore by this point, and immediately took all the charges from Hopkins' junior officers at face value. He was suspended from command and dismissed from the navy a year later without a court-martial. The overwhelming consensus from historians is that Hopkins was an inept commander and ill suited by temperament and capacity for the job given him by Congress, but that in the handling of his dismissal he was "treated shabbily" and very much a victim of politics as well as his own shortcomings. Despite his failures and oft-cited contempt for Congress' management of the navy, he was still dismissed from the service without any kind of hearing or even a full account of the charges against him.[53] In any case, if it is true, as the men trying to evict him from the navy alleged, that he was prone to profanity-laden tirades against Congress, he was far from the only officer in the Continental navy to rage against his civilian superiors.

Nothing generated so much bad blood between the naval officer corps and Congress as the initial seniority list. Congress made the mistake of issuing a series of captains' commissions early in the war without bothering to define seniority. This was a deliberate oversight, not an unintentional one, as it passed a resolution in the spring of 1776 authorizing the Marine Committee to recommend names for captains' commissions, and explicitly stating that the committee could not determine rank, as Congress intended to settle that question at a later time.[54] By the time it finally got around to establishing relative rank, several officers had already distinguished themselves, and they naturally assumed their contributions would be rewarded in the form of seniority. Once the Marine Committee began considering the question in earnest, the fact of their deliberations soon became an open secret, and status-conscious officers waited tensely for the outcome.[55] Their tension shortly turned into rage. The first officers' list actually demoted some of the country's naval heroes, bumping John Paul Jones from fifth on the Continental navy's first fleet to eighteenth overall. John Barry and Lambert Wickes, two others who had a clear record of success, also placed surprisingly low, at seventh and eleventh, respectively.[56] The rationale behind the rankings had little to do with past achievement. Only one captain from George Washington's early naval force made the list, and likewise only one officer had any kind of naval experience in the Royal Navy. Embarrassingly, Congress itself could not even explain how it established the order of this list, with a Congressional committee appointed in 1781 to look into the matter conceding that they "could not fully ascertain the rule by which [the captains' list] was made, as the relative rank was not conformable to times of appointment or dates of commission." The committee even suggested that Congress might alter the rankings on a more sensible basis, though nothing came of this.[57] The anger that snubbed officers felt was understandable, but Congress also had to deal with the political realities of a collection of just-barely "united" states fighting a war. Southern delegates had to be appeased (hence James Nicholson, of Maryland, sat at the top of the list), and states expected that one of their own would command ships constructed within their borders, meaning seniority had to be shaped to keep the "right" officers in command of their respective vessels.[58]

Recognizing the limits of its naval oversight, Congress sought to improve the situation through the creation of two navy boards. The first, initially called the Navy Board but later retitled the Navy Board of the Middle Department, was established on November 6, 1776, and assigned to "execute the business of the navy, under the direction of the Marine Committee."[59] Consisting of three men based out of Philadelphia, this board also proved inadequate to cope with the multitude of details in running a navy, and in April 1777 Congress created a second board to oversee the New England states.[60] This board was dubbed the Navy Board of the Eastern Department, and it went on to enjoy a greater measure of autonomy than its predecessor in Philadelphia, thanks to its distance from the Congress.[61] The two boards' initially vague mandate received some clarification in July, when the Marine Committee sent orders to the Eastern Board spelling out its responsibilities (these rules presumably mirrored those given to the Middle Board). The first duty assigned was to bring oversight to ship construction in all states falling under the board's purview. They were to keep careful registers of ships, stores, and people—both officers and men—in naval service. They also had authority to rein in the officer corps, being tasked with directing "the economy of all Continental Vessels" and keeping watch over ships' accounts. They also had the authority to order courts-martial "in all cases where the Commanding officers shall refuse, or neglect the same."[62]

Although the chain of command seemed straightforward, the Marine Committee also tended to undermine the boards. Members of the committee interacted directly with officers and naval agents without communicating with the regional board, meaning that agents "sometimes discovered that they were serving in a single task two or three naval masters."[63] Further complicating matters were the boards' lack of authority over state naval forces, and the fact that, despite being civilian agencies delegated by Congress to oversee military affairs, the boards were apparently assumed to be under George Washington's command; at the very least Washington was authorized to give orders to captains of the Continental navy, seemingly with the ability to overrule the navy boards.[64]

Perhaps no incident highlights the muddled chain of command involving the boards better than John Barry's clash with his superiors over the sinking of two naval vessels. The conflict originated at the Navy Board of the Middle Department. Though it consisted of three men, the dominant figure in the board was Francis Hopkinson. An esteemed attorney as well as successful poet, Hopkinson assumed the dual roles of chairman and secretary for the board. His remarkably successful career in law included a visit to London, and he had developed an expertise in maritime law prior to the Revolution. Elected to the Continental Congress by his home state of New Jersey, Hopkinson was one of the signers of the Declaration of Independence, and while he seldom argued before Congress, he proved an industrious member behind the scenes. The other two members, John Nixon and John Wharton, both possessed a measure of maritime experience, but whether through industriousness or force of personality, Hopkinson became the clear senior member of the board.[65]

Though his standing vis-à-vis Washington was unclear, Hopkinson entertained no doubts about his authority over his naval officers. "All Officers . . . belonging to the Navy of the United States . . . are hereby directed to give personal attention to the Navy Board every Monday and Thursday . . . to receive the orders of said Board," reads one of Hopkinson's first directives to his officers.[66] Still, some decisions proved too sensitive for anyone to make. When it came to choosing who would lead the naval defense of Philadelphia in the fall of 1777, Congress was unwilling to favor its own officer, John Barry, over the commander of the Pennsylvania state navy, John Hazelwood, fearing that doing so would upset the delicate relationship between congressional and state authority, and Hopkinson likewise avoided weighing in on the matter. For much of the ordeal, Barry and Hazelwood worked with the question of their relative rank unsettled. Washington sent his instructions for the riverine defense of the capital to Hazelwood, and never wrote to Barry, indicating he favored Hazelwood's claim to authority, but he also declined to make a definite statement on the matter.[67]

In the weeks leading up to the British attack on Philadelphia, Barry was hard at work outfitting the *Effingham* and the *Washington*, but getting them ready in time for the defense of the city was proving impossible. It could not have helped that Washington continually seized his men for use elsewhere. Hopkinson usually took whatever of Barry's men the general wanted, but on at least one occasion he had no qualms about flatly refusing a request for men from Washington.[68] By October 1777, with the British assault on the capital imminent, the ships remained far short of being any use in the city's defense, leaving Barry no choice but to sail upriver and miss the battle.[69] Frustrating though it was, this fate probably benefitted his reputation, for by that point the capture of Philadelphia by the British was a foregone conclusion.[70]

With the capital taken, Washington could only seek to minimize the damage to the American cause. His foremost objective was to prevent the British from gaining any more of the colonies' resources. With this end in mind, and in hopes of putting Barry's seamen to his own use, he recommended to Hopkinson that the *Effingham* and *Washington* be sunk at a spot on the river where it would be possible to raise them at a later time. Washington presented the idea as merely a suggestion, noting that he did not consider himself "a Judge of such matters," but he thought such a course "highly expedient."[71] It then fell to the navy board to implement Washington's recommendation. Its murky status in relation to the general, however, posed problems.[72] Initially, Hopkinson hesitated in complying with Washington's idea. Though he assured Washington that "your desires shall always be a Law to us," he thought the vessels' defenses perfectly sufficient to forestall any British attack, and argued that it would be premature to scuttle them until the threat was much more imminent—the same assertions that Barry would later present to the board.[73] Though Washington disagreed with Hopkinson's assessment, he clearly felt uneasy about imposing his will on the board. Rather than order Hopkinson and Wharton to comply with his wishes, Washington wrote another letter arguing at length for the prompt destruction of the ships. He cited the shortage of manpower to defend the vessels and the need for these few men in other operations. Considering the risks of maintaining the vessels against the scant reward of keeping them, he repeated his suggestion that they be sunk. That Washington entertained serious doubts about his authority to make such a decision is clear from the tone of his letter. "If I have stepped out of the line of my duty to make this request, I am persuaded that you will excuse it," he wrote.[74] Washington's concern with stepping "out of line" did not, however, keep him from writing again, the same day, to reiterate his desire that the ships be scuttled.[75]

Washington uncharacteristically reached his decision without first consulting others closer to the situation. Hopkinson, of course, counseled against sinking the ships, and Barry certainly would have offered the same advice, considering he later insisted as much to the Navy Board. For his part, Washington studiously avoided using the word "order" in his communications with Hopkinson, and he may have assumed that the Navy Board would overrule him if it felt so inclined. Hopkinson, however, apparently did not feel secure challenging the general again, and set aside his own judgment. The frigates would sink.[76]

At no point did either man consider consulting Barry himself, the military officer most familiar with the situation and certainly qualified to give an assessment of the vessels' safety. Instead, Hopkinson brusquely informed Barry that the only two ships under his command were to be scuttled immediately.[77] Horrified, Barry rushed to the navy board's temporary headquarters to protest his orders. "[Conscious] of the Secure Situation of our ships," Barry later wrote, he felt it his "duty to expostulate with the Navy Board before they were rashly destroyed." He expressed certainty to Hopkinson that were "General Washington fully acquainted with the Security of the ships he would not order them to be Sunk, and further that they might be made ready for Sinking should the worst happen." In case Hopkinson believed he lacked the authority to reverse the decision, Barry "offered to go to his Excellency the General and give him full information on all that had been done."[78]

Hopkinson refused, despite the fact that Barry was recommending to him almost exactly what he had proposed to Washington earlier that day. Moreover, he let Barry know in a manner the proud captain found utterly humiliating, denigrating his knowledge of maritime matters and issuing the directive in a condescending tone.[79] Flying into a rage, Barry informed Hopkinson that he "knew more about a ship than General Washington and the Navy Board together." Perhaps realizing how scandalous such a remark sounded, he then appealed to the hierarchy of civilian control, claiming that the Marine Committee ordered him to command the ship, and that the Committee outranked both Hopkinson and Washington (true), making it impossible for him to sink the ships unless he received orders to do so directly from the Marine Committee. Such an assertion rested on shaky legal interpretation, for the Marine Committee created the navy board and vested it with substantial authority, and the board had already endorsed Washington's recommendations, though Barry was probably unaware that it did so hesitantly. For his part, Hopkinson countered the captain's legal reasoning by shouting, "You shall obey our orders," and forcibly evicting Barry from his office.[80]

Whether Barry really put any stock in his argument that the Marine Committee's orders superseded Hopkinson's or simply used that as a desperate ploy to avoid a task he found distasteful is impossible to say. However, upon leaving Hopkinson's office he set about sinking the vessels as directed. As a final insult, Hopkinson came at the last moment to oversee the actual scuttling of Barry's ship. Unlike his earlier loss of temper, the captain dutifully stepped aside.[81] In response to a query from Washington as to whether the ships remained afloat, Hopkinson assured him that "your Orders were immediately complied with" and "punctually executed." Indeed, he expressed "great Concern that your Excellency should for a Moment suspect us of neglecting your earnest Instructions after having so solemnly assured you that we would strictly obey them." Hopkinson even went out of his way to reassure the general that he would never think of consulting Congress, the civilian head of government and the body he ostensibly reported to, before complying with any of Washington's directives.[82]

Hopkinson was later dismayed to learn that at almost the same time he and Barry argued over whether to scuttle the vessels, Congress, believing that Washington's recommendation had not yet been carried out, quickly passed a resolution urging that both ships be preserved and the strategy for their defense that the Navy Board had originally proposed be implemented instead—exactly what Barry had suggested.[83] While it was too late to comply with Congress' wishes on that score, Hopkinson instead complained about Barry's treatment to the Marine Committee, resulting in the necessity of an inquiry into the matter. Barry acknowledged having hesitated to comply with the order to sink the ships, citing his duty to prevent the needless loss of precious resources. However, he adamantly denied having refused to comply in "indecent terms," as Hopkinson claimed. He concluded with the assertion that, as a captain, he merited being treated "with complesance, and as a gentleman," and that he "should think [himself] unworthy of the Commission the Honorable Congress has been pleased to give me could I tamely put up with different treatment."[84] The Congress concluded that Barry had indeed treated his superior "with indecency and disrespect" and ordered him to acknowledge such to the board, and Hopkinson in particular, but issued no further punishment than that.[85] While apologizing to Hopkinson no doubt seemed galling to Barry, the ruling amounted to little more than a slap on the wrist, certainly far less than Hopkinson had sought. If Barry even complied with this directive, he left no record of it, nor did Hopkinson, and at least one historian speculates that the apology never happened.[86]

The same unclear division of authority and responsibility that tormented the navy boards afflicted the American commissioners in France, who served as yet another branch of administration for the Continental navy. For officers who found themselves on French shores, Benjamin Franklin, John Adams, and Arthur Lee were the designated American contacts; these three men functioned as something of a parallel Marine Committee/Board of Admiralty—an unofficial third Navy Board based out of Paris.[87] An ocean's distance from Philadelphia gave the commissioners a level of independence from Congress in overseeing naval affairs that the navy boards in the United States never approached. This independence, of course, did nothing to alter the fact that, as America's diplomatic agents to an essential ally, they had a host of duties, and the Continental navy was decidedly not the most important. Indeed, all three occasionally grew irritated at badgering captains who seemed to think their foremost reason for being in France was to secure ships and supplies for cruises.[88]

Their autonomy in overseeing naval affairs did not extend to the French Ministry of Marine either. The commissioners, like the new nation they represented, were consistently short of funds, and after the treaty of alliance in 1778 they depended on France to provide ships, arms, and supplies. Recruiting seamen was actually much less of a problem than in America, "for there was," according to one historian, "human driftwood in every port of Christendom, of divers nationalities, willing to ship under any flag."[89] The loyalty of such crews was, of course, less than perfectly reliable, but at least it made signing a crew the least onerous aspect of getting a ship to sea. Securing the other essentials for any cruise from the French Ministry of Marine meant that France necessarily had the ability to shape naval plans and veto proposed operations. Franklin bluntly conceded as much to John Paul Jones, writing him that "as the Court is at the Chief Expense, I think they have the best right to direct," when it came to the captain's cruising orders.[90] Even when they operated in close conjunction with the French, the ultimate power to get things done (or not) rested squarely with the government in Paris. At one point, Franklin and French Minister of Marine Antoine de Sartine envisioned a bold plan to terrorize British coastal cities, but the King of France intervened in the planning stages, turning a doable and potentially spectacular raid into a hopeless scheme for invading the British Isles. The entire mission died well before it ever came close to getting underway.[91]

This was the most dramatic plan that eventually got scrubbed, but signs that the commissioners would have to balance their own naval oversight with French desires appeared much sooner. John Adams reached Paris in 1778 and learned that a major port had three American agents all doing the same job in competition with one another. In addition to the agent chosen by Franklin, there was another sent by the Continental Congress, and a third appointed by the French government. This was hardly an isolated case, as several ports had more than one American representative at odds with each other.[92] The division of authority between American and French leaders was not always so starkly displayed, but it was an ever-present reality. John Paul Jones never hesitated to appeal directly to the French Minister of Marine for ships and support, outlining his grand plans and strategic visions to Sartine without going through the commissioners. American naval officers in France also, in turn, received orders directly from the French government.[93] The three commissioners were diplomats first and naval overseers second, and so any activity they undertook involving American naval forces had to be done in such a way as to insure continued harmony with an indispensable ally.

Relations between the commissioners and naval officers were often strained. The ever-diplomatic Benjamin Franklin cultivated a remarkably good relationship with John Paul Jones, and probably did as well as anyone in constraining and guiding that strong-willed officer. Yet whether with Jones or anyone else, the commissioners had to deal with the reality that their naval resources fell far short of their glory-hungry officers' ambitions. This created a minor international incident at one point. While France was still officially neutral, Gustavus Conyngham was allowed to sail his privateering vessel out of Dunkirk on strict orders not to seize any more British shipping during the return voyage; to do so would clearly demonstrate France's support of the American rebels before King Louis XVI was ready. Conyngham not only disregarded these orders, he used French sailors as part of a prize crew for one of his captures. The British protestations of outrage and French anger temporarily strained relations between Franklin and the one ally that the colonies could ill afford to lose.[94]

The commissioners also had frequent headaches sorting out squabbles between captains and their junior officers. When John Paul Jones accused one of his lieutenants, Thomas Simpson, of insubordination, he had Simpson placed under arrest pending a court-martial. At first, this only entailed being confined to his cabin aboard a prize ship, but later he was transferred to a filthy French prison. Jones hectored the commissioners for a trial, but of course this required officers, an insufficient number of whom were available in France at the time. Meanwhile, more than seventy officers and men petitioned the commissioners on Simpson's behalf, accusing Jones of tyrannical treatment and complaining, plausibly, that he had arrested Simpson unfairly and that the lieutenant was a man of "unspotted Character" who consistently behaved himself "in such a manner as to command the Respect and Esteem of all who had the happiness of his Acquaintance."[95] The commissioners apparently found Simpson's outpouring of support persuasive, for they quickly wrote to Jones that his treatment of the offending lieutenant seemed "to carry in it, a degree of severity, which cannot be justified by Reason or Law;" and diplomatically instructed the irate captain to free his prisoner immediately.[96] Jones complied but also vented to the commissioners that it was impossible to manage an effective fighting ship with insubordinate officers and mutinous sailors.[97]

Unfortunately for Jones, this was not the last time he had to come to the commissioners with a crisis created by a mutinous subordinate. The next offender was Pierre Landais, a former officer in the French navy who had received a commission and honorary citizenship from Massachusetts at the outset of the war. Landais won his place in the Continental navy not only thanks to his prior experience, but also to his careful cultivation of the right connections. Landais ingratiated himself to members of Congress who were hostile to Benjamin Franklin, and this faction believed that the French officer could soon rival the Marquis de Lafayette in popularity, hopefully diminishing Franklin and his proteges in the process.[98] It did not take long for those who interacted closely with the Landais to form a different opinion of him. John Adams found him jealous, suspicious, and ill tempered in the extreme, and besides all that a poor officer who mistreated his subordinates, was incompetent, and, perhaps worst of all, lazy and indecisive. Adams, with impressive prescience, predicted his career would end in ruin.[99]

The commissioner's dim view of Landais notwithstanding, the Marine Committee had given him command of the frigate *Alliance* and he was assigned to Jones's squadron. The two quickly came to despise one another, with Landais at one point boarding Jones' flagship, *Bonhomme Richard*, and berating the commodore in front of the crew before announcing that he would no longer obey any orders he disliked. He proved he meant those words shortly thereafter by ignoring Jones's directive to attend a council of officers, instead breaking from the squadron and sailing off on his own without permission. During the now-legendary Battle of Flamborough Head, in which Jones captured the British frigate *Serapis*, Landais capped off his insubordination by opening fire on Jones's ship while it was locked in combat.[100]

Landais faced a certain court-martial for his conduct during the battle, but his fortunes were revived thanks to the internal squabbles of the Paris commissioners. Benjamin Franklin was disgusted by Landais' appalling conduct and swore he would not trust the Frenchman with another ship under any circumstances. Franklin and his fellow commissioner, Arthur Lee, had become bitter enemies by this point, however, and so any man the good doctor hated had a friend in Lee. While Jones was in Paris lobbying to get his men the pay and prize money due them, Lee and Landais schemed together for the latter to retake command of the *Alliance*. Lee contended that since Landais was commissioned by the Congress, Jones could not relieve him of command, even for firing on an American ship. This strained legal reasoning would never have held up, of course, had not Landais also rallied the crew and many of the officers to his side while Jones was away.

When Franklin got word of the situation, he alerted Jones but did not intervene in any real way. Perhaps he assumed the captain could handle such blatant mutiny on his own, especially since the *Alliance* would have to sail out under French guns, and the government of France was apparently prepared to open fire if Landais made the attempt. Jones backed down though, this time to Franklin's annoyance rather than at his prompting. He claimed he let Landais sail away without a fight from humanitarian motives, not wanting to see French guns firing on American sailors. No one believed him, then or later.[101] Jones let the *Alliance* go because he had no desire to command it and was happy to be rid of Landais, who was court-martialed and removed from the navy shortly thereafter. The cashiering of such a troublesome officer notwithstanding, the whole messy affair was yet another example of the impotence of the American government in dealing with is naval officer corps. This incoherent chain of command had very practical consequences for naval operations. In late 1777, members of Congress conceived a bold plan to send American frigates to the Indian Ocean, where they could wreak havoc on Britain's trade with China. The operation never took place. "Better order must be established in our marine, and the ships' companies better sorted, before it will be safe to attempt enterprises at such a distance," Arthur Lee reported back to Philadelphia. The Continental navy was simply not capable of operations that "require a certain extent of ideas in the captain and entire obedience in the crew."[102] The commissioners in Paris were in no position to enforce such order and discipline, but then neither was any other person or body tasked with overseeing the Continental navy. Such grand plans would have to await a more professional service under a more effective government.

By the fall of 1780 the Continental navy's reputation was badly battered, despite the occasional heroics of men like Barry, Whipple, and Jones. Certainly a young privateer captain by the name of Thomas Truxtun took a dim view of it. Truxtun's performance had been impressive; he was among the most successful privateers in the war, and his stolen supplies and arms proved essential to Washington's army.[103] Never one to underestimate his own worth, Truxtun was apparently so pleased with his own accomplishments that he determined his own ship more meritorious than anything in the whole Continental navy. At least he indicated as much when he refused to lower his command pennant when in port next to John Paul Jones' ship *Ariel*. This was in blatant defiance of Congress' orders that all American ships show proper acknowledgment of the American flag flying aboard commissioned ships in foreign ports. Truxtun's actions were no inadvertent error either; he passed close by the *Ariel* coming into port and "shewed no mark of respect to the Continental Flag & Commission . . . or even shewing any mark of Politeness." While the two ships were together in the port, Truxtun raised an additional broad pennant as a further sign of his disregard for the Continental navy ship. Jones was infuriated by this insult to both himself and his country's navy, and when he sent an officer over to instruct Truxtun to lower the pennant, the messenger returned and reported that Truxtun's crew had "menaced" him and informed him that Truxtun's orders were to "treat with contempt and disobey any Order or request to haul down the Pendant." Only when an armed boatload captained by Jones' lieutenant sailed for Truxtun's ship was the offending pennant lowered, and then only temporarily.[104] Jones sent the Board of Admiralty a blistering account of Truxtun's blatant disrespect, calling for some sort of reprisal for the privateer captain's "Insolence" in "bidding defiance to Congress and the Continental Flag." Congress looked the other way; Truxtun was a successful privateer and the overburdened government had more pressing issues than upholding the honor of its navy. That open contempt for the laws of the Continental Congress and one of the nation's most successful naval officers could be overlooked says much about the Continental navy's status by that point in the war.[105] Jones refused to accept that reality without comment. In addition to alerting Congress he fired off a letter to Truxtun, lecturing him on the honor due his government and its navy. "It is not me you have Offended," he concluded. "You have Offended the United States of America."[106]

The Continental navy, and the Congress that ran it, were fair game for offense by that point. William Ellery of Rhode Island, one of the few delegates who had consistently involved himself in naval affairs from the beginning of the war, looked despondently on what was left of the force in 1781, as the Board of Admiralty was in its final days. "The next time America goes to war, I hope she will have a respectable navy," he wrote to a member of the navy board at Boston, adding that the "few remaining ships do not deserve that name."[107] John Adams took a similar view. Pondering the fortunes of the navy he helped create, Adams lamented in 1780 that when "recollecting the whole history of the rise and progress of our navy, it is very difficult to avoid tears."[108]

Yet Adams shared Ellery's hope of a more "respectable" navy for his country. Building a force that could meaningfully "distress our foes" would call for far more attention from Congress, however. The keys, in Adams' mind, were "the augmentation of ships, the multiplication of seamen, the improvement of discipline, and the formation of officers." Building a corps of the right kind of officers was essential, and the immediate and long-term needs of the navy on this point were in conflict. Adams of course understood that, at that moment in the war, commerce-raiding and avoiding major battles were the best options for the rebel colonies. In thinking more broadly about the kind of navy the new nation would need in the future, Adams still firmly believed that officers "who have a thirst for glory and a wish to distinguish themselves in brilliant battles ought not to be discouraged."[109]

John Paul Jones would not survive to see the new American navy birthed under the Constitution, but a generation of officers who shared his vision of the United States as a powerful maritime nation committed themselves to earning the respectability that Ellery and Adams hoped for. One of the foremost among them would be none other than Thomas Truxtun. Although he sneered at Jones and the Continental navy flag at the end of the Revolution, Jones' lecture apparently got through to him at some point and he became an ardent defender of the honor of the U.S. Navy.[110] Fortunately, his civilian superiors shared that vision. Going forward, the Washington administration firmly rejected oversight by committee for the new navy; a single executive oversaw naval forces under the direction of the president, first in the form of the secretary of war, and after 1797 via the Secretary of the Navy. The first civilian leaders of the navy, like the officers they oversaw, prioritized building a force that could demand the respect of its European counterparts, and that included advancing officers who showed the "thirst for glory" that Adams desired. All this, however, would have to wait over a decade for Congressional and public will for any navy at all.

# –2–

# "To This Great National Object"

## *The Creation of the United States Navy, 1783–1797*

**AUGUST 24, 1785.** After nearly a month of suffering through "the horrors of a miserable captivity," James Leander Cathcart struggled to keep his sense of despair at bay. His ship, the American commercial vessel *Maria*, had been seized by Algiers on August 1, easy victims of Mediterranean predators thanks to the well-known impotency of the new United States of America. Cathcart and the rest of the crew had been stripped of their clothing and belongings, given nothing but a pair of trousers "swarming with myriads of vermin," and fed barely enough food to survive before being sold into slavery. He eventually had the relatively good fortune of being put to work in the Dey of Algiers' palace, unlike the crew of another American ship, the *Dauphin*, whose captured sailors were cast into the dreaded quarries to perform backbreaking labor. Richard O'Brien of the *Dauphin*, who had been taken into captivity a day before Cathcart, reached out to Thomas Jefferson in Paris and asked him to make their dire situation known to Congress, pleading that "Oure Sufferings is Beyond Oure Expressing or your Conception." Without immediate relief, O'Brien feared his crew would starve.[1] Had Cathcart and O'Brien been able to peer into the future their despair would have exceeded their worst imagination; they and their fellow Americans would languish in slavery for another eleven years, and half of them would perish without ever seeing their homes again.[2] Although it was free, the infant United States was far from secure. With an empty treasury and no navy, the nation's commercial shipping made an inviting target, and no threat to vulnerable ships was more notorious than the Barbary corsairs.

The Barbary states consisted of three semi-independent regencies of the Ottoman Empire on North Africa's Mediterranean coast: Algiers, Tunis, and Tripoli. The independent Kingdom of Morocco was the fourth of the so-called Barbary Powers; its predation of European shipping functioned more or less the same. Their economies hinged on seizing the ships of other nations and enslaving their crews. Massive ransoms and annual tribute from any country that wanted to send ships near the region generated revenue for rulers. The Barbary Powers had preyed on European shipping for generations, since before the "Old World" was even aware the American continent existed, but they were also shrewd in the sums they demanded as part of their protection racket. Periodic wars with various European nations consistently proved that it was much cheaper for the Barbary's victims to buy security than to fight for it. Nations with the military might to crush the Barbary Powers and free the Mediterranean for commerce actually found the corsairs quite useful. For Britain in particular, Barbary piracy served to weaken the maritime economies of rivals, so much so that it was said if Algiers did not exist, it would be to Britain's advantage to create it.[3]

The seizure of the *Maria* and *Dauphin* was a crisis for a country in its infancy struggling to establish itself on the world stage. Of more immediate concern, it was a major disaster for a nation desperately short on funds. The source of the American captives' misery was not indifference; no less than George Washington, Thomas Jefferson, and Alexander Hamilton were deeply troubled by the whole situation, and thought at length about how to remedy it. The painful reality was that any Continental navy ships left after the Revolution had been given away or sold, and the nation was defenseless at sea; it had no way to safeguard its commercial ships from depredations in the Mediterranean, or anywhere else for that matter. The infant republic had to face the harsh truth that if it wanted to be any kind of commercial nation, it would have to pay the costs of safeguarding that commerce.

The creation of the U.S. Navy grew directly out of the crisis on the Barbary coast. And while the dissolution of the Continental navy after the Revolution invited attacks on American shipping, it also gave the new nation a chance to start fresh and correct the errors made in the Revolutionary War regarding maritime forces. The new navy would have more stable oversight, and a more direct chain of command. This did not mean that all was perfect upon the navy's creation. Congress initially balked at creating a separate Navy Department, and even the quite modest fleet authorized was not guaranteed to survive until another international crisis intervened. The Washington and Adams administrations insured the new navy's survival, but in the process of creating the force, seeds of future tensions between the officer corps and the government were planted that would blossom in significant civil-military crises before John Adams left office.

Although the United States emerged victorious against Great Britain, the end of the war found the Continental navy at its nadir. Only two ships were left, the rest either in British hands or at the bottom of ocean. The economy of the new nation was not in much better shape, and an expensive building program to launch a viable navy was out of the question. Robert Morris, who had assumed the job of running the navy by virtue of his willingness to take it when no one else would, ultimately chose to sell off the two remaining ships. Even as the United States was being born, its navy disappeared.[4]

Unemployed, most of the officers of the Continental navy returned to life as merchant captains. John Paul Jones drifted across the Atlantic to Russia, hoping to use a commission in the czarina's navy to gain the full measure of glory he never quite found in his own country.[5] Far more typical were the experiences of John Barry and Thomas Truxtun. Both used their skills as seamen in commercial voyages to Canton, China, where they mingled with numerous other patriots from the recent war with Britain, and often dined convivially with their former adversaries. Although highly lucrative, the Canton trade—or any voyages by American merchant vessels—posed hazards; merchant captains drilled their crews to defend the ship if pirates attacked, particularly if they sailed anywhere near the Mediterranean. The ever-present threat posed by the Barbary corsairs could not fail to remind veterans of the Revolution that the country they had helped create lacked the ability to protect its commerce at sea.[6]

The only hope of the country creating a new navy rested with the Constitution drawn up in Philadelphia in 1787. By and large, naval veterans enthusiastically supported the charter. Joshua Barney gave speeches campaigning on behalf of pro-Constitution delegates in his home state, firmly convinced that repealing the Articles of Confederation offered the best hope for his country; he was certainly also aware that it gave him the best chance at a commission in a federal navy.[7] While many who had served in the Continental navy favored the new charter, few went so far to see it approved as John Barry. Watching from the gallery at the Pennsylvania ratifying convention, Barry was disgusted when Antifederalist delegates, aware that they lacked the votes to prevent ratification, left the convention. Their departure prevented the establishment of a quorum, so a vote could not take place. Barry, likely with the collusion of Speaker Thomas Mifflin, led a gang of sailors to the inn where a few of the truant assemblymen dined peacefully, prematurely celebrating the success of their plan to block the Constitution. The convention lacked only two delegates for a quorum, and Barry's gang unceremoniously seized James McCalmont and Jacob Miley, two ringleaders of the Antifederalists, and dragged them—quite literally kicking and screaming—back to the state house. Relatively unhurt, the two recalcitrant delegates found themselves locked inside and forced to watch as their colleagues voted in favor of ratification.[8]

If the Revolutionary War hero expected gratitude for his extralegal activities, he was soon disappointed. To Barry's chagrin, McCalmont brought charges against him, which Benjamin Franklin, Thomas Mifflin, and even Barry's good friend Charles Biddle felt obliged to support, despite their great relief at Barry's actions. The matter quickly passed, however. Once the Constitution became the law of the land, none of its supporters could stomach the thought of an actual reprimand for Barry, despite the highly dubious legality of his actions, and the charges were dropped.[9]

The Constitution that Barry so strongly supported laid the foundation for a future United States Navy, while explicitly ensuring civilian control over any such force. The delegates vested the president with power as "Commander in Chief of the Army and Navy of the United States," while restricting the power to "provide and maintain a Navy," and "to make rules for the government of land and naval forces" to Congress.[10] Although it was obvious the militia system was woefully ineffective, the attitude of the times mandated some sort of compromise between federal and state power over soldiers on land; militia forces might be ineffective against foreign enemies, but the states regarded them as indispensable in blocking overreach by their own government. This political tension coupled with deep-rooted fears of standing armies made it impossible for the federal government to assume complete power over the states' militia forces (although Congress did gain the power to impose a measure of discipline on the militias and take command of those called into federal service[11]). At sea it was another story; the delegates ensured that any navy would be the sole prerogative of the federal government. By prohibiting states from granting letters of marque or maintaining ships in a time of peace, the new charter guaranteed that the constant squabbling between the Continental navy and the various state navies that mired the Revolution would not be repeated in future wars.[12]

The role of a navy also came up in the national debate over ratification. In *The Federalist*, Alexander Hamilton, James Madison, and John Jay argued strongly in favor of a naval force, citing Congress' ability to create one as a key reason for supporting the new Constitution. Only in a strong union could the individual states and regions come together to achieve "this great national object, a NAVY," one that would ensure the freedom of America's seagoing commerce and prevent envious European nations from "clipping the wings by which we might soar to a dangerous greatness."[13] This, of course, formed a crucial part of the Antifederalists' objection to the Constitution, since they feared the diminution of state power it promised. The ability of Congress to create and administer a navy was one of the Antifederalists' main targets, with Southerners in particular fearing that such a force would grant inordinate power to New England states, where shipping dominated the economy. More broadly, opponents blasted a navy as frightfully expensive, and therefore requiring massive taxes to sustain—the very thing the country had just declared independence to oppose. Not only that, it threatened to draw the nation into Europe's regular wars, with all the taxation, armies, and centralization of power that came with them.[14]

Finally, opponents of the Constitution argued that creating a navy also meant creating a naval officer corps. Military leaders, whether they command forces on land or sea, have "a different interest from and opposed to the civil power," argued one Antifederalist delegate.[15] While naval forces' role at sea physically separated them from the government and population, thereby making them less of a threat to liberty, opponents of the Constitution still feared the creation of an officer corps whose values would be antithetical to ideals of the Revolution.

On top of all this, Antifederalists argued that a navy was simply unnecessary, when the Atlantic Ocean acted as a perfectly good barrier against invasion.[16]

The Federalists ultimately triumphed, and the Constitution became the basis for a new American government. Yet the objections to a navy still carried considerable weight, and a maritime force did not follow automatically after ratification. Opposition still ran strong, and the fragile financial state of the new government precluded the immediate construction of a fleet. For many leaders of the new nation, however, an American display of force at sea was only a matter of time. Federalists like Alexander Hamilton saw the navy as indispensable in protecting American commerce and obtaining respect from European powers. Washington shared his treasury secretary's sentiments, as did first Secretary of War Henry Knox. While opposition to the navy almost entirely came from those who shortly joined the Jeffersonian-Republican party in opposition to the Federalists, not everyone in this camp was of one mind on the issue. A significant minority of those who became Jeffersonian Republicans and later vehemently opposed building a navy were supportive at the time, and recognized a very real need. Permanent navies, according to the political ideology of the day, did not threaten liberty the way standing armies did, since they were necessarily separated from most of the country and could not be used to enforce the will of a tyrant against the liberties of the people.[17]

Even Thomas Jefferson, who later reduced the American navy as president, believed a small force was necessary and advocated for its creation. The impetus for Jefferson's thinking was the need to combat rampant piracy in the Mediterranean, the same piracy that had resulted in more than a dozen Americans being enslaved in Algiers (including Cathcart and O'Brien).[18] Meekly paying tribute to obtain the prisoners' freedom and secure American commerce rankled Jefferson's free trade sensibilities, but he was far from alone in recognizing that with no naval force at all, there was nothing to prevent North African rulers from demanding whatever extortionate rates they wanted (a fact the British were quick to point out to all four Barbary states). The crews of the *Maria* and *Dauphin* experienced the reality of American weakness in brutal fashion as their captivity dragged on year after year. In 1793, the number of Americans enslaved in Algiers skyrocketed. Word reached the Washington administration in November that Algerian cruisers had seized eleven American ships and had enslaved in excess of one hundred American sailors.[19] The impact on American shipping was immediate and catastrophic; once-thriving commerce in the Mediterranean vanished. "Seamen who had braved the most awesome winter gales the North Atlantic had to offer were paralyzed by the fear of enslavement in North Africa," notes historian Ian Toll. "Vessels bound for the Straits of Gibraltar could not be manned at any rate of pay." The crisis threatened to devastate the already weak American economy. "Maritime insurance premiums doubled, and then tripled, U.S. government bond prices collapsed, and merchant houses were bankrupted."[20]

This news finally forced Congress to take decisive action. On March 27, 1794, it passed the Act to provide a Naval Armament (also known as the Naval Act of 1794), creating the United States Navy. The legislation authorized the building of a mere half-dozen ships, to begin immediately. Despite the American citizens enslaved within the Barbary regencies at the time, stiff opposition still ran through much of Congress, and the act passed only narrowly. Moreover, it ended ominously for naval advocates, promising that "if a peace shall take place between the United States and the Regency of Algiers," construction of the frigates must cease immediately.[21]

The creation of the U.S. Navy prompted a flurry of letters from more than a hundred applicants seeking officers' commissions. Selecting the first officers to lead the nation's incipient maritime force fell to President Washington and Secretary of War Henry Knox. Given his sterling Revolutionary War record, John Barry was an obvious choice for the most senior officer in the new Navy (John Paul Jones had died two years prior), and Washington and Knox sought his advice on appointments for the other five frigates. By doing so, they set a precedent that the future Navy Department would routinely follow. Civilian officials charged with selecting naval officers looked to those same officers to nominate their peers. In this case, the three men seem to have enjoyed a cordial working relationship. Barry praised Washington for ignoring "powerful interests" backing some unworthy candidates; "the President from the first was determined to come as near to justice as was in his power" and he selected the first officer corps based solely on each man's merit.[22]

By "powerful interests," Barry meant that the selection process for naval officers would be less politicized than for the Army. As one prominent historian noted, in the Federalist Era "commissions at all levels, as in England, could be bought—not with money necessarily, but with political influence."[23] Good connections mattered, of course, for Washington could not ignore politics altogether. Yet even the best connections would not suffice for a man who was unqualified. When Alexander Spotswood, the husband of one of Washington's cousins, wrote asking for a commission for his son, Washington rejected him on the grounds that men "who served with great reputation through the whole of the last war" had already applied in large numbers, "grounding their pretensions upon merit."[24] For Washington, the most important qualification for the job was proof of excellence in commanding ships at sea, not political bona fides or good breeding.

There were indeed plenty of veterans from the Continental navy (though a good number of these need not have bothered applying based on their performance), and to overlook that experience for political calculus would have been unseemly for a new republican government. The deeper truth was that selecting naval officers was simply different from selecting army officers. The conventional wisdom of the day held that a competent army officer brought most of the necessary skills and expertise with him to command. Leaders, civilian and military, assumed that well-educated gentlemen, men who expected and received deference in civilian life, could step in to command and gain whatever special knowledge they needed with ease. The navy was altogether different. Status as a gentleman was important, but not just any gentleman understood seamanship. A sailing vessel was one of the most complex technologies of its day. The British navy took in boys as young as eight, and rarely older than fourteen, and required them to spend years learning the science and art of seamanship before allowing them to advance to lieutenant.[25] The U.S. Navy would later take on young men without maritime experience as midshipmen to be trained up under experienced captains (Washington did tell Spotswood he *might* be able to appoint his son as a "second or third Lieutenant" at a later time). For the highest ranks, however, the new navy needed men thoroughly familiar with how to manage a ship as well as a proven record of commanding effectively. Barry believed the Washington administration succeeded, cheerfully reporting to Nicholson that "the appointments have given general satisfaction."[26]

The first six captains chosen were, in order of seniority, John Barry, Samuel Nicholson, Silas Talbot, Joshua Barney, Richard Dale, and Thomas Truxtun.[27] Seniority was based on each man's standing in the Continental navy at the close of the Revolution.[28] Truxtun, who would go on to tower over the others in the historical record, carried the distinction of being the only one who had not served on that force, having spent the war privateering. Truxtun also appears to have enjoyed the least political patronage, with no record of his receiving the endorsement of a prominent figure as part of his application to the service. Of course, given that Truxtun interacted with Barry when the two made merchant voyages to Canton, it is perhaps not entirely true that he had no political connections; he may have enjoyed the strongest connection of all: a friendship with the man helping the administration make its decision on who should receive captain's commissions. Regardless of how he got his commission, Truxtun did more than all the others to establish the Navy's reputation and prepare it for the future.[29]

Internal bickering in the Navy began before the first keel was laid. The seniority of the first six captains was determined by their order on the list, and this became an immediate source of controversy. As soon as he learned that he ranked behind Talbot, Barney flew into a rage. He fired off a lengthy letter to Knox demanding that he be elevated to what he considered his proper place in the order of seniority. Barney started by arguing that Talbot, who was serving in Congress at the time, had used his political connections to secure the highest possible rank for himself. Furthermore, Barney bolstered his claim to seniority by undercutting his rival's war record, insisting that Talbot had never actually commanded a ship at sea during the Revolution. This was inaccurate; Talbot, like Barney, had commanded more than one privateer over the course of the war, and he had also served as a lieutenant-colonel in Washington's army, most famously capturing a British floating battery and also severely damaging the British 64-gun *Asia* in New York Harbor using a fireship. In addition to an enviable record in the army, he had been appointed as captain in the Continental navy late in the war. Here Barney found a technicality that he could latch onto. Despite his numerous services to his country elsewhere, Talbot had never actually had the opportunity to command a ship after being appointed captain, due to the abysmal state of the Continental navy by the time he received his commission. Meanwhile, though he never attained the *rank* of captain, Barney had in fact commanded a few small ships at sea during the Revolution, earning him the honorary *title* of captain. He concluded that this merited him a higher station than Talbot in the new national navy.[30]

Secretary of War Henry Knox was not interested in Barney's complaints, and even less interested in setting a precedent of negotiations between the War Department and its officer corps. He brusquely responded that the order of rank was settled. Barney then returned his commission; although he had campaigned hard for the creation of the U.S. Navy, and for a spot in its officer corps, he had no intention of serving in a position he considered degrading. With Barney gone, President Washington awarded a commission to James Sever.[31]

Meanwhile, almost as soon as Congress approved the captains, the navy nearly disappeared. A successful treaty with the Regency of Algiers was ratified by the Senate in March of 1796, thus removing the immediate need for a naval force. According to the Naval Act of 1794, construction on the ships should have ceased immediately and the officers returned to civilian life. However, North Africa was no longer the only source of danger to American shipping. Relations had soured between the United States and its Revolutionary War ally, France. The Treaty of Amity and Commerce signed by the two countries during the American Revolution stipulated that each would come to the other's aid in future wars. In 1793, France had occasion to claim this clause, when Great Britain declared war to reverse the work of the French Revolution. Washington recognized that involving the United States in the conflict would be the height of folly, given the country's weakness and financial struggles. His declaration of neutrality infuriated the French, as did the new Treaty of Amity, Commerce, and Navigation, Between His Brittanic Majesty and the United States of America (the Jay Treaty), which many in France—and the United States, for that matter—saw as an economic alliance with Britain. The French Revolutionary government began authorizing privateers to seize American ships, which they could do with impunity thanks to inability of the American government to protect its merchant fleets.[32]

With the cries against French depredations becoming incessant, a compromise allowed work to continue on three of the frigates.[33] The War Department chose the vessels under construction in Philadelphia, Boston, and Baltimore—those closest to completion—and paused the other three.[34] John Barry, Samuel Nicholson, and Thomas Truxtun, the officers assigned to oversee construction of these vessels, retained their jobs. Their counterparts were not so lucky. Dale, Talbot, and Sever remained on the roll as captains but with no ships to command or duties to perform. Having already had to squeeze three ships from a tight-fisted Congress largely opposed to any naval establishment, the Washington administration found no justification for keeping these men on the payroll and released them from the American Navy.[35]

Dale returned to the merchant marine upon losing his ship—and his salary.[36] Talbot accepted the post of "agent for impressed seamen" and set out on a frustrating and largely fruitless sojourn to the West Indies, where the British routinely seized American sailors for their own navy. Talbot managed to secure the release of a few victims of British impressment who were indisputably American citizens, but he suffered continual frustration working with arrogant and otherwise occupied British officials. Following that, he too spent time in the merchant service.[37] The two captains' decision to pursue other endeavors is certainly understandable; at the time, neither man had any way of knowing when or if the government would ever require his services. Their time away from active duty in the military would, however, have serious implications in the future, and, in Talbot's case, nearly bring the U.S. Navy to a halt at the moment of America's greatest success against France.

While Washington managed to convince Congress of the need to complete the naval force already begun, a separate government department devoted to naval affairs was out of the question, and oversight remained with the War Department. As long as Henry Knox was Secretary of War, this arrangement worked well, for Knox was a capable and careful administrator.[38] His duties were also limited to overseeing construction of a mere six (later reduced to only three) frigates. There was no functional navy to man or to plan strategy or operations for. So far as the construction of the frigates was concerned, Knox delegated most of the responsibility to the officers themselves. Barry, Nicholson, and Truxtun were appointed superintendents of their respective ships and charged with constructing, equipping, and manning the ships they were to command, though they maintained regular communication with the War Department.[39]

With Knox's retirement from public life in January 1795, the civilian oversight of the new navy grew considerably weaker. Timothy Pickering served briefly as Secretary of War, but his tenure was uneventful as far as naval matters were concerned. Finally, Washington's old friend James McHenry assumed the duties of Secretary of War on January 27, 1796.[40] The choice proved unfortunate. McHenry lacked Knox's prestige and Pickering's administrative abilities. His most remarkable trait was what one historian dubbed an "easygoing" manner that was ill suited for the myriad responsibilities and powerful egos a man in his position faced.[41] Alexander Hamilton initially considered him "*very well-disposed*, but *very unqualified*," and later became convinced that "McHenry is wholly insufficient for his place, with the additional misfortune of not having himself the least suspicion of the fact!"[42] In time, Hamilton became the de facto Secretary of War, operating the War Department himself as the head of the Provisional Army, a situation not wholly dissatisfying to a man of Hamilton's ambition.[43] Despite McHenry's less than sterling record and qualifications, when John Adams assumed the presidency in 1796, he felt it best for the sake of national unity to retain Washington's cabinet, and McHenry kept his job.[44]

Meanwhile, the federal government's lethargy in building up a fleet to defend American commerce rankled Northern merchants. Increasing French depredations frustrated citizens of the nation's vital shipping centers: Baltimore, Boston, and coastal New England. That frustration mingled with patriotic fury when the so-called XYZ Affair became public. American emissaries to France were approached immediately upon arrival by agents, codenamed X, Y, and Z, who informed them that substantial bribes would be required before any negotiations could begin. When Adams made these overtures public, war fever swept the nation.[45] Fueled by anger at French haughtiness, and possibly to encourage greater action by their government, private citizens began taking up subscriptions to build warships that would then be put to the federal government's use.[46] Such generosity, while certainly helpful for a country seeking to build a navy from scratch, posed a real threat to civilian control. Washington, Knox, and Hamilton had tried desperately to rid themselves of the militia system specifically because localized forces diminished central control, and the potential that the towns, and especially the subscribers, who provided these ships would also want to dictate their use must have given pause to the new president, particularly since he had no Navy Department and an already overworked and unreliable Secretary of War at the time.[47] Fortunately, the subscribers proved willing to let their government use the ships as it wished, though they did exert some influence over the captains assigned to "their" vessels.[48] For example, the citizens of Philadelphia were instrumental in Stephen Decatur Sr. receiving command of the ship built by their subscriptions, which they christened the *Philadelphia*.[49]

The subscription warships were only one of many signs that the Adams administration's management of the U.S. Navy was lacking. The problem was not with Adams, one of the most enthusiastic supporters of a navy dating back to the earliest days of the Revolution. The truth was that managing both the Army and the Navy was too big a job for any one man, and particularly for Adams' ineffective Secretary of War. The rapid growth of the Navy to meet the crisis with France demanded a separate Navy Department. Fortunately, Adams would soon have the chance to name a sterling appointment to run the Navy, a man who would not only oversee a thorough defeat of French privateers, but also play a major role in shaping the naval officer corps for a generation to come.

# –3–

# "To Rid Our Navy of Such Men"

## *Benjamin Stoddert and the Creation of the Navy Department, 1798–1801*

**JANUARY 1, 1800.** A new century dawned inauspiciously for the American Navy. On the first day of 1800, eleven barges manned by more than four hundred pirates "armed with muskets, sabers and boarding pikes" swarmed the U.S. Navy schooner *Experiment* and its merchant convoy of four ships in the Caribbean "with the intention to board each of the vessels." In fierce action lasting in excess of five hours, the *Experiment* repelled three boarding attempts, and sank at least two of the attackers, but in the process also lost a pair of the ships in its charge. Particularly painful was the loss of the schooner *Mary*, whose captain was "inhumanely murdered" by the attackers. While the capture of two ships entrusted to his care frustrated the *Experiment*'s commander, Lieutenant William Maley, it was obvious that they were unavoidable given the becalmed waters and the overwhelming number of pirates launching the attack. Edward Stevens, the U.S consul general in San Domingo, was on board the *Experiment* the entire time and reported back that he was shocked any of the American ships, including his own, had survived the attack.[1]

By all accounts at the time Maley acted with prudence and courage, and made the best that could possibly be expected of the situation. His impressive performance never brought him any glory though. Within a year, he had been stripped of his commission and fired from the Navy.[2] As a final indignity, long after his death a story began circulating that he spent the entire battle in the hold of his ship. David Porter had served under Maley during the attack. In 1876, Porter's son, the Civil War hero David Dixon Porter, published a claim that Maley had turned coward at the sight of so many enemy ships and immediately ordered his crew to surrender without firing a shot. The heroic Porter, so the story went, led a mutiny that confined the commanding officer belowdecks, and then it was Porter, not Maley, who spearheaded the defense that saved half the convoy.[3]

The story is almost certainly false, though the younger Porter apparently accepted his father's account in good faith, and whether the elder Porter was guilty of slander or genuinely misremembered events is open to question (in his old age, he may have conflated Maley and another captain who was dismissed for cowardice after fleeing battle).[4] Maley's actual offense was capturing neutral vessels, repeatedly, as well as drunkenness, open quarrels with subordinates, and grotesque mismanagement of government funds and property. Such a lengthy list of scandalous behavior would doom any officer's career, but there was never a hint of cowardice in Maley's short stint in the Navy, even from those working to get him cashiered.

Still, Porter's version of events is telling when it comes to the first generation of naval officers in the United States. Porter crowns himself with glory by claiming to have committed mutiny, a crime that would normally lead to hanging—hardly something one would expect an aging captain to brag about to his son, particularly a son who was following in his footsteps as a naval officer. Yet Porter had come of age at a time when the U.S. Navy feared timidity far more than insubordination, and if the attack on the *Experiment* had gone exactly as Porter described, it is unlikely Secretary of the Navy Benjamin Stoddert would have censured him. Stoddert knew when to assert his authority, but while he happily jettisoned officers for incompetence, insubordination in itself was virtually never a firing offense. Indeed, Maley's case is telling. Even when presented with overwhelming evidence of the lieutenant's unfitness, Stoddert hesitated to let him go, simply because he had shown himself an active and spirited officer. Only when Maley's repeated seizures of neutral ships became unbearable did Stoddert finally dismiss him.[5]

For Stoddert, the foremost concern in building the officer corps was that men of action—men who would take daring risks and zealously seek to advance the nation's reputation abroad—should govern American ships. While he encouraged discipline on board ship and grew annoyed when officers failed to follow his orders, Stoddert worried far more about idleness and excessive caution than perfect subordination when evaluating captains. Writing to John Barry, Stoddert commented that a "spirit of enterprise and adventure, cannot be too much encouraged in our officers under your command, nor can too many opportunities be afforded the enterprising to distinguish themselves." Although such actions carried great risks for the country's undeniably few vessels, Stoddert's primary concern was not to avoid losing ships. "We have nothing to dread," he told Barry, "but inactivity."[6]

Stoddert's inclinations led him to something of a hands-off approach in his oversight of captains. Beyond providing broadly outlined orders, Stoddert allowed them considerable discretion in all matters of naval governance. He routinely consulted them on his decisions, and he tolerated behavior that came perilously close to insubordination, especially from officers whom he considered zealous and active. This mindset, and the attitudes it created among the officer corps, caused him difficulty late in his tenure, but slothful, careless, and overly cautious captains produced a far greater measure of grief. If Stoddert came to regret his excessive delegation by the close of the war, he also did an admirable job culling the ranks of captains whose timidity failed to bring credit to their country.

Stoddert's administration, and the officer corps that rose to prominence under him, played a defining role in the naval history of the United States. His term as secretary was crucial for the precedents it set as much as for the actual decisions he made. While naval administration evolved a great deal after Stoddert, it was he who determined the kind of character America sought in its naval officers, and all subsequent captains through the War of 1812, for good or ill, came from a mold that Stoddert established: aggressive, courageous, sensitive to any insult to their own or their country's honor, and nearly impossible to control.

John Adams assumed the presidency uniquely suited to address foreign policy concerns, having spent time as an American envoy in courts across Europe. He needed all that expertise, for he took office just as the war scare with France was beginning. The war effort finally gave Adams the widespread public support and the political capital he needed to build up the Navy. In addition to reviving construction on the three frigates abandoned during the Washington administration, the federal government set about purchasing merchant vessels for conversion into warships.[7] The task of overseeing all this, along with the final stages of construction on the three frigates, proved too much for the Secretary of War. McHenry's obvious inability and the growing size and responsibility of the Navy made it imperative that Congress create a Navy Department, and it finally did so in the spring of 1798. However, Congress left the exact prerogatives and powers of the head of the department vague. It was careful to note that the secretary's principal duty was to execute orders given him by the president, and otherwise transferred any powers over naval matters once held by the Secretary of War to him. It was assumed, though never explicitly stated, that naval officers would be subject to the orders of the Secretary of the Navy, but the act that established the Department of the Navy offered no guidance on the exact boundaries of the captains' authority, or on any practical matters relating to the oversight of the officer corps. The day-to-day details of the Secretary of the Navy's relations with the officer corps were left for the first secretary—and his successors—to work out on their own.[8]

Adams faced a daunting task in trying to find someone to accept the post. The federal government had little to offer talented men, and any capable secretary could certainly make far more money in private business. Adams' first choice, George Cabot, declined, citing his own lack of qualification. Cabot also noted his "life of indolence" for the previous two decades, which he felt rendered him physically unfit for the demanding workload of a cabinet officer. He did, however, offer up an assessment of the qualities the young republic needed in its first Secretary of the Navy. Besides the obvious need for someone holding "considerable knowledge of maritime affairs," the secretary should also possess a strong understanding "of the human heart" in order to effectively evaluate, motivate, and maintain his officer corps.[9] For all his doubts about his own fitness for the job, Cabot proved remarkably prescient. The man eventually chosen struggled with the personalities, foibles, and stubbornness of his officers as much as strategy, procurement, or seamanship.

Rebuffed by Cabot, the president then offered the job to merchant Benjamin Stoddert of George Town. Though not the man most coveted for the job, few could have questioned Stoddert's qualifications. A native of Maryland, he enjoyed a modestly successful merchant career before the Revolution and was commissioned as a captain in the Continental army during the war, where he suffered a severe wound at the Battle of Brandywine. He then honed his administrative skills as secretary for the Congressional Board of War. Throughout the conflict, the young Marylander received near universal praise; Colonel Thomas Hartley, who commanded Stoddert on a bloody expedition against hostile Native Americans, gushed in his report that "all the parties will acknowledge the greatest merit and bravery of Captain Stoddert. I cannot say enough in his favor; he deserves the esteem of his country." Stoddert's postwar mercantile career proved equally successful, although (like many of his contemporaries) land speculation cut deeply into his finances.[10] It seems the only person ill at ease with Stoddert's nomination was Stoddert himself. "I hate office—I have no desire for fancied or real importance," he complained to one friend, and after acquiescing to Adams' offer, he lamented that "in conferring the appointment of Secretary of the Navy upon me, the president could not also confer the knowledge necessary for the Secretary of the Navy to possess, to make him most useful to his country."[11]

The self-doubts and insecurities that Stoddert brought to the capital dissipated as he grew more confident in his abilities, but Stoddert always relied heavily on subordinates to manage naval affairs. In part, this was an unavoidable aspect of the primitive communications in the era. The great distances and slow mail service meant that "Stoddert . . . had to trust the local navy agent and vessel commander. Rarely was there a second opinion to guide the secretary."[12] Moreover the Navy Department had no apparatus for recruiting, training, or evaluating its officers in its early years and all these tasks fell, by default, to the officer corps itself. If Stoddert was dependent on subordinates, he also expected peak performance from those he trusted, and seldom hesitated to sharply reprove those who failed to measure up. In his life before government service, Stoddert could be exceedingly blunt with merchant captains who failed to meet his expectations. In words he would repeat many times as Secretary of the Navy, he expressed "very great mortification and surprise, that your ship still remains in the country" to a lackadaisical merchant captain, and delivered a stinging rebuke to an associate for mutual financial loss that, he claimed, "proceeded from . . . *your failure in your engagements.*"[13]

Stoddert's relations with his officer corps were mixed—a combination of soaring praise for some, deep trust with many, and an infuriating lack of communication or cooperation with others. But through it all, the civilian side of the civil-military relationship remained remarkably unified; Adams maintained a close working relationship with Stoddert. They conferred regularly in person, and Adams was always intimately involved in guiding naval policy. Stoddert, for his part, was unswervingly loyal to the president; even late in the administration when much of the cabinet turned on Adams, he had a faithful ally and friend in Benjamin Stoddert.[14] As secretary, Stoddert was careful to give Adams the chance to view his major letters to captains, which consistently received the president's stamp of approval.[15] He was also extremely scrupulous about keeping Adams informed of all the department's affairs, apologizing on the rare occasions when the speed of events forced him to act without consulting with him first.[16]

For his part, Adams consistently trusted Stoddert in naval matters. He overruled Stoddert infrequently, with the notable exception of the Truxtun-Talbot controversy (more on that later). Even then, he expressed regret at doing so. The two saw eye-to-eye on how the Navy should be managed and what expectations the department should have for its officer corps. Adams established the strategy for the conflict and seems to have provided considerable input on the details of ship movements, but he left the interaction with the officer corps to Stoddert. Adams inserted himself directly into the use of the Navy on only one occasion, ordering the *Merrimack* to sail and notifying Stoddert afterward, hinting in the letter of his displeasure at the number of vessels still in port.[17] This episode stands out in the historical record for its rarity. Correspondence between captains and the president is almost nonexistent, for Adams never gave the slightest hint that the Secretary of the Navy lacked his trust. That said, Stoddert's autonomy was hardly boundless; he consulted regularly with Adams in Washington, and his letters to officers routinely cite Adams' explicit wishes or orders. Throughout the Quasi War with France (1798–1800), it was Stoddert who signed the orders and communications to the officer corps, but he and Adams spoke with one voice.

For Stoddert, the foremost priority was that his officers be zealous in advancing the infant Navy's reputation, and he repeatedly stated his desire to purge those who failed to measure up; his desire to "rid the service" of the unfit comes up over and over again in his letters. "Our navy at this time when its character is to form, ought to be commanded by men who, not satisfied with escaping censure, will be unhappy if they do not receive and merit praise," he commented to Adams, adding, "I hope and I believe that there are several such men in the service."[18] Disgrace worthy of removal was not limited to cowardice in battle or neglect of duty either. Stoddert showed no patience with captains who dallied in getting to sea over difficulties he considered surmountable. Annoyed that one of his ships remained in port long after it should have sailed, despite multiple warnings, Stoddert complained, "I have always entertained an opinion that men who suffer trifling difficulties to interpose between them and their duty are unfit for public service. It shall be my endeavor to rid our navy of such men." Stoddert felt inclined to assume the worst when a captain failed to get to sea in a timely fashion. Although he acknowledged to Adams that he was unsure what circumstances kept Christopher Perry from sailing in distant Newport, the delay still diminished his trust in the captain. "Men of real merit," he commented, "always know how to get over difficulties."[19] He reiterated the same idea to Josiah Parker later, complaining that the country "had better have no navy than have it commanded by indifferent men, and it shall be my study to rid the service of such men." The consequences of timidity or sloth among the officer corps weighed heavily on his mind; the tiny fleet of a new and relatively weak nation depended on the character of its leadership to deter attack and generate respect for the United States. Officers of "zeal and spirit" might be able to "make up for want of great force by great activity." But if not, "we had better burn our ships, and commence a navy at some future time when our citizens have more spirit."[20] In writing to his captains, the first secretary promised he had a "determination to honor and reward, by promotion . . . the meritorious officers," but he again reminded them of his commitment to "rid the service of men who disgrace it."[21]

His hopes for the high quality of his officer corps were challenged by the massive expansion prompted by the Quasi War with France. Christopher McKee estimates that the corps under Stoddert ballooned from the three remaining captains to more than seven hundred officers in the four years the United States was at war with France.[22] There were two means for Stoddert to choose the officers who could lead America's Navy in the aggressive manner he desired. One was to select from among a host of applications himself. Unlike Washington's initial search, practical seamanship counted for surprisingly little to Stoddert. He and his successors did not care if an applicant had never left shore or even seen the ocean. He depended on the current officers to train newcomers. Far more important were an applicant's established personal character and quality education, and also good references.[23] Stoddert wanted not only men who were energetic and industrious, but who also exhibited staunch physical courage. As he explained to one correspondent, "Bravery is a quality not to be dispensed with in the officers. Like charity, it covers a great many defects."[24] In choosing from among a host of applicants which potential midshipmen best fit these criteria, Stoddert relied heavily on letters of recommendation from prominent citizens who knew the applicant personally.

For aspiring officers, having good connections to prominent citizens was a major asset. Yet there was one class of persons whose recommendations Stoddert valued far above all others: officers themselves. Stoddert looked to his senior officers to fill the ranks by appointing their own subordinates.[25] "I wish you would select, and nominate to me, suitable characters for your officers," he wrote to one captain, stipulating only that "men of courage, abilities, and patriotism, and such men only" be added to the ranks of "our infant Navy."[26] While a captain's appointment of junior officers had to be formally confirmed later, in practice the secretary rubber-stamped any acting commissions granted by his captains, and openly told his officers that such would be his practice.[27]

Beyond merely appointing their subordinates, Stoddert also looked to captains to maintain the quality of the officer corps, pressing them to punish those who merited it while also giving him detailed reports of anyone ready to move up in rank. He even encouraged Silas Talbot to bypass him and go directly to the president with the names of those the captain wanted appointed as midshipmen, assuring him that Adams would readily approve all recommendations. Stoddert also proved willing to delegate the task of pruning the officer corps to his most senior commanders. In the same letter to Silas Talbot, Stoddert urged him to try everything in his power to induce a few "unworthy" lieutenants to resign.[28] Stoddert felt strongly that meritorious officers should join with him in nudging out their peers who failed to measure up. In an enclosed missive to Talbot's apparently frustrated subordinates, Stoddert reiterated his theme of acting "to rid the service of them who disgrace it," this time urging that it was "the duty of all the other officers" to do so.[29] But Stoddert also proved willing to defer to his officer corps when they left men in place that he felt the service would be better off without. When a court-martial acquitted a young lieutenant of sleeping on duty, Stoddert clearly believed that the evidence was sufficient to cashier him but chose not to reject the court's findings.[30]

Even ashore, Stoddert was in no sense a micromanager, and he seldom bothered with details of constructing and outfitting ships. He did, however, expect careful returns on all expenses and strictly ordered captains to provide them.[31] Like Knox, Stoddert believed that the men who commanded ships at sea knew best to supervise their construction; the autonomy he allowed naval officers was little different from that given merchant captains, who also usually oversaw the outfitting, and sometimes the construction, of their vessels. Like all his predecessors at the War Department, Stoddert faced a daunting workload with a limited staff of five clerks, making delegation even more of a necessity than the communications of the era already dictated.[32] He could even be flexible on naval regulations when he felt circumstances dictated. In one case, he told a captain that although employing boys on ships was forbidden, he would allow him to do it anyway, copying a common practice in the British navy.[33]

The area where Stoddert maintained his authority to the greatest degree was in ship movements and overall naval strategy. Stoddert formulated the strategy for waging the war against France, and he oversaw the movements of the Navy accordingly.[34] Yet he by no means shut his officers out entirely in this realm either. He was willing, at times, to grant captains discretion on where they sailed.[35] That the leeway he granted them came in part from his own inclinations and not solely from pressure brought to bear by the officer corps can be seen in Alexander Murray's response to his orders. Murray felt honored by the "extensive and unconfined latitude" he enjoyed, "leaving me at large to act as my judgment shall dictate." The freedom granted Murray had a salutary effect, with the captain moved to assure his superior, "I will not disgrace your confidence," a vow he reaffirmed later with a promise to "achieve something of moment that will meet with your approbation."[36] Early in the war, Stoddert even sought Truxtun's advice on "the manner of employing our force."[37] He also leaned on his officers for more general oversight of the Navy. When Stoddert considered revising the naval regulations originally penned by James McHenry, he assigned Barry, Truxtun, Dale, Stephen Decatur Sr., and Thomas Tingey to recommend new regulations.[38]

As far as what was expected of officers at sea, Stoddert's constant reminders to act aggressively did not always yield positive results. A zealous desire to win laurels for oneself and the country could be a double-edged sword, as many captains proved less careful than the administration would have liked in determining whether a ship was from a neutral nation before seizing it.[39] "Mistakes of this kind," Stoddert complained, "will lead us into quarrels with all the world." Having entrusted great authority to his officer corps, Stoddert felt the need to rein them in based on repeated errors on this score, reminding them that captains "must be governed by laws, and by their instructions founded on laws." Even at sea, a captain could not consider himself law—though he could come close with his own crew—but must remember that his duties were to the president. Furthermore, Stoddert expressed great displeasure at officers writing to friends and even to newspapers with commentary on the American war effort and executive management of the Navy. Doing so clearly violated the duty of a military officer to his government, provided the enemy with valuable information, and generally proved "injurious not only to the public interest, but to the officers themselves."[40] The practice of writing to newspapers seems to have ended once Stoddert directed his captains to cease doing so, though he continued to receive unsolicited advice from officers on a variety of matters for his entire tenure.[41]

The action that elicited the most anger from Stoddert by far was that of captains returning home early from cruises. This remained a constant problem throughout the war. Stoddert groused to one correspondent that if it had "not been for the unlucky return of so many of our vessels, there would be nothing to regret in the conduct of our navy."[42] John Barry, the senior captain and Revolutionary War hero, ranked among the worst offenders. Stoddert was "mortified" that Barry neglected a key part of his instructions in where to sail, cut short his cruise, and after his return lingered in port far longer than the secretary would have liked. Barry also proved lax in maintaining communication with the Navy Department, and his continued sloth in getting to sea and engaging the enemy prompted Stoddert to remind him to "set an example of activity and enterprise" for younger officers, lest they too begin displaying similar lethargy in performing their duty.[43] But Barry was not one of the younger officers; the normal effects of age coupled with the toll that years at sea had taken on his body had drained the energy out of one of the heroes of the Revolution.[44] His contemporaries understood this, with Stoddert considering him "too infirm for service," and complaining to Alexander Hamilton that he was "old and infirm."[45] Thomas Tingey somewhat less tactfully referred to him as "an old wife" in private conversation.[46]

If his highest-ranking captain caused him grief, the second on the list was even worse. Unlike Barry, Samuel Nicholson possessed a spotty Revolutionary War record.[47] His career in the Quasi War, on the other hand, proved far more consistent: his every voyage was a disaster. Nicholson repeatedly failed to make any effort at discerning the national origin of the ships he seized, to the point that Stoddert even toyed with having him arrested after one particularly egregious violation of neutrality.[48] If Nicholson's only offense had been lack of care in seizing vessels, that would have been frustrating enough, but he also displayed a tendency to return early from cruises and dallied in setting sail again even after he received orders to do so.[49] Moreover, he presumptuously ordered a subordinate captain to join his squadron, despite orders to the contrary from Stoddert.[50]

However vexing Nicholson could be, Stoddert held back from removing him from the service. His humanity clashed with his desire to rid the navy of incompetents, for he knew that Nicholson lacked income to support his large family, and he could not bring himself to leave Nicholson's children destitute. There was also the matter of the problematic captain's political clout. Stoddert cited his "respectable family" as a reason for overlooking this most blatant instance of him seizing a neutral ship; the subscript was that the captain's relations had enough influence to make life difficult for Stoddert if he tried to kick Nicholson out of the Navy. Whatever the reason, rather than firing his second-ranking officer, Stoddert stationed him where he could do no harm, granting him shore duty supervising ship construction on the pretext that he had been separated from his family for so long while at sea (although not as long as his orders actually directed).[51]

Isaac Phillips was not so lucky. He committed the opposite mistake: where Nicholson was too quick to act against another nation's vessels, Philips displayed too much timidity—and received no leniency whatsoever from the Navy Department. On November 16, 1798, while cruising off Havana in the *Baltimore*, Phillips encountered a Royal Navy squadron under the command of Captain John Loring. Loring hailed Phillips and asked him to come on board his flagship, the *Carnatic*. With the two countries at peace, and fighting a common enemy, Phillips probably saw nothing amiss in this and readily allowed British messengers to row him over. Any hopes he had of a friendly encounter vanished once he arrived on board. Loring, a native of America, had been a Loyalist and prisoner of war during the American Revolution. He joined the Royal Navy as soon as he obtained his parole. His hostility to his native country hung over all that followed. Although Phillips was clearly a commissioned officer in the U.S. Navy and the *Baltimore* a government ship, Loring dismissively asked, "Who is Ben Stoddert?" and claimed he had never heard the name before. Loring then made it painfully obvious that he felt not the least concern for whether the United States even had a navy, let alone whether the ship before him was part of such and announced that he would be taking desperately needed seamen for his own ship from among Phillips' crew. Whatever verbal protests the American officer might have made fell on deaf ears, and Phillips meekly returned to his own ship and obeyed British orders to assemble his crew and hand over his muster role. He watched in dismay as Loring's men carried off fifty-five tars, almost a third of the *Baltimore*'s crew.[52]

Perhaps reflecting on the enormity of his actions afterward, Loring did send fifty of the seamen back the following day. This small token made it easier for Phillips to sail his ship back to the United States, but it did him no good beyond that. Stoddert exploded when he read the report, telling his soon to be unemployed captain that "it is impossible to find an excuse for . . . your tame submission to the orders of a British lieutenant, on board your own ship." It was bad enough that Phillips had failed to put up any kind of defense against being boarded, but he had "descended further, and actually obeyed [the British officer's] orders to have all hands called, and to give him a list of their names." For such "degrading" conduct, President Adams summarily dismissed Phillips from the service, and revoked his commission as an officer.[53] Although the power to dismiss an officer rested solely with the president, Adams acted on Stoddert's recommendation. Stoddert made this point perfectly plain in a later letter, telling a correspondent, "If [Phillips] has been hardly dealt with I am to blame, not the president, who judged from my representation."[54] A spirited letter from Phillips defending his conduct got no sympathy from the secretary. Even if he lacked the force to prevent the British from taking his men, Stoddert informed him, Phillips should have maintained a vigorous defense and, if defeated, struck his flag and surrendered his ship as well as his crew.[55] Obeying orders from another nation's officer, and thus making the American navy subordinate to Britain's, was unforgivable.

Despite the obvious hopelessness of his case, Phillips continued to campaign for his old job, or at least to punish Stoddert and Adams for dismissing him. He enticed several of his subordinates on the *Baltimore* to resign in protest to his dismissal. Although this delayed the ship sailing again, Stoddert shed no tears at their loss.[56] The example made of Phillips apparently had a salutary effect. When a British officer came on board the *Ganges* in February of the following year, Captain Thomas Tingey boldly informed him that he would not muster his crew, as he "considered all my crew Americans by birth or adoption." Tingey, a former officer in the Royal Navy, knew from experience exactly what was expected of a captain when his country's sovereignty was at stake. He informed the British officer that his men could not produce individual protections commonly carried by American seamen at the time, because their protection was the American flag flying from atop the vessel. Just in case his crew felt any doubt as to their safety, Tingey called all hands on deck after the British left and reiterated that not one of them would be taken unless the British first slew him in combat. He received a rousing three cheers from his crew and praise from the president.[57]

While Tingey's boldness impressed Stoddert, his favorite among his officers was Thomas Truxtun, supposedly the least qualified of the initial six captains. Despite his infamous display of disrespect to the Continental navy, Truxtun enjoyed a close relationship with Stoddert and embodied his civilian superior's ideal of a naval officer. He served his country not out of any pecuniary interest, but to perform great deeds that would outlive him. "Does any man enter into [naval service] for the sake of subsistence," he rhetorically inquired of his brother officer, Richard Dale. The answer, to Truxtun, was perfectly self-evident: "Are not glory and fame the grand incentives?"[58] He possessed tremendous courage in battle and zeal in pursuing the enemy. In part, this was a function of his desire for personal fame and honor, but he also took his duty to his profession very seriously. After holding the Continental navy in contempt, he was determined to ensure that his country's new naval force commanded the respect of Europe. That meant building the Navy on the British model, and Truxtun sought to emulate the Royal Navy in establishing an American tradition at sea.[59]

Emulating Royal Navy discipline, however, did not always sit well with his crew. He began his first cruise by facing a potential mutiny, and the angry seamen only relented after being threatened with court-martial and execution.[60] Tellingly, he learned of the mutinous plotting from Stoddert, who forwarded him a letter sent by anonymous members of the *Constellation*'s crew to Congress. The speaker of the House had no interest in intervening between a naval officer and his sailors, and forwarded the message to Stoddert, who likewise preferred to let Truxtun handle the matter himself.[61] The Adams administration, and its Jeffersonian-Republican successors, showed far more concern for a stable military hierarchy at sea than the Continental Congress had, and officers in the early U.S. Navy thus enjoyed much greater latitude in their dealings with seamen than had their Revolutionary predecessors. At the time, and for decades afterward, captains faced almost no interference whatsoever from civilian authorities on the treatment of their crews. If seamen had any grievances, their only option was to appeal to the captain of the ship; any party above him that they reached out to would likely just ignore them, or, at this case shows, warn the captain and leave them to face his wrath. There were unwritten limits, of course. An unofficial contract existed between officers and men, a common understanding of the expectations and privileges of the crew, but when they felt their officers had violated this contract, sailors' only options were mutiny or desertion, both of which carried substantial (even life-threatening) risks.[62]

Likewise, there was none of the democratic ethos of the Revolution in Truxtun's relations with his junior officers. Truxtun complained endlessly of the lazy, intemperate, and often insubordinate bunch he took on his first cruise, but rather than appeal or negotiate with them, he expressed the view that the Navy's only recourse was to "purge well at first," a view that Stoddert agreed with wholeheartedly.[63] In contrast to Phillips' scandalous behavior, Truxtun placed a subordinate officer under arrest for allowing just one of his men to be taken by the Royal Navy.[64] But merely performing the bare minimum of one's duty was inadequate in Truxtun's mind. In speaking to one lieutenant, he cited the infancy of his country's naval service in urging his lieutenants not to be "idle and indifferent spectators of what is going on"; rather, they should instead display a "minute attention to duty."[65] Truxtun eventually created a book for superior officers to list all their complaints against inferiors, which he planned to forward to Stoddert regularly.[66] He keenly felt the youth of the U.S. Navy, and the need for officers devoted to its reputation, urging his lieutenants not to expect the comparatively luxurious treatment of their peers in European navies, but instead to tell themselves, "I prefer the attention I owe the infant marine of my country, to every indulgence, and pleasure," at least until such time as the service had established itself.[67]

Truxtun's autonomy over his subordinates extended to who was allowed to make up the junior officer corps. He reserved for himself the discretion regarding which officers to push out of the service and which to retain. He chose not to bring charges or report to Stoddert when a troubled midshipman struck a superior officer during a confrontation.[68] He even ignored Stoddert's and Adams' repeatedly stated desire that only men of proven character and good reputation be named officers, appointing the son of a close friend in hopes that naval service would transform him into "a useful member of society."[69]

Truxtun's relentless discipline of his officers and crew paid off. Despite his seemingly constant complaining about their laxity and sloth, he worried that other captains would become jealous at how quickly his subordinates received promotions.[70] His officers eventually recognized that they were fortunate to have him as a mentor, even to the point of declining independent commands to remain under his tutelage.[71] The *Constellation*'s captain may have thought little of the men under his command, but they performed well enough to make their ship the first in the republic's Navy to capture an enemy vessel. In a fierce action on February 9, 1799, the French frigate *L'Insurgent* surrendered to Truxtun. The battle was a remarkable victory for the infant Navy of the United States. The *Constellation* lost only one man killed, compared to seventy French sailors. Truxtun was justly proud of what he and his men had accomplished, and he basked in the profuse praise of his country upon reaching home with his prize.[72]

The lone death among the *Constellation*'s crew was a seaman named Neal Harvey. He was slain not by French guns, but by one of his own officers. After apparently giving evidence of cowardice in battle (exactly what he did is unclear), Lieutenant Andrew Sterrett ran him through with a sword. Sterrett felt no qualms about his actions after the fact, boasting to his brother, "We would put a man to death for even looking pale on board this ship."[73] While the Republican press blasted Harvey's killing as deliberate murder, the administration took no action, and indeed it is unlikely a president from the

Jeffersonian party would have retaliated against Sterrett either. It was the responsibility of the officers to squash any displays of cowardice among their men, and summary execution in battle was a perfectly acceptable practice in the British and French navies of the time. Later, in the War of 1812, David Porter gave a thirteen-year-old midshipman orders to shoot a sailor who fled in the heat of battle.[74] While naval regulations imposed a requirement for a court-martial to punish men with more than a dozen lashes (a requirement routinely ignored), in the heat of battle a captain's authority was even more absolute, and Sterrett's decision to kill Harvey brought no repercussions from Adams or Stoddert.

Meanwhile, in the heady aftermath of victory, Truxtun took to critiquing the administration's handling of the war effort. In his report to Stoddert, he famously announced that French Captain Michel-Pierre Barreaut "tells me I have caused a war with France, if so I am glad of it, for I detest a thing done by halves."[75] Truxtun's inclusion of his opinion of government policy clearly crossed the line separating the military force and its civilian government. Moreover, it identified Truxtun with the radical wing of Adams' Federalist Party, which broke with its president and loudly clamored for a declaration of war, even as Adams strove to keep the conflict contained. Alexander Hamilton, who acted as the leader of the radical Federalists, hoped to shore up his own power by openly challenging the president's desire to avoid war.[76] No doubt he was delighted to read the administration's policy publicly critiqued by the Navy's premier captain. Truxtun's thinly veiled criticism of his own government flouted the authority of civilian control of the military. With the Navy short on victories and in desperate need of popularity, and with Truxtun a national hero, the department apparently chose to overlook his implied criticism.[77] Like Sterrett's slaying of Harvey, the matter was ignored.

Truxtun's euphoria over his capture was short-lived. With the war expanding—if still not declared—the government recalled Richard Dale, Silas Talbot, and James Sever to service in the summer of 1798. Talbot was already preparing to return to sea when Truxtun captured the *L'Insurgent*. Ostensibly, Talbot outranked Truxtun. He had been ahead of him on the initial list of captains and had never resigned from the Navy. Truxtun, however, was by far the most successful of America's captains, and he felt that his accomplishments—and Talbot's time away—made him superior in standing to Talbot. While he had willingly agreed to be last among captains at the outset of his career, sensitivity over the issue of rank set in very soon thereafter. As early as 1796, he was horrified at the slightest rumor that Talbot might return to the Navy, citing both the British and French precedents that active duty officers surpassed in rank those who spent time away from service.[78]

In truth, the question of relative rank had vexed Stoddert from the beginning of his administration.[79] In September of 1798 he dealt with officers contesting the chain of command. Rather than explicitly order two officers to accept their relative standing based on the dates of their commission, he told them that such standing would remain in place until Adams ruled with finality.[80] Alexander Murray, one of the captains involved in that dispute, soon needed additional soothing, after he wrote to Stoddert to protest being placed under Truxtun's command. Murray's objection, Stoddert claimed, "gave me real pain," and he assured his injured officer that "nothing was ever farther from my thoughts, or the thoughts of the president, than to do any act, which might imply a distrust of you."[81] While he was nothing but conciliatory here, within a few months his patience for officers complaining about their rank seems to have worn thin. He mildly rebuked a master commandant for complaining about his standing vis-à-vis officers commissioned to newly constructed ships. Stoddert informed him that he should be satisfied with his condition, although the letter is nonetheless primarily an attempt at conciliation.[82] Even though he could sharply reprove any officer who displeased him, with those he favored Stoddert found it difficult to issue directives he knew they would object to, and in matters of relative rank he preferred to conciliate, or else pass the issue on to the president.[83]

Conciliation was impossible when it came time to rank the three captains recalled to service, and Stoddert knew immediately that it would be difficult—he hoped not impossible—to keep any of them from resigning in protest. "Talbot and Dale," he warned Adams, "contend for the rank given them by first appointment in 1794: And without obtaining it, I fear neither will continue in the service." However, "if they do obtain it, I fear Truxtun, a man of equal merit, will not."[84] Adams held off on making a definitive statement on the matter, instead deferring to the Navy Secretary's judgment.[85] For his part, Stoddert queried the rest of the cabinet (whether on his own initiative or at Adams' request is unclear), and all agreed that Truxtun now outranked both Dale and Talbot.[86]

That was enough for Stoddert. Dale initially threatened to quit rather than be subordinate to Truxtun, but after extensive pleading Stoddert convinced him to remain in the service. Still, after withdrawing his threat to resign his commission, Dale demanded leave for a lengthy merchant voyage to India, which the Navy Department granted him, despite the country being at war.[87]

Talbot was another matter. Stoddert pleaded with him throughout the summer of 1799 to accept a commission as the fifth captain in seniority, repeatedly promising that he would do everything in his power to keep him from serving anywhere near Truxtun, and thus rendering the question of their relative rank moot. He also pointed out that due to Barry's age, Nicholson's shore-bound assignment, and Dale's furlough, he would be the second-ranking captain actually at sea. It was simply an unfortunate circumstance, Stoddert insisted, that had allowed Truxtun to leap over Talbot, but now that the matter was done there was no reason for the returning captain to feel the least bit slighted. Staying in the Navy, even at a lower relative rank than he had before "never can be interpreted to reflect the smallest discredit to your reputation."[88]

Even as he negotiated with Talbot, Stoddert painted a somewhat disingenuous picture of the situation to Truxtun in a desperate effort to only have one captain at a time threatening to resign from the service. He wrote his favorite captain assuring him that his status in the Navy was perfectly safe. "I do not think you need to be under the least uneasiness on the subject of rank," he promised, for the "heads of all departments concur in my opinion, that you must rank from 1794—Talbot from 1798."[89] He was happy to report that Dale had already agreed to serve with his rank relative to Truxtun altered, and he was confident that the matter would soon be settled for good. "Talbot," he cheerfully forecast, "I expect will also acquiesce."[90] Truxtun apparently took him at his word, but in the process, he could not resist taking another shot at Stoddert's personnel policies. When he learned that Dale had negotiated a furlough out of the deal, he sent a not-particularly subtle rebuke to Stoddert for allowing an officer to leave the service while his country was at war.[91]

Apparently realizing the cabinet was stacked against him, Talbot sought allies, marshaling the influence of his most prominent political connections to lobby on his behalf. Henry Knox's relationship with Talbot dated back to the Revolution, and Talbot had appealed to their friendship in 1794 when he sought a commission in the new navy. Talbot now turned to him again for help in the controversy with Truxtun.[92] Talbot also called on Alexander Hamilton, the former Treasury Secretary, right-hand man of George Washington, and de facto commander of America's Provisional Army to present his case before the president.[93] This was likely not the wisest move, since Adams and Hamilton were embroiled in a nasty feud at the time.[94] Still, when the situation came to a head in the coming months there could be no doubt that Talbot possessed powerful friends.

There was also the matter of Talbot's actual commission. The crux of Stoddert's argument in Truxtun's favor was that although Talbot had been officially offered, and accepted, a spot in the Navy as a captain, by the time Congress got around to actually sending out the paper commissions, Talbot, Dale, and Sever were already out of the service. Accordingly, Stoddert sent him a commission dated 1798 and listing Talbot as fourth in rank behind Barry, Nicholson, and Truxtun. He also promised that he had brought the entire issue to Adams' attention and that the president would rule with finality on relative rank at a later time. In the interim, he once again promised not to force Talbot to serve anywhere near Truxtun where their disagreement on relative rank would become an issue in practice.[95]

Talbot ignored the new commission and Stoddert's promises—the only thing that would satisfy him was restoration to his original rank above Truxtun. Bypassing the Secretary of the Navy altogether, Talbot took his appeal directly to President Adams. In turning to the chief executive, he brought out his trump card: a threat to resign if the president refused to rule in his favor. This distressed Adams greatly, for Talbot was to assume command of the *Constitution* and sail as soon as possible to protect vulnerable American commerce. "Your refusal to accept the commission has ruined all my designs," Adams lamented to the recalcitrant captain. The president of the United States practically begged Talbot to serve with the question of relative rank undecided, echoing Stoddert's promise that he would never order him to sail anywhere near Truxtun, so the rank question would be a moot point. He and Stoddert both also promised to have the question settled by a council of officers at a later time, hoping that following the dictates of their fellow officers, rather than civilians, would be more palatable.[96]

Talbot refused to budge. "Neither my honor nor my reputation [will] permit me to be commanded by Captain Truxtun, because he [is], in fact, a junior officer," Talbot wrote back. If "from political or any other motives whatever" the administration was determined that Truxtun must outrank him, then he would have no choice but to "freely relinquish my present station, and retire to private life."[97] Having made his threat to resign abundantly clear, Talbot also met with Adams personally to plead his case. Given the earlier clash involving Joshua Barney, it was only human for Talbot to feel frustrated by the repeated campaigns to belittle his Revolutionary War service. In meeting with Adams, he made absolutely sure the president knew in exhaustive detail all that he had done and how important his services were in the war against Britain. He rehashed every single contribution he had made to the war for independence, and insisted that he deserved as much acclaim for his own martial services during the Revolution as Truxtun did for his victories against the French.[98]

Adams was convinced—or at least he was ready to have the whole messy affair over with. After meeting in person with Talbot, he wrote Stoddert a lengthy letter, elaborating all of Talbot's contributions in the Revolutionary War. In "talents, services, and general merit . . . Talbot will not suffer by comparison to any officer," Adams assured his Navy Secretary.[99] While Adams was no doubt sincere when he claimed to have reached his decision from "mature deliberation" and "impartial consideration of the whole subject," there was another factor that worked in Talbot's favor. In his first missive to Stoddert announcing he was favoring Talbot, Adams noted that the *Constitution* needed to sail immediately, and with Talbot at the helm it could. Had the government allowed him to resign, the entire war effort would have faced a serious setback.[100]

It fell to Stoddert to break the news to Truxtun.[101] To no one's surprise, the hero of the *Constellation* immediately tendered his own resignation. He felt insulted that the Navy did not fully appreciate his accomplishments, and he was every bit as committed to his own sense of honor as Talbot. "It as little becomes my character to yield my rank against what I think a well-founded right as it would my ship to an enemy unequal in force. I have therefore thought it proper to quit," he informed his officers on the *Constellation*, in the process undermining the selfless attention to duty he had worked so hard to instill in them.[102]

Truxtun did not, however, fade quietly into the sunset. One of his fellow officers, though upset at his decision to leave the service, took heart when he saw "in today's paper that he will still act as his own trumpeter."[103] "He might more aptly have been likened to a full brass band," comments Truxtun's generally sympathetic biographer. The wounded captain made sure his side of the story was not lost to the American public, loudly proclaiming his ill treatment to anyone who would listen. In the meantime, he was left to spend a few months simmering in his home at Perth Amboy, New Jersey.[104]

"This avarice of Rank in the infancy of our service is the Devil," Stoddert groused to Hamilton after losing his most successful officer.[105] Still, however frustrating Truxtun and Talbot's conduct might have been, the infant Navy had a limited number of experienced, successful captains to draw from, and none was more successful than Truxtun; the service simply could not afford to let him go. Upon receiving his irate captain's letter of resignation, Stoddert talked it over with Adams, and they both decided to ignore it and wait for his temper to cool before launching a campaign to entice him back into the service. They somehow convinced George Washington himself to invite Truxtun to Mount Vernon, where the Father of his Country urged him to reconsider leaving the Navy, especially when the nation was at war. Stoddert then personally went to Truxtun's home and asked him to return to the service. Whether bored with civilian life, believing himself indispensable to his country, or genuinely moved by the secretary's appeal, he agreed, but only on the condition that he never be ordered to serve under Talbot. This Stoddert granted.[106]

Having enticed Truxtun back into the service, Stoddert hastened to prevent any other officers from leaving over rank issues. Had he and Adams accepted Truxtun's resignation, and then readmitted him to the Navy, several others would have passed him in seniority before he returned. By bringing him back with his relative rank intact, the administration risked triggering another round of resignations. Thus, Stoddert's first move after readmitting Truxtun was to write a soothing missive to Stephen Decatur (father of the more famous Stephen Decatur, who was a young midshipman at the time), urging him not to also resign over relative rank. Once the other officers knew that the president had not accepted Truxtun's resignation, Stoddert expressed confidence that "it cannot give a moment's uneasiness" to them that they still ranked beneath him. Perhaps recognizing this statement for the wishful thinking that it was, he also appealed to Decatur's sympathies, describing the "great pain" he and Adams would feel if other valued officers left the Navy in protest.[107]

Even with the clash between Truxtun and Talbot settled, Stoddert's duties grew increasingly overwhelming. He briefly held dual roles as head of the Department of War and the Department of the Navy; at the same time, the massive increase in the size of the Navy during wartime had not brought a corresponding increase in his staff. He proposed creating a board of naval officers empowered to handle most of the logistical management of the service—under his authority, of course—but nothing came of it. In addition to overseeing the activities—and occasionally soothing the egos—of his officers, Stoddert often acted as a liaison between his officer corps and Congress. His duties included regular reports to the House of Representatives and Senate on naval activities, but he also advocated on behalf of the officer corps, especially in appealing for them to receive better pay. He also fought ultimately futile battles with a parsimonious Congress for the creation of the rank of admiral and a program of naval expansion, including construction of 74-gun ships of the line.[108] In addition to all this, he faced constant pressures from merchants, who always seemed to feel that he provided them with insufficient protection, and who cared little how many ships he actually had available to convoy them.[109] Defending himself before accusations of inadequacy or deliberate failure to protect all of America's commerce wore on him, and the strain began to show in his relations with his officers.

In the midst of such a workload, Stoddert understandably expected his captains to continue showing the initiative that he so prized. He was annoyed when officers looked to him to issue orders for steps that he felt they could easily take on their own authority, especially in terms of dealing with their own subordinates. He wrote James Sever to express his hopes that actions "so obviously dictated by common sense" had been taken without waiting for specific orders from him, and further urged Sever to deal as severely as necessary with a problematic junior officer, in hopes of driving him to either resign or commit some offense that would provide a pretext for cashiering him.[110] His concern with the sensitive feelings of captains also diminished; in writing a letter to Talbot, he crossed out a section reassuring him of the president's confidence in his abilities, and sent only a fairly terse list of directives instead.[111]

Even Truxtun did not escape censure. When he wrote the secretary asking for permission to court-martial several mutinous seamen, Stoddert testily informed him that he should have taken the initiative to do so himself, without consulting the department. Furthermore, he informed Truxtun that "I do not like this method of appealing to the head of the Department by officers who are themselves competent to the object of appeal."[112] The following day, he wrote Truxtun again, even going so far as to tell him to start acting as an admiral, incorrectly assuming that Congress would shortly create that rank. "You must act," Stoddert informed Truxtun, "with all the authority . . . as if you had command of the whole navy."[113] In the coming weeks, he must surely have berated himself for this choice of words.

Congress did not create the rank of admiral, at least not for another sixty years. Moreover, Truxtun took his injunction to act as though he controlled the entire Navy to heart, quite thoroughly. The following month, Truxtun approved a court-martial sentence and signed it "Thomas Truxtun, Vested with the power of Commander-in-Chief of the Navy of the US."[114] At the Norfolk shipyard, Truxtun brusquely ordered shipbuilder Josiah Fox to drop everything and attend to his ship, deliberately countermanding a written order from Stoddert that another ship had priority.[115] Finally, seeing Captain Alexander Murray's vessel idle in port awaiting instructions from the department, Truxtun ordered him to sail immediately, giving him instructions on his own authority, which, he believed, included command of "the whole Navy." Unfortunately, Murray sailed in the opposite direction Stoddert intended. The Department of the Navy needed him to relieve Talbot at Cape François, and when he left before orders reached him, Stoddert scrambled to find another officer to allow Talbot—and the large number of his seamen whose enlistments had expired—to return home.[116]

A horrified Stoddert sharply reprimanded Truxtun, informing him of Murray's intended duty in Cape François and adding that his hasty departure meant that his ship sailed without valuable supplies. Stoddert also, apparently for the first time, thought to instruct one of his officers on the details of civil-military relations. "I am extremely mortified," he complained, at the "unwarrantable" and "in every way improper" step taken by Truxtun. Seemingly reversing his earlier instructions, Stoddert noted that certain decisions "belong to the Executive exclusively." He warned, "You must avoid such interference in the future."[117] Within a week, though, Stoddert cooled down, and sent a very conciliatory letter to Truxtun, assuring him that the Navy would be able to work out all the confusions resulting from Murray's early sailing, and expressing a wish that Truxtun visit him in Washington if he decided to return from Norfolk by land.[118] He may have realized that he ultimately had no one to blame but himself for the episode with Murray, and likely felt some guilt for his outburst at an officer who genuinely believed he was fulfilling his superior's wishes. That Truxtun took a somewhat loose view of civilian authority should have been obvious by that time though, and by mellowing his earlier expressions of dismay, Stoddert may have missed an opportunity to pull his favorite officer off a road that would ultimately end in his ignoble exit from the service.

Meanwhile, the conflict with France dragged on, and Truxtun had no choice but to keep detesting the war effort, for Adams never ceased waging it "by halves." Even as Alexander Hamilton schemed to seize the power of the presidency from him and field a massive army, Adams sought a peaceful solution to America's differences with France. He succeeded in 1800. The two countries signed a new treaty, ending the undeclared conflict with absolute finality, although it would take years to sort out all the competing claims for damages.[119] For the remainder of his life, Adams regarded the peaceful resolution of hostilities with France as one of his greatest legacies, but at the time it cost him dearly. Having infuriated the radical wing of his own party, Adams fell to Thomas Jefferson in the election of 1800, and his cabinet prepared for a transfer of power.[120]

Adams and Stoddert knew all too well that Jefferson's backers included many of those most hostile to the creation of the Navy in the first place, and that the new president had won the election on promises of a dramatic reduction in federal spending. They spent their last days in office scrambling to lay a foundation that could survive the Jefferson administration. Stoddert reluctantly conceded that the peacetime Navy should sell all but thirteen of its frigates, but he could not resist trying again to get Congress to build 74s. Knowing the Jeffersonians would insist on reducing the officer corps, he campaigned for those released to receive half-pay for life, financed by the sale of the Navy's unneeded ships. Congress balked at much of Stoddert's proposed plan, instead allowing half-pay only for those officers who were retained but not on active duty. The captains released from the Navy received nothing. Jefferson also retained fewer captains than Stoddert would have liked, and the outgoing secretary lamented to Alexander Murray that the number retained was "too small to include all those who would do honor to any service."[121] Furthermore, the United States would not send out a 74-gun ship for almost two decades, and of the thirteen frigates retained, seven were stored "in ordinary" until such time as they might be needed.[122]

Although Stoddert did not leave the Navy as powerful as he would have liked, he did bequeath it an officer corps capable of future greatness. Barry and Nicholson, rendered ineffective by age and incompetence respectively, had been stationed on shore where they could do no harm. Both died in uniform without ever again setting sail. More importantly, captains who displayed cowardice or simply lacked drive had been made into examples. Phillips and Maley offered ample excuses for their poor decisions, but Stoddert was singularly unimpressed and removed both men. On the other hand, he readily tolerated threats to resign and hypersensitive egos from officers who brought credit to the service. Truxtun, for a time, was allowed to remain on the Navy rolls, even as he refused to perform any duties associated with the job. Even after he returned, he dictated to the department what orders he would accept, refusing to serve in any capacity that might cross paths with Talbot.

Stoddert not only tolerated behavior such as this, but also encouraged it by consistently calling for zeal and then ignoring overzealous behavior that bordered on (or obviously was) insubordinate. Those that met his expectations played a major role in choosing subordinates, determining strategy, and enjoyed near-total autonomy over their crews. Robert Smith, who followed him in the Navy Department, inherited an officer corps that was daring, bold, and zealously determined to combat any enemy. On the other hand, he had to manage a group of officers who showed a willingness to include their civilian superiors and each other among their list of enemies. Thomas Jefferson and Robert Smith assumed command of a competent but highly contentious officer corps, and like Stoddert, they would spend much of their time struggling to control it.

# –4–

# "To Make an Impression of Our National Character"

## *The Navy in the Tripolitan War, 1801–1807*

**AUGUST 1, 1801.** A British flag drooped in the mild breeze from the mast of the American schooner *Enterprise*. Lieutenant Andrew Sterrett was engaged in the common practice of disguising his ship's nationality to improve his chances of luring his prey close. Seldom has the ruse worked more perfectly. Early that afternoon, an unsuspecting Tripolitan corsair, the *Tripoli,* came alongside Sterrett and gleefully informed him that they were seeking American merchantmen to capture. Their excitement turned to horror as Sterrett dropped the British flag and replaced it with the Stars and Stripes. The American lieutenant hurriedly called his men to battle, later boasting that "the officers and men throughout the vessel behaved in the most spirited and determined manner, obeying every order with promptitude and alertness." They needed all their fighting prowess, for the ensuing battle lasted for over three hours. Three separate times the Tripolitans tried to board the *Enterprise,* and each time they were repelled "with great slaughter." Repeated feigned surrenders caused the Americans to hold their fire, only to give the enemy time to regroup and strike again. Incredibly, none of Sterrett's men were killed in the fighting, and their tenacity paid off when the now significantly smaller Tripolitan crew finally surrendered in earnest.[1] "The carnage aboard was dreadful," Sterrett reported. Twenty men, a full quarter of the crew, lay dead, and another thirty were wounded. The ship itself sustained crippling damage, and was little more than a hulk.[2]

But it was still the Bashaw of Tripoli's hulk. Sterrett found himself in the awkward position of having just captured a vessel of a nation not technically at war with his own. Congress had not declared war on Tripoli, and the ever-scrupulous President Thomas Jefferson refused to grant his officers authority to take enemy vessels as prizes, even if they engaged them in self-defense. And so, even as Sterrett basked in the glow of victory, he prepared to release his capture, but only after throwing its guns overboard and stripping it of the ability to do much of anything beyond limp back into the port of Tripoli.

When word of the *Enterprise*'s exploits reached Washington, Federalists and Republicans alike were quick to heap praise on Sterrett and his men. Jefferson, however, was far more controversial. Infuriated Federalists wondered how the president could have possibly allowed such a weapon of war to slip through America's fingers and back into the hands of its enemies. The president's political opponents were quick to attribute incompetence—or worse—to Jefferson for what had happened, but in truth Sterrett's orders were a natural result of a new nation still figuring out how its institutions would function. Jefferson entered office with a strict view of the war-making powers the Constitution granted the president, and the war effort against Tripoli suffered in its first year as naval officers struggled under limitations imposed by the government. Ultimately, Jefferson's views of presidential authority evolved but little, as Congress, including Federalists, explicitly authorized a much more aggressive campaign against Tripoli.

Aggressiveness proved very agreeable to most naval officers. Stoddert succeeded in purging the officer corps of timid, cowardly, or simply lazy officers, and a rising generation of lieutenants and young captains displayed the zeal for duty and honor that the first Secretary of the Navy so prized. Robert Smith, Stoddert's successor, took a similar view of what constituted a good naval officer. While he did not write as extensively about the need for a passionate and vigorous defense of the nation's honor, his track record of praise and penalizing clearly cultivated the same attitudes among young officers as had Stoddert's. This came at a cost—in the Mediterranean, junior officers seemed to fight with each other as much as the Tripolitans, and many promising young gentlemen had their lives cut short by duels. This was bad enough, but Smith also came perilously close to losing some of his most valuable captains over questions of honor. John Rodgers almost fought duels in the theater of war that could have, very easily, left the squadron without a suitable commodore. Fortunately, he backed off both times, but upon returning from the Mediterranean after the war ended, Rodgers and Captain James Barron threatened to defy the Navy Department's orders and leave their respective stations to meet on the field of honor. Creating a bold and courageous officer corps was only the first step; the Navy now had to channel those traits into engaging the enemy, not one another or the Navy Department.

In the war with Tripoli, civil-military relations included a new aspect. Rather than only interacting with the president or, most often, his civilian representative in the Secretary of the Navy, officers now engaged with civilian diplomats to a much greater degree. The representatives Adams sent to France to end the Quasi War had little direct interaction with the Navy, but in the Barbary Wars American emissaries worked alongside naval officers, and the division of responsibilities was seldom explicit. In general, however, both sides fully understood where the initiative lay. Civilian diplomats waited for authorization from the commodore in command to begin negotiations. While naval officers freely entered into the diplomatic realm, negotiating directly with Barbary rulers and helping to establish acceptable terms, the Jefferson administration's civilian emissaries had little say in how the war was conducted. Successive commodores in the Mediterranean enjoyed good relations with American consuls, and often forged very effective teams in pursuing U.S. interests, but responsibility and authority always tilted in naval officers' favor.

The Navy played a significant role in Jefferson's presidency even before he took office. The election of 1800 ended in a tie between Jefferson and his supposed vice president, Aaron Burr. While Burr initially indicated he would step aside if all Republican electors cast votes for him as well as Jefferson (who no one doubted was the true Republican candidate), he later reneged and tried to use the uncertainty to his own advantage. A Federalist-dominated House cast ballot after ballot, without producing a decisive winner.[3] Key Federalist leaders approached both candidates through intermediaries, seeking concessions in return for votes. Gouverneur Morris openly informed Jefferson that the presidency would be his if only he would promise, among other things, not to abolish the Navy. Jefferson sharply rejected this advice, saying he would "never go into the office of president by capitulation, nor with my hands tied by any conditions."[4] Nevertheless, Jefferson appears to have tacitly authorized Samuel Smith to assure Federalist James Bayard that he would preserve the Navy if elected, and those promises at least helped members of the defeated party stomach the thought of Thomas Jefferson as their new president. After thirty-six ballots, he finally received the required votes.[5]

With the election settled in his favor, Jefferson could finally begin assembling a cabinet. Among his first decisions was one that must have chilled the Federalists who allegedly voted for him based on an implicit promise to preserve the Navy. Albert Gallatin, the man Jefferson chose to be head of the Treasury Department, was among the most vocal and uncompromising opponents of the Navy. He had vigorously opposed its creation as a member of the House, and was zealous to see debt reduced and public expense minimized as a member of Jefferson's cabinet.[6] Jefferson himself, however, had far milder plans for reducing naval spending than his critics feared. He entertained no illusions of disbanding the Navy, as so many Federalists accused, and he even intended to use the fleet in the Mediterranean from the start of his presidency. Jefferson trusted Gallatin's fiscal responsibility, but he had no intention of making the Swiss financial wizard the only voice in his administration.

Finding someone to counter Gallatin proved difficult, however. Jefferson first offered the job to Samuel Smith, a staunch Republican in the House of Representatives who enjoyed a thriving merchant shipping business. But Smith wanted to keep his seat in Congress, and refused. His brother Robert followed, and John Langdon turned down two separate offers. An increasingly frustrated Jefferson practically begged merchant William Jones to take the job, but Jones could not bring himself to leave his business unattended. "I think I shall have to advertise for a Secretary of the Navy," Jefferson moaned to Gouverneur Morris, before finally enticing Samuel Smith to serve as interim secretary until a permanent replacement could be found.[7] To avoid jeopardizing his standing in Congress, Smith refused any pay for the job and continued with his legislative duties.[8]

Meanwhile, the situation in the Mediterranean was unraveling rapidly. The United States always proved slow in delivering its promised tribute to the Barbary powers, and as it grew in economic strength during the Washington and Adams administrations, Barbary rulers naturally expected more lucrative treaties. For Yusuf Karamanli, the Bashaw of Tripoli, the incentive to declare war was even greater. Yusuf seethed at the American agreement with Algiers, which recognized the Algerines as the preeminent power in the Mediterranean and granted them greater tribute than any other North African principality. War with the United States—an untested power who, the British assured him, was incapable of a major military operation—gave him a chance to solidify his hold and the throne and increase his country's wealth and standing. Tunis and Morocco likewise began acting aggressively toward the infant republic, hoping for a better deal while also testing the new nation's strength and resolve.[9]

Rumblings of war trickled in to the capital early in Jefferson's tenure, but he hoped it would be possible to avoid open conflict. In the spring of 1801, he made plans to send a small squadron to the Mediterranean to assess the situation and bring back a report. Crucially, if any of the Barbary powers had declared war on the United States, the ships were authorized to defend American commerce and "sink, burn, or otherwise destroy" enemy vessels, but there was no no mention of taking them as prizes—the clause that ultimately forced Sterrett to let the *Tripoli* go.[10] Based on his reading of the Constitution, Jefferson doubted whether he had the power to do anything more than this without congressional approval, and in any case he preferred not to burden his administration with a foreign entanglement so early, distracting him from a domestic agenda of republicanizing the government and restraining an army whose loyalty was, he feared, in question.[11] To lead this fact-finding mission, the administration turned to the man who remained the most celebrated figure in the Navy: Thomas Truxtun.

The Jefferson administration quickly discovered that Truxtun could be just as much of a headache as an asset to the service. The hero of the *Constellation* was the obvious choice to command a squadron to the Mediterranean. He was the most successful captain to emerge from the Quasi War, and he was also recognized as the most effective mentor for rising young officers. But his aggressive temperament became, once again, a double-edged sword. Almost as soon as Jefferson moved into the presidential mansion, Truxtun raised the issue of relative rank again, rehashing in his usual excruciating detail how he deserved higher standing that Talbot, and asking Jefferson to move him up the captain's list. He acknowledged that he was (rather blatantly) violating the chain of command, but justified it by insisting he was "writing to you this letter as Mr. *Jefferson* and not as President Jefferson"—although of course it was only President Jefferson who could grant his request. Jefferson said as much in his reply, pointing out that even though Truxtun's "communication was expressly made to me in my private character, yet it is only as a public officer that my opinion can be of any consequence." His opinion: Adams was perfectly qualified to rule on the matter, and "it is expedient that questions of rank once settled . . . should not be disturbed again," otherwise no military could function.[12] Truxtun remained behind Talbot for the time being, although his rival left the service just four months later, no doubt to Truxtun's great relief.[13]

Truxtun again butted heads with the new administration when he received his orders for the Mediterranean. Upon learning that Jefferson lacked any definite idea if the nation was at war, and intended the squadron only as a means of gaining intelligence and providing its seamen with experience, Truxtun balked. "Peace can afford no field for me on the ocean," he complained, and he only wanted command of the squadron if it was authorized to "act decisively." The member of Jefferson's cabinet charged with overseeing the launch of the squadron had no interest in a major confrontation with one of the nation's most popular war heroes. This happened while Jefferson was still in search of a permanent Secretary of the Navy, and Samuel Smith was juggling his congressional and Navy Department duties, while only being paid for one. He allowed Truxtun to decline command of the Mediterranean Squadron without resigning his commission—to, in essence, refuse one set of orders in hopes more agreeable ones would be forthcoming.[14] Besides his desire to avoid having it out with Truxtun, Smith followed the practice of the Royal Navy, which for most of the eighteenth century routinely granted its officers the right to decline any command that they considered threatening to their honor as gentlemen.[15]

After Truxtun's refusal, Richard Dale commanded the squadron, setting sail in early summer of 1801. Upon returning just under a year later, he brought the unwelcome news that Tripoli had indeed declared war on the United States, and that Sterrett and the men of *Enterprise* had already fought a battle with a Tripolitan cruiser.[16] Even after Sterrett's fight with the *Tripoli* opened the war, Dale had struggled with what to do next. His orders authorized him to defend American commerce and "chastise" the enemy, but said nothing beyond that. Throughout the summer and fall of 1801, Yusuf entertained limited communications with Dale, in which he indicated at least some interest in a temporary truce, but the commodore did not believe his tightly restricted orders allowed him to enter such a parley, and the opportunity passed.[17] If Dale did not consider himself able to negotiate at all, his view of his ability to wage war was little better. He contented himself with blockading the port of Tripoli as best he could with inadequate resources. Dale perceptively informed his government that a complete blockade was impossible, especially without gunboats to stop smaller ships from hugging the coastline where the water was too shallow for frigates to attack. Moreover, he believed a blockade would not force an honorable treaty in and of itself, and he asked his superiors to authorize an attack on the Tripolitan capital.[18]

There is no way to know what would have happened if Dale had been authorized to act as both a diplomat and military officer. It seems unlikely that the Bashaw would have agreed to any terms the administration would have accepted, given the difficulties the next three commodores had ending the war. In any case, at the time the aspect of Dale's instructions that came back to haunt Jefferson was the failure to authorize taking prizes or prisoners. While the nation rejoiced at Sterrett's heroism in defeating the *Tripoli*, the fact that he let her go took most of the shine off his victory. While the Navy's officers studiously refrained from commenting on their president's policies in this case, the Federalist Party was under no such obligation. Still seething over losing power in the recent election, Federalists pounced on the president for sending the Navy against a hostile nation with—in their minds—inadequate authority to actually engage the enemy. Alexander Hamilton led the charge, firing off no less than eighteen articles in the pro-Federalist *New York Evening Post*. The president's decision-making, Hamilton asserted, "ought to alarm all who are anxious for the safety of our government, for the respectability and welfare of our nation," further accusing Jefferson of "making a most prodigal sacrifice of constitutional energy, of sound principle, and of public interest to the popularity of one man." Jefferson's view of his authority to wage war, Hamilton argued, amounted to "nothing less than this, that *between* two nations there may exist a state of complete war on the one side—[and] of peace on the other" (emphasis in original).[19]

Jefferson was no doubt annoyed at his longtime enemy's attacks, but he also recognized that securing an honorable peace with Tripoli required negotiations backed by much greater force. He immediately made plans to send another, more powerful squadron against Tripoli, this time with the power to wage war. He appealed to Congress for authorization to take Tripolitan vessels as prizes, establish an effective blockade, and generally do whatever was necessary to force the Bashaw to grant peace on acceptable terms. Congress granted Jefferson everything he asked for.[20]

For the next squadron, it was not Samuel Smith who issued the orders, but his brother Robert. After declining the post once, Robert Smith had finally agreed to act as Jefferson's permanent Secretary of the Navy the previous summer.[21] After such a lengthy delay in finding a secretary, Jefferson had begun to grow desperate, and appealed to Samuel to intercede with his brother on the administration's behalf. The elder Smith's appeal apparently worked, for Robert accepted the job on July 13, 1801.[22] One historian speculates that Robert Smith's main qualification for the job was that he could draw on his brother's advice.[23] Even less flattering, it was hard for observers to avoid thinking the younger Smith's main qualification was that he had caved and taken the job when everyone else refused. Neither assessment is fair. Robert Smith had ample exposure both to government and the sea. He served lengthy terms in the Maryland house and senate, and at one point he had the chance to join the state supreme court. His law practice focused heavily on admiralty and maritime cases, not surprising given he hailed from Baltimore, one of the most significant coastal cities in the nation, and his family had long ties to the sea.[24]

Although initially reluctant to take the job, Robert Smith went on to become one of the most significant Secretaries of the Navy in history.[25] He proved an extremely capable and energetic administrator, but he never had unfettered control of his department. Jefferson took a keen interest in naval affairs, and every major decision on commands, strategy, and deployments bore his personal approval. Like Adams and Stoddert before them, Jefferson and Smith enjoyed an excellent working relationship, and they were generally of one mind on naval matters, including how to deal with the Barbary corsairs. The glaring exception was Jefferson's gunboat program. Smith had doubts about it, though he ultimately followed the president's wishes without much objection.[26]

Within days of ordering the new squadron to take on Tripoli, Smith lost the services of two of the nation's most distinguished captains. Firmly committed to the position, the younger Smith was prepared to take a harder line with his captains than Samuel had done, and this trait manifested itself almost immediately. Having led the first expedition with skill and insight, Dale seemed a logical choice to take the next squadron against Tripoli. Smith tapped him to return to the Mediterranean in the winter of 1802. In the same letter that ordered him to begin preparing to assume command of the squadron, Smith broke the news that the reduction in the officer corps following the end of the Quasi War meant that there was no captain junior to Dale who could serve as flag captain. Traditionally, the commodore would have an officer under him to handle the day-to-day affairs of running the flagship, freeing the commodore to devote all his time and energies to the overall squadron. Given the Navy's recent contraction, Smith informed Dale that this tradition would have to be set aside, and he would have to balance both commanding his own ship and the fleet as a whole.[27]

Dale objected, writing back to Smith and suggesting that if only Congress would create the rank of admiral, *any* other officer in the Navy would be his subordinate and therefore eligible to serve as flag captain. If such Congressional action was not forthcoming, Dale sought the same privilege Truxtun—and most British officers—had enjoyed, to decline command of the squadron. Robert Smith, however, was not interested in British precedents or overly concerned about what privileges officers had once enjoyed. "Congress will not . . . pass a law this session authorizing the appointing of Admirals," he brusquely informed Dale, before adding that "from the tenor of your letter I perceive it is also necessary to state to you, that no Officer of the Navy can consistently be allowed to decline at his will & pleasure a service to which he may be ordered by the President."[28]

This was too much; believing his prerogatives as an officer were being violated, Dale immediately tendered his resignation. Smith was sympathetic, responding with praise for Dale's long service to his country and wishing him success as a private citizen. What he did not say in his response is telling though. There was no mention that perhaps some arrangement was possible that could entice Dale back into the service, nor did he plead with the aggrieved captain to reconsider. A more marked difference from the way Adams and Stoddert approached the clash between Truxtun and Talbot is difficult to imagine; Dale said he wanted out, and that was that as far as Smith was concerned.[29]

Eager to get the expedition to sea, Smith hastily ordered Truxtun to take command from Dale, rightly calculating that wartime service would be more to the aggressive captain's liking. Truxtun, however, was even more upset than Dale about the lack of a flag captain. Besides, he found the idea that there was no officer suitable to command a ship that Smith could order to serve under him more than a little insulting—he was, after all, the preeminent officer in the Navy, and anyone else should be honored to serve as his flag captain. With his status on the line, he sought to force Smith's hand. Making no effort to conceal his motives, Truxtun informed the secretary that he had "a reputation to lose which I am very tenacious of," and demanded a flag captain to command the *President*. If he could not have this, "I must beg leave to quit the service."[30] Much to his dismay, Smith responded to him in the exact same way he had to Dale. He accepted Truxtun's resignation without hesitation, and sent another officer, Richard Valentine Morris, to replace him.[31] Truxtun's storied naval career was at an end, this time for good.

For the rest of his life, Truxtun adamantly insisted that he had not actually intended to resign his commission, only to decline command of the squadron, just as he had done a year prior. His defense hinged on the idea that a captain could decline any particular set of orders he disliked, and that when he begged "leave to quit the service," a complete resignation was actually the furthest thing from his mind. In a pamphlet distributed to counter supposed attacks on his honor made by the *National Intelligencer*, Truxtun insisted that had Robert Smith ordered him again to set sail, he would have done so despite the absence of a flag captain. What he had written at the time indicates otherwise; Truxtun quite explicitly said he wished to "quit the service," not "the squadron," and it is difficult to imagine Smith interpreting this as anything other than a resignation. Most likely, Truxtun did intend for Smith to interpret his letter as a resignation, but he never meant for the secretary to accept it. He had, after all, quit the Navy once before, and in the end got back into the service with no loss of rank and all his demands met. It is not surprising that he tried such a successful tactic again the next time he felt the department did not fully appreciate his contributions. Times had changed by this point, however. Stoddert had pleaded with him to return to the Navy when the department was desperate for good captains. Now, the officer corps was smaller, but America's troubles were also focused in the Mediterranean, not spread out across the oceans wherever French privateers roamed. More importantly, every remaining captain was perfectly competent to command a squadron, and thus all of them were expendable. Truxtun was, in some ways, a victim of his own zealous desire to train up a competent generation of junior officers. Whatever his contributions to the service, he was not indispensable anymore.

Still, Truxtun's years-long campaign on his own behalf apparently moved Robert Smith at least somewhat, for in 1805 the secretary dusted off the proposal for a panel of officers that Adams and Stoddert toyed with when Truxtun was at loggerheads with Talbot. Smith wrote to Stephen Decatur alone at first, explaining Truxtun's argument and asking for Decatur's opinions. Decatur responded unequivocally that he did not "consider it in the power of an officer to resign any particular service he may be ordered to, however hazardous or disagreeable."[32] Smith then sent a circular letter to four of the Navy's senior captains. He asked the brothers Samuel and James Barron, Edward Preble, and William Bainbridge to give their professional opinion on Truxtun's claims and encouraged them to discuss the matter among themselves. The verdict was unanimous: Truxtun had specifically stated that he wanted out of the service. His letter could only be interpreted as a resignation, and therefore he was no longer an officer in the United States Navy.[33]

The unanimous response from the leading voices in the Navy shows how much attitudes had evolved by the end of the Tripolitan War. There was, of course, something of an incentive for Decatur, the Barrons, Bainbridge, and Preble to reach the conclusion they did—had Truxtun returned to the service, he would have come back superior to all of them in rank. Still, with one voice they not only acknowledged Truxtun's plain intent to leave the service, but also rejected the idea that he could have simply declined a specific command even if that was all he wanted to do. A growing professional ethos within the officer corps was strengthening the sense of subordination to civilian authority, and Truxtun's breed of officer who viewed orders as conditional was increasingly unwelcome.[34]

Whether or not Smith and Jefferson anticipated a years-long quarrel with Truxtun, at the time of his resignation their most immediate concern was finding someone who could take the desperately needed Mediterranean squadron to sea. They assigned the squadron to Captain Richard Valentine Morris. Even after Federalist criticisms, Morris' instructions, like Dale's original orders, limited him to defending American commerce from attacking corsairs and blockading the coast of Tripoli. He managed to fall short of even those restricted orders, however.[35] Bringing along his wife, young son, and personal servant, Morris dallied in Gibraltar for two months, enjoying the fine company of his naval brethren from Britain while the coastline of Tripoli remained open. Upon finally leaving Gibraltar, he took a less than direct course for Tripoli, escorting American and Swedish merchant ships, a decision for which the owners were no doubt grateful but which did little to aid the overall war effort. He then stopped off at Leghorn, where he *again* lingered longer than was absolutely necessary and arrived at Tripoli in late January of 1803, only to return to Gibraltar in March, just when the weather was optimal for Tripolitan cruisers to go out against American merchants. Finally, a disgusted Jefferson ordered Morris home to give an account for his lax efforts. He departed the Mediterranean for home on May 10, 1803, leaving John Rodgers in temporary command.[36]

Morris' lackadaisical blockade infuriated the president. "His progress from Gibraltar has been astonishing," Jefferson complained to Gallatin. "I know of but one supposition which can cover him; that is, that he has so far mistaken the object of his mission as to spend his time convoying." Even if Morris did interpret his orders that way, which seems unlikely given Smith's explicit instructions to maintain the blockade, Jefferson would not have been satisfied. Morris, the president went on, received "latitude" and "discretion" in his instructions based on the supposition that "he had an ambition to distinguish himself." In other words, the administration gave him vague orders assuming he possessed the desire for fame that animated so much of the officer corps, and that he would therefore make the most of any opportunity to engage the enemy.[37] Like Adams and Stoddert before them, Jefferson and Smith expected naval officers to pursue distinction zealously and give evidence of a willingness to risk their personal safety in combat. Young officers who were too brash or hot-tempered might be forgiven, even if they killed each other on the field of honor. But a mature commander who seemed too intimidated or lazy to wage warfare was inexcusable. Any officer who displayed such a lack of vigor with his country's reputation on the line was unworthy of his commission. Smith was equally incensed at the commodore's lack of communication. "We can obtain no information [from Morris] on what he is proposing to do. We have to generally rely upon others with respect to his movements," vented Smith to

John Rodgers. Not only had Smith just learned secondhand of Morris' having left Gibraltar—where he should not have been in the first place—but "neither do I know where he is or what he is proposing to do."[38] As soon as Morris set foot on American shores, Smith ordered a court of inquiry into his conduct.[39]

The court did not issue the ultimate rebuke on one of their own, ruling that Morris' actions did not result from "any deficiency in personal courage." While this was no doubt a relief to the commodore, the verdict still stung. It conceded that he rendered some "essential services" to the Navy, but he nevertheless failed to "throw any degree of luster upon our arms." Simply performing the minimal requirement of his duties, without gaining honor for the service, was not enough. The court ruled that Morris might have been an acceptable commander of a single ship, if another stood in authority over him, but was unfit for command of a squadron. While it could have been worse, the court's findings were damning enough, and Morris resigned in shame. In the meantime, John Rodgers was left in temporary command in the Mediterranean until a replacement for Morris arrived.[40]

That replacement was Captain Edward Preble. Sharp-tempered, aggressive, and thoroughly committed to his duty, Preble embodied both Stoddert and Smith's ideal naval officer. Political considerations, however, did intrude somewhat into his selection. The captain, despite leaning toward the Federalists in his political outlook, managed to build a close personal friendship with the Secretary of War, Henry Dearborn, a friendship that probably played a decisive role in Preble receiving command of the squadron.[41] After a lengthy illness that nearly ended his naval career, he threw himself into the task of waging war on Tripoli with enthusiasm.

Preble's aggressive temperament was a welcome change for Jefferson and Smith after Morris's disastrous stint in the Mediterranean, and they made it clear in their orders to the new commodore that they expected him to execute his campaign with zeal. Preble's instructions included a stipulation that the "conduct for some time past pursued by our squadron in the Mediterranean has, unhappily, not been calculated to accomplish the object of government nor to make an impression on the enemy of our national character. We have therefore transferred to you the command of our forces in that sea in full confidence that you will maintain the dignity of your station and the FLAG of your country will not be dishonored in your hands."[42]

Preble clearly took this directive to heart, and he pounced on the first opportunity to show that he was made of sterner stuff than his predecessors. Late one evening while off the coast of Cadiz, Spain, an alert lieutenant spotted an unidentifiable ship through the haze. Hastily summoned from his quarters, Commodore Edward Preble hailed the strange sail. "What ship is that?" he inquired, only to have the same question thrown back at him. "This is the United States' frigate *Constitution*. What ship is that?" he called back, again without receiving an answer. Annoyed, Preble shouted at the mysterious vessel, "I am now going to hail you for the last time. If a proper answer is not returned, I will fire a shot into you." The captain of the other ship finally revealed himself, announcing that he was Sir Richard Strachan of the Royal Navy's *Donnegal*, which boasted eighty-four guns. "If you fire a shot, I will return a broadside," he warned the American commodore, then curtly commanded him to "send your boat over."[43]

Preble's mercurial temper ignited. Jumping atop the netting, he thundered back at the British, "This is the United States' ship *Constitution*, forty-four guns, Edward Preble, an American commodore, who will be damned before he sends his boat on board of any vessel!" He then gave orders to his gunners, loud enough for the British to hear, to "blow your matches boys!" Minutes later, a lieutenant from the *Donnegal* frantically rowed over and offered his captain's apologies for the misunderstanding. The British vessel, he explained, had not expected to encounter an American, and, fearing that the *Constitution* was French, Strachan found it necessary to stall while his crew scrambled to quarters. Preble accepted Strachan's apology, and the two went their separate ways.[44]

The incident may have seemed insignificant, but Preble's performance had a profound impact on his crew. Not always the most popular of officers, Preble earned a healthy measure of respect from his subordinates by refusing to be cowed by a British vessel.[45] He also showed that he had the fighting spirit Jefferson and Smith had been looking for in a Mediterranean commander.

Also on board Preble's flagship was Tobias Lear. After spending over a decade as George Washington's personal secretary, Lear was now a fixture in the Jefferson administration, which had previously dispatched him as an envoy to San Domingo.[46] Lear's primary appointment was as consul general at Algiers, still the strongest of the Barbary regencies. He was also invested with "full power and authority" to negotiate treaties with both Tripoli and Tunis.[47]

The alleged "full" power to negotiate was not as expansive as he might have wished, for Jefferson declined to go into any great detail on the division of authority between the civilian consul and naval commodore. Lear replaced James Leander Cathcart who had fallen out of favor with Algiers, and he held the same ambiguous expectation of cooperation that the administration had imposed on Cathcart and Richard Valentine Morris. Morris had been instructed to "cultivate the best understanding with [Cathcart], and communicate frequently and fully, and cheerfully cooperate with him in all points relating to his mission." Crucially, Morris had not been entrusted with power to make peace, only to cooperate while Cathcart did so.[48] Preble was likewise ordered to "cordially cooperate" with Lear "in all such measures as may be deemed the best calculated to effectuate a termination of the war with Tripoli." Preble's orders contained an implicit clause that his duty was to bring military force to bear while Lear alone held the power to make peace.[49] Ultimately their effectiveness hinged on being willing to cooperate, as Lear's status as civilian representative gave him no authority to direct military operations, and in practice Preble held the initiative until the Bashaw was willing to engage in negotiations.

Early in the fall of 1803, Preble arrived in the Mediterranean, where he found Rodgers in temporary command. The two butted heads immediately. Rodgers had been as frustrated by Morris's handling of the war effort as anyone in Washington, and when he learned he had temporary command of the squadron, he eagerly looked to capitalize on the chance to perform great deeds for his country, and win glory for himself in the process.[50] But by the time he fought through foul weather from his station at Leghorn to the American station at Gibraltar, Preble was already there, and his moment to shine had passed. Smith had done them no favors in creating a murky chain of command, with Rodgers senior to Preble but technically recalled, and the junior Preble in command of the squadron, except for the ships Rodgers commanded for his voyage back home. Rodgers did not sail for home immediately, however, instead lingering to aid in putting tense relations with Morocco to rest.[51]

The needs of their country clashed with the two naval officers' prickly sense of honor, and for a time it was unclear which of these two values would prevail. The issue that finally made Rodgers lash out was Preble's decision to fly the commodore's pennant from his flagship, the *Constitution*. Rodgers felt insulted by this. Preble, who was by nature more conciliatory, wrote to assure him that he only flew the pennant so that the ships of his squadron would know where their commander was located, and not seek out a ship from another squadron for orders. He assured his fellow officer that the flag "is not hoisted for the purpose of injuring your feelings," and that he had "no disposition to be on such terms . . . as to injure the interests of our country." Preble expressed hope that Rodgers would let the matter rest.[52]

His hopes proved in vain. "Permit me to observe," Rodgers sniped back, "that this is not an affair between private individuals, and that my feelings *as an officer* have been most sensibly injured." Preble need not bother citing the will of the government to justify his pennant either. "I do insist that, if the date of your commission is subsequent to mine, *it is not in the power even of the government* to place you . . . in a situation . . . of treating me with disrespect" (emphasis added). Such language almost invariably would have preceded a challenge, but Rodgers held back from this drastic step, citing "the interest of our country." He promised to take the matter up again with Preble at a time when they were not on a distant station overseeing a war. In the meantime, he agreed to meet with Preble to discuss strictly naval and diplomatic matters.[53] The two apparently did set aside their differences for the sake of duty, but Rodgers left the Mediterranean simmering over this perceived insult; his willingness to make his honor subordinate to the good of the service was exhausted the next time an officer failed to show him proper respect.

Having set aside their animosity, Rodgers and Preble turned their attention to Morocco. Although technically at peace with the United States, Morocco had dispatched two ships to prey on American commerce, apparently in hopes of securing a more advantageous treaty. In consultation with James Simpson, the American consul at the Moroccan city of Tangiers, Preble decided it was time to show the Barbary States that not all his countrymen were in the mold of Richard Valentine Morris. "I am fully aware that it is in our interest to have peace with Morocco" Preble wrote back to Smith, but added that the Moroccans must never believe the United States was so weak and "over anxious" that it would take peace "on any terms they choose to dictate." Preble was determined to show his country's strength and secure the respect of the Barbary powers along with peace, insisting to Smith that "cringing to those barbarians will not answer."[54] Preble made sure no one could accuse him of cringing. He arrayed the full military might of the U.S. Navy off the Moroccan coast, then pressed the Sultan, Maulay Sulaiman, to affirm his 1796 treaty with the United States. After a few tense days, Sulaiman relented, and Preble and Rodgers happily went their separate ways, the former drawing confidence from the fact that his tenure in the Mediterranean was off to a wildly successful start.[55] The two civilians present, Simpson and Lear, took part in the negotiations, but their contribution was confined to "able advice and assistance."[56] It was clear that Preble was, at the very least, an equal partner with Lear in the entire process, while Rodgers also added his stamp of approval to the return of two captured Moroccan vessels.[57]

Besides his tense relationship with Rodgers, Preble also had to deal with the rest of the officers under his command. As with Stoddert, Smith preferred to stay out of interofficer relations, and Dale, Morris, Preble, and later Samuel Barron all had essentially complete freedom in their dealings with subordinates. During his tenure in command, Preble took it upon himself to purge unfit junior officers from the service. He never presided over a court-martial during his stint in the Mediterranean, finding it much simpler to write a letter of resignation for any officer he deemed beyond salvaging and hand it to the offender to sign.[58] He could show mercy as well, however. While on shore leave in Syracuse in December of 1803, Midshipman Walter Boyd became roaring drunk and displayed blatant public intoxication, even abusing several locals. Exactly what Boyd did is unclear from the report sent to Commodore Edward Preble, only that he was guilty of some form of "abuse." His attacks were not only against the civilian inhabitants of Syracuse, however. Two lieutenants, either also on leave or sent to find Boyd, ordered him back to his ship, whereupon Boyd began verbally assaulting them as well. When one officer, Lieutenant Jonathan Thorn, grabbed him, Boyd tackled his superior and it took three other officers to drag the riotous sailor back to his ship. Preble immediately placed him under arrest.[59] After sobering up, Boyd sent the commodore a contrite letter, and promised to conduct himself honorably from that point on.[60] Apparently seeing promise in the young man, Preble granted him a second chance.

Alcohol was not the only thing that could get young officers in trouble. Their own sense of honor, mixed with minute quarters and boredom, could be deadly. The Mediterranean squadron saw an explosion of duels, often for the pettiest of slights. One young man died for refusing to remove his hat upon entering a room; others traded shots over a spilled container of ink ruining a new vest, and another lieutenant sacrificed his life "for the preference in a simple game of billiards."[61] Prevailing views on honor made it difficult for men to avoid duels even when they wanted to. When Midshipman Richard Somers laughed off his friend telling him he looked "like a fool" in his new hat, the rest of his messmates persecuted him relentlessly for his supposed cowardice. He was only able to prove his manhood by challenging all six of them to duels in succession. The affair was called off after Somers traded shots with three of his persecutors, but only because the aggrieved midshipman was too delirious from blood loss to keep going.[62] Midshipman Joseph Bainbridge almost created an international incident when he killed the personal secretary of the British governor of Malta.[63] The crop of junior officers sent to the Mediterranean were the "men of spirit and enterprise" that Stoddert had so eagerly sought, and when they found themselves unable to wage war against the enemy, they soon turned their weapons on one another. Moreover, with personal honor at stake, no man could refuse a challenge and hope to preserve his reputation in the officer corps.

While it was surely frustrating for Smith to learn that so many of his promising young officers were falling to each other's bullets, he never took any steps to address the problem. Captain Alexander Murray proposed amending the naval regulations to stipulate harsh penalties, including the revocation of commission, for anyone who participated in or failed to prevent a duel.[64] Nothing came of it. Other captains did take steps to curb the practice. Even Stephen Decatur, a man who eventually died in a duel, issued standing orders after he became a captain that all disputes among his subordinates had to be referred to him for arbitration before resorting to the field of honor.[65] Yet the Navy Department accepted this as a frustrating but unavoidable aspect of the officer corps. After all, the kind of naval officers that Stoddert and now Smith sought out—men of zeal, courage, and aggressiveness—were just the sort of men most prone to engage in duels. While they were by turns frustrated and grieved by the loss of promising youths, they never inserted themselves into matters of personal honor among the young gentlemen under their authority.

Preble had little to say about dueling among the officers of his squadron, for he had much larger concerns: bringing Tripoli to heel and proving his country's mettle to other watching nations. Much to his dismay, his grand plans for the assault on Tripoli soon suffered a devastating setback. In October 1803, fate dealt one of the Navy's unluckiest commanders its cruelest blow yet. William Bainbridge had already suffered the indignity of losing a schooner in the Quasi War (he was heavily outnumbered and escaped without censure) and having his ship forced into transporting cargo for the Dey of Algiers prior to the Tripolitan War. Having returned to the Mediterranean in command of the frigate *Philadelphia*, Bainbridge strayed too close to shore in his pursuit of a Tripolitan vessel. The ship grounded on the rocks and refused to budge. The men of *Philadelphia* desperately tried to get their ship free, but to no avail, and soon Tripolitan cruisers surrounded them. Fearing that he faced a choice of surrender or blowing up the ship and all on board, Bainbridge chose the former. "I never presumed to think that I had the liberty of putting to death 306 Souls because they were placed under my command," he insisted to Preble.[66] To his great humiliation, the Tripolitans freed *Philadelphia* and sailed it triumphantly into the harbor just hours after he surrendered.

Preble was mortified when he learned of *Philadelphia*'s fate. "Would to God, that the officers and crew of the *Philadelphia* had one and all determined to prefer death to slavery," he bemoaned, concluding that "it is possible such a determination might have saved them from either."[67] The commodore eventually softened his view of Bainbridge, particularly after the captive officer managed to smuggle secret communications out of Tripoli and became a vital source of intelligence.[68] In the short term, however, Preble's more pressing concern was depriving Tripoli the use of one of his own country's finest frigates. In a daring late-night raid on February 16, 1804, a young lieutenant named Stephen Decatur led a party into Tripoli Harbor where they set fire to the *Philadelphia*'s magazine and transformed it into a gigantic fireball lighting up the city. When the smoke cleared, the frigate was a smoldering hulk. In an instant, Yusuf Karamanli lost his prize and Stephen Decatur became a household name.[69]

No one was more thrilled with Decatur's victory than Edward Preble. He fired off a letter to the Navy Department recommending Decatur for promotion to captain.[70] Jefferson and Smith were only too happy to comply, and Decatur received his commission in the next set of letters to reach the Mediterranean. Not everyone was pleased with this outcome, however. In fast-tracking Decatur's advancement, the Navy Department allowed him to skip over several other lieutenants who had entered the service before him—including Andrew

Sterrett, the man who had heroically captured a Tripolitan vessel back in 1801.[71] Charles Goldsborough, chief clerk of the Navy Department and a close confidant of Secretary Smith, anticipated the problems Decatur's promotion would cause, and he (possibly at Smith's prodding) wrote a private letter to Preble suggesting Decatur decline the promotion. Such a noble "deed would justly bear the character of sublimity," Goldsborough promised, before offering an only slightly delusional vision of the other lieutenants rushing forward to insist that Decatur be promoted over them. Yet the real value of the new naval hero declining his justly earned laurels was that "it would be the means of avoiding those bickerings & heartburnings which his promotion will create."[72]

The Navy got its bickerings and heartburnings aplenty. Decatur did not decline the promotion, and it is doubtful Preble even bothered to suggest it. Just as Goldsborough feared, Sterrett flew into a rage when he learned Decatur had been promoted while he still languished at lieutenant. He immediately resigned in protest, informing Smith that it was "incompatible with the correct principles of Honor to serve under" an officer who had previously been junior to him.[73]

Robert Smith was distressed to see him go. "Your high reputation as an officer and a Seaman and your distinguished energy might and probably would ultimately have raised you to the highest honors in the Navy," Smith lamented to him. "I regret much therefore that you have deemed it proper to resign." As with Truxtun, however, Smith refused to bargain with even the best officers who wanted out. "I cannot refuse, however painful it may be, to accept your resignation," the secretary concluded, and with that Sterrett was back in private life.[74] Robert Smith's sadness over his departure was no doubt sincere; days later he proudly presented Sterrett with a ceremonial sword voted to him by Congress for his capture of an enemy vessel, adding that his delight in presenting the award grew out of "the high sense entertained by your Country of your gallant conduct."[75] Smith's high praise for the departed lieutenant may have stemmed in part from regret that he had not promoted Sterrett faster, but regardless of his personal feelings about the young officer and the future value he might have been to the service, the Quasi War practice of haggling with officers about relative rank and begging them to remain in the service was over.

Meanwhile, Preble still had a war to fight. Even as he was celebrating Decatur's destruction of the *Philadelphia*, a new crisis emerged that again distracted his full energies from forcing Yusuf Karamanli to capitulate. He received deeply troubling intelligence that Tripoli's neighbor Tunis was preparing to declare war against the United States as well. With a more potent Navy than Karamanli's, Tunis posed an even more serious threat to American commerce, and Preble knew his squadron would be overwhelmed taking on both simultaneously.[76] He appealed to the Navy Department to send more ships. He did not, however, betray any hint in his letters to the department that he was intimidated by the challenges facing him; in fact, he seemed to revel in them. "Give me the means," he concluded, "and I will [render] the purchase of peace or the payment of tribute totally unnecessary in this Eastern World."[77]

Faced with the threat of two wars that would overwhelm his already inadequate fleet, Preble shifted his anchorage to Tunis harbor and sought to ease tensions there. Fortunately, the destruction of the *Philadelphia* seems to have put the Tunisian government in a more conciliatory mood.[78] In this instance, Preble happily handed the problem over to his civilian counterpart. The commodore placated the Bey of Tunis enough to convince him to table his grievances until Lear arrived from Algiers.[79]

Once he was confident his country's relations with Tunis were stable, for the moment at least, Preble hastened back to Tripoli to resume securing an honorable peace there. The three-hundred-plus Americans from the *Philadelphia* now in the Bashaw's hands did not help matters—Karamanli saw them as a trump card that would force the pesky new naval power to yield on his terms. Preble also learned what most of Europe had been forced to come to grips with: the geography of Tripoli made it a brutally difficult nation to force into submission. The coastline was both elevated and extremely rocky, making bombardment pointless; it was also too shallow for large frigates to approach. While the blockade was reasonably effective, assaulting the city itself was nearly impossible. A gunboat attack on the city yielded six captured Tripolitan gunboats and a hundred dead Tripolitans, but made no impact whatsoever on control of the harbor, or on the Bashaw's sense of security. An attempt to sail a fireship into the harbor and blow it up ended in failure when the ship exploded prematurely.[80] With each passing day, Karamanli became more confident he could dictate terms if he held out long enough.

And it was clear that Preble would be the one to accept or reject terms. Tobias Lear, in part based on the changed circumstances after the destruction of the *Philadelphia*, remained at Algiers and left Preble fully in charge of the war effort. That included the commodore offering peace proposals himself through a third party. Bonaventure Beaussier, the French consul at Tripoli, tried to mediate between Preble and Karamanli, but his job was made exceedingly difficult by Preble's deep mistrust of France's newfound goodwill toward America less than five years removed from the Quasi War.[81] Preble had his instructions, but he also had a clear conception of his own regarding what kinds of terms were acceptable. "I value the character of my country too highly to consent to a peace which the most powerful nation in Europe would blush to make," he wrote to James Leander Cathcart, the onetime slave in Algiers who now served as another longsuffering American representative in Barbary.[82] Preble consistently delivered demands that the Bashaw was unwilling to meet, indeed that Beaussier told him explicitly would be nonstarters with Tripoli's ruler.[83] Meanwhile, Lear functioned as little more than an observer, and a distant one at that.

Preble suffered a crushing blow in late spring of 1804 when word arrived from Washington that he was being replaced as commodore of the squadron. The decision was a difficult one for the administration, since Jefferson and Smith felt nothing but "unqualified approbation" for his "activity, judgment, and valor." Yet with the loss of the *Philadelphia* Jefferson had no choice but to send reinforcements, and once again the issue of relative rank reared its head. There was no officer senior enough to command the new squadron linking up with Preble in the Mediterranean, yet junior enough to serve under Preble. Instead, Samuel Barron, who sat above Preble on the captains' list, commanded the squadron.[84] When the new commodore arrived in September, Preble had the option of remaining with the squadron under Barron's command or returning home, and to no one's surprise he chose the latter.[85]

The new command structure suffered from more bruised egos and command intrigue. John Rodgers, still eager to earn fame and glory against the Barbary powers, served as Barron's second-in-command. Third was Captain James Barron, the commodore's younger brother and one of the most promising young officers in the Navy. The two brothers mingled freely, and Rodgers—not without reason—seethed that the younger Barron was sidestepping him and co-commanding the squadron. Tensions ran high among the three officers for the next several months.[86] Samuel's poor health only exacerbated the problem. With the elder Barron weak and, Rodgers judged, ineffective at commanding the squadron, Rodgers' belief that James Barron was actually exercising authority that should have been his grew in tandem with Samuel's frailty. Meanwhile, Lear's role remained unchanged—he was still tasked with negotiating peace with Tripoli, but could only begin when the commodore of the squadron believed the time was right and authorized him to do so.[87]

Along with the change in command of the squadron came another new development. William Eaton, formerly a captain in the U.S. Army and resident diplomat in Tunis, finally received permission to recruit Yusuf's brother, Hamet Karamanli, for an expedition to depose the troublesome Bashaw and establish a regime friendlier to the United States. Eaton and Samuel Barron sought to force the Bashaw to terms while Lear prepared to negotiate an end to hostilities.[88] This three-headed command structure was bound to create tension, all the more so since Eaton had a long history of friction with the Navy. He had repeatedly accused naval officers of neglecting their duties to him, and once took it upon himself to provide Secretary of State James Madison with a detailed account of every shortcoming displayed by his brethren at sea that he encountered (in fairness, many of his criticisms were not inaccurate, especially with respect to Morris).[89] He also wrote Alexander Murray to censure his conduct, prompting the captain to remind him that this was well outside his authority; "Our government," Murray responded, "will determine whether I was right or wrong in my proceedings."[90]

Finally free to launch his daring expedition, Eaton enjoyed great success. A force under his and Hamet's command captured the city of Derne, second only to the capital of Tripoli in importance, in April 1805. They immediately prepared to launch an attack on the capital. Jefferson, however, had never actually planned to assume responsibility for propping up a new government in Tripoli. Hamet had already failed as ruler of Tripoli once before, when he was deposed by his brother, and he lacked Yusuf's ability to manage affairs of state effectively. America's alliance with a potential usurper was intended solely as a way to put pressure on Yusuf, a fact Eaton never fully appreciated. While Eaton gleefully prepared to march on Tripoli, Yusuf Karamanli, suddenly in a more conciliatory mood with his brother threatening, began backing off his more outlandish demands. Samuel Barron concluded that it was time for negotiations, in part because he feared further attacks on Tripoli might prompt

Yusuf to slaughter the crew of the *Philadelphia* in retaliation. He gave Lear the go-ahead to engage Yusuf in talks. To Eaton's fury, the United States reached an accord that left Yusuf on the throne and even allowed him to extract a face-saving ransom for his prisoners.[91]

The United States paid $60,000 for the crew of the *Philadelphia*, despite Eaton's certainty that Yusuf Karamanli was on the brink of total defeat. Eaton then despondently evacuated Derne, leaving Hamet to face Yusuf's wrath with little hope of American support. The change in fortunes was "as strange a reverse in so short a time as was ever recorded in the disasters of war," he complained, lamenting that he had been "thrown from proud success and elated prospects to an abyss of hopeless wretchedness."[92]

Eaton vigorously proclaimed in pamphlets and correspondence that he could have secured a treaty without a penny in tribute or ransom, if only Barron and Lear had supported a final attack against Tripoli.[93] Once the Senate ratified the treaty, Eaton shifted his attacks to anyone who had supported it, and highlighted the country's shameful abandonment of Hamet. His outrage was fired by his awareness of his friend and former ally's ongoing hardships. Eaton kept up regular correspondence with Hamet for the remainder of his life, and advocated tirelessly for any financial support he could find. He wrote John Rodgers in 1805 asking him to grant Hamet an interview and telling him that the former U.S. ally was considering another operation against his brother with the help of the Kingdom of Two Sicilies. Nothing came of that, and three years later, Hamet desperately appealed to Eaton for help when his family was in dire straits financially.[94]

In his dismay over the treaty, Eaton found an ally in Preble, who wrote him to commiserate over the humiliating terms. The "sacrifice of national honor which has been made by an ignominious negotiation" sickened the former Mediterranean commander, and Preble expressed hope that the Senate would recall Lear and appoint Eaton in his stead.[95] Preble's commiseration with Eaton, however, came only in the form of private condolences; he never voiced any opposition to the treaty in public. Whatever his personal misgivings, he loyally stood by his government.[96]

As for Rodgers, he finally got his chance to crown himself with glory after the war with Tripoli ended. Although Preble had quieted tensions with them less than a year before, threats of war again emanated from Tunis, and Rodgers determined to settle U.S. affairs there permanently (and perhaps release some of his frustration at never getting a chance to command attacks on Tripoli). The issue in question was the capture by the American squadron of a Tunisian ship and its two prizes that had been trying to enter Tripoli while the port was under American blockade. Hamuda, Bey of Tunis, demanded the vessel's return. Rodgers flatly refused. While Rodgers insisted that the United States only wanted peaceful relations with Tunis, "Your subjects have assassinated that friendship," and "appear not to be sensible that any respectful considerations are due from them to the United States."[97] The Bey "has been in the habit of threatening us with war," Rodgers wrote to the chargé d'affaires at Tunis, but the Bey failed to understand that America was different from the other nations he bullied into tribute. If the Bey "provokes [the United States] to war, he will feel in less than six months from its declaration, that the wars he has hitherto been engaged in were, on the part of his enemies . . . lenity and affection."[98] Rodgers brought the full American force into Tunis harbor on August 1, 1805, and gave the Bey a day and a half to capitulate or face bombardment.[99]

Once again Lear was present and ostensibly heading negotiations, but it was clearer than ever where the initiative lay. Rodgers set the tone with his initial communication with Hamuda, threatening war and setting the terms of a peaceful settlement. After a brief exchange of communications between the Bey and Rodgers, Hamuda agreed to allow Tobias Lear to come ashore and engage in peace talks. Even then, Rodgers continued to set the terms of relations between the two countries. He informed Hamuda that avoiding a full blockade and naval offensive required him to choose one of three options: (1) sign a promise of perpetual peace in the presence of British and French ministers, (2) provide a security and send an official minister to America for future negotiations, or (3) "make such alterations to the treaty as [Lear] may require." Failure to submit to one would prompt Rodgers to impose all three. Hamuda reluctantly settled on sending a minister to the United States, and Rodgers sailed for home.[100]

Later, Jefferson indicated he was not particularly happy with Rodgers' aggressive treatment of Tunis, and he sent a conciliatory letter to the Bey, bearing both his and Secretary of State Madison's signatures.[101] Whether Rodgers ever knew about the president's displeasure is unclear, but it had no impact on his later career. He remained one of the most trusted and influential officers in the service.

By the dawn of 1806, U.S. interests in the Mediterranean were secure, and Jefferson looked to scale down the Navy. Rodgers was eager to return home, both because his young bride-to-be awaited him, and because he was convinced his honor needed defense. While he moved on from his spat with Preble, Rodgers never let go of his bitter grudge against James Barron, certain that the younger Barron had convinced his brother to hold out on yielding command of the squadron. Rodgers was hardly inclined, then, to overlook what he regarded as a slanderous attack on his character. In May 1806 reports reached him that newspapers back in America had accused him of drawing his sword and viciously running through one of his subordinates in a fit of anger (or shooting the unfortunate man dead, depending on the paper). He returned to the United States in the summer of 1806 determined to take revenge on all whom he believed had "injured" him, and he had no doubt that James Barron was the guilty party.[102] Furious, he wrote to Barron, assuring him that he was more than ready to meet him and "account for his claim."[103]

By late 1806, the conflict between the two had degenerated into a seemingly inescapable morass. James Barron insisted he fought for "vindication of his brother's honor,"[104] while Rodgers felt he had no choice but to take to the field of honor or face permanent disgrace. Rodgers named Thomas Tingey as his second, while Barron chose Franklin Wharton, both fellow naval officers. Fortunately, before the two could schedule an "appointment," illness seized Barron, and the matter had to be delayed.[105] In the meantime, the entire messy episode became known among the officers of the Navy and officials in Washington. Barron wrote in January of 1807 that the delay "has produced a family of opinion . . . greatly injurious to my character," and insisted that his health had recovered and the duel must take place soon, lest he be forever branded a coward.[106]

As the affair between two of his most senior officers reached its climax, the Secretary of the Navy finally broke his silence. Yet Smith was unwilling to address the approaching duel directly. Instead, he vaguely informed Barron that his "services will soon be required for purposes other than those to which they are now directed," an oblique reference to the preparations for meeting

Rodgers on the field of honor. He then pointedly ordered Barron to "give all your attention to the gunboat building under your direction . . . you will of course remain where the boats are building, and you will not move from that place without special orders from me."[107] Smith gave a similar directive to Rodgers, thereby making it impossible for them to meet in person without an act of blatant insubordination.[108] Yet that is precisely what both were prepared to do. So insistent was Barron that the two meet, he expressed a willingness to violate orders to bring the matter to a close.[109] Like Truxtun, Rodgers and Barron felt that they had no duty to follow orders if they believed doing so would tarnish their reputations. At a minimum, adhering to the commands of the Navy Department was a decidedly secondary consideration.

The duel was scheduled to take place at Havre de Grace, with Rodgers incredibly hoping "that it will be with such circumspection as to prevent the knowledge of his friends or the civil authorities," despite the fact that the forthcoming meeting was by this point common knowledge in the Navy Department.[110] However, where the wishes of the secretary in Washington failed, the intervention of fellow officers succeeded in preventing bloodshed. The two men's seconds desperately labored to bring about a peaceful settlement, and delays from Barron's illness and separation had, as Tingey hoped, given time for the principals to reflect on the enormity of their actions.[111]

John Stricker, a fellow officer, wrote to Rodgers that he believed the controversy "might be settled without resorting to arms." Apparently, he had talked the matter over with Barron as well, and informed Rodgers that his potential opponent was having second thoughts about "calling" on him, but still felt insulted by "the style of your reply" to his letter. By merely conceding that "your reply was the hasty suggestion of the moment—the effect of an instantaneous irritation that was excited by so unexpected a notification," he could settle the matter. Stricker felt confident that Rodgers could do so without a diminution of honor, and "put an end to an affair of much concern to your friends—and particularly so to the secretary of the navy." Rodgers succumbed to the prodding of his friends, and conceded to the terms outlined by Stricker. The seconds published a pamphlet, including the full text of Stricker's letter and a heading assuring readers that Barron's and Rodgers' friends considered the terms "highly honorable to both parties."[112] The two men managed to avoid a duel and comply with the secretary's wishes, but more importantly, they could assure their brother officers that they did so of their own volition and in perfect keeping with the standards of honor.

How much credit does Robert Smith deserve for the peaceful settlement? It seems probable that, despite their claimed intention to ignore his orders and trade shots in secret, Smith's intervention at least influenced both Barron and Rodgers to settle the matter peacefully. Neither ever said so, however, and agreed to set aside their differences only after being pushed to do so by their seconds. Smith was apparently just relieved not to lose either man, and let the matter rest, though he must have known of their plans to fight in defiance of his orders. Two captains agreeing that their honor could be satisfied without resorting to arms in so long-standing a dispute was undoubtedly precedent enough. Besides, Smith had long ignored constant dueling for far more trivial causes among his younger officers, and he was apparently disinclined to set a precedent of civilian interference in such matters with two celebrated naval heroes. Like Stoddert, he wanted an effective officer corps that did not irreparably damage itself through constant dueling, but that remained committed to the era's ideals. By not dueling, Barron and Rodgers satisfied Smith's wishes as far as an effective officer corps was concerned—they knew when to show appropriate restraint. By showing their willingness to duel unless absolutely certain settling their differences would leave their honor intact, they proved that American naval officers were in no way weak or contemptible, a crucial point for a young nation still trying to prove itself.

# –5–

# "A Government Rigorously Frugal and Simple"

## *The Navy and the Jeffersonian Republicans, 1805–1812*

**FEBRUARY 20, 1801.** Few men knew the inner workings of the Navy Department more intimately or cared more deeply about its success than Charles W. Goldsborough. Initially Stoddert's clerk, he was subsequently appointed chief clerk of the Navy Department, and went on to become one of its most influential men, serving in a variety of capacities until 1843.[1] He even acted as interim Secretary of the Navy during the James Madison administration.[2] All that was still to come in February of 1801, however, and at the time Goldsborough foresaw only a bleak future for his beloved Navy in the aftermath of Jefferson's election. Writing anxiously to Edward Preble, he feared "a new order of things is now to be adopted" and the policies "heretofore pursued by the Administration, under which we have enjoyed protection, security, peace and prosperity, are to be changed—our political ship is about to be launched . . . with an unskilled pilot at the helm." Goldsborough could offer no hint of optimism, abruptly closing his missive with a lament that "I forebear any reflections on this subject, as they cannot be otherwise than painful."[3]

Goldsborough's fear is understandable, even if it proved unfounded. No one, Federalist or Republican, doubted Jefferson's staunch commitment to slash government spending, and that trimming, or gutting, the Navy would be a major means of saving money. For Federalists, there were added fears that he shared his party's opposition to the very existence of the Navy.

By the end of his administration, however, Jefferson's image among naval officers and naval advocates had improved considerably. Goldsborough himself became a close confidant to his boss at the Navy Department, Robert Smith. Captains drifted toward Republicanism in their politics, and some even showed genuine support for Jefferson's gunboat program—more support, in fact, than many subsequent historians.[4] Jefferson's succession by his good friend and longtime ally, James Madison, cemented the Jeffersonian-Republican party in power.

Jefferson and Madison are justly criticized for the thoroughly unprepared state of the U.S. Navy going into the War of 1812, although in fairness they labored under a host of political and fiscal constraints. In terms of the kind of naval officers their administrations cultivated, the Republicans carried over Stoddert's ideas almost entirely. They elevated and rewarded officers who showed zeal for the country's honor, all while showing far greater patience with insubordination than they ever did with timidity or inactivity. That said, the growing professionalism of the officer corps is readily apparent during the years leading up to the War of 1812. Thanks to the Peace Establishment Act and Jefferson's apolitical attitude toward choosing officers, the Navy grew increasingly independent of partisan politics in these years. Moreover, this professional ethos is evident by the fact that, despite highly controversial actions from the Jefferson administration, these years never witnessed any serious civil-military crisis.

In the buildup to the election of 1800, Jefferson summed up his views on military policy neatly, telling like-minded politician Elbridge Gerry, "I am for a government rigorously frugal and simple, applying all possible savings of the public revenue to the discharge of the national debt." So far as this concerned the military, Jefferson well understood the need for national defense, despite what his more hysterical Federalist critics might have claimed. Yet he did not believe a large (and expensive) permanent military establishment was needed to protect the nation. "I am for relying, for internal defense, on our militia solely until actual invasion." His views on the Navy were similarly defense-oriented. He wanted "such naval force only as may protect our coasts and harbors from such depredations as we have experienced." He was decidedly opposed, however, to "a standing army in time of peace which may overawe the public sentiment; nor for a navy which by its own expenses and the eternal wars in which it will implicate us, will grind us with public burdens and sink us under them."[5] Fearing that a Federalist-minded officer corps not only failed to share these objectives, but also wanted to subvert the government, his priorities for the military were not only cutting expenditures, but also making sure Army and Navy alike were led by officers who shared correct republican principles.[6]

Jefferson took office convinced that the Federalists had plotted to subvert the Revolution and establish a quasi-monarchical (or a purely monarchical) government.[7] The officer corps on land and sea was filled almost exclusively with Alexander Hamilton's allies; it was a staunchly Federalist force.[8] In light of this, Jefferson feared the overwhelming majority of officers were overly sympathetic to a strongly antidemocratic form of government—not to mention an unhealthy association with Great Britain. His first order of business was thus to republicanize the highest echelons of the military. Jefferson and his Secretary of War, Henry Dearborn, used a reduction in the Army to purge blatantly Federalist officers, and more than a few who were simply unfit to hold commissions. They then began establishing a small, effective, politically reliable officer corps. At the center of this vision was a military academy at West Point, which could provide the nation with much-needed trained engineers and also make sure the future leadership of the Army was deeply ingrained with the values of civilian control and republican ideology.[9]

In the Navy, reforming the officer corps proved easier. Jefferson never considered a naval academy similar to West Point, but he and the Smith brothers were able to use the Peace Establishment Act of 1801 to shape the existing set of officers to their liking. Under the terms of the act, the Navy underwent a drastic reduction in officers, with a total of almost three hundred exiting the corps. Knowing Jefferson's intentions to cut spending on the Navy, the Federalist Congress passed the act in the waning days of the Adams administration, with considerable input from Stoddert. The hope was that by reducing the Navy in a measured way, they could prevent Jefferson from gutting it altogether. Whether Jefferson envisioned even more severe cuts before he assumed office is unknowable, but the terms of the act were apparently to his satisfaction. The task of reducing the officer corps to comply with the new limits fell largely to Samuel Smith, with his brother Robert finishing the job upon assuming permanent oversight of the department. Both acknowledged that not all those slated for removal were unworthy of their commissions, and it was a painful duty to cut several "meritorious" officers.[10] Moses Brown, a captain who served heroically in the Quasi War, received a form letter from Acting Secretary Samuel Smith within weeks of the new president's inauguration, informing him that his vessel had been sold and that he was now unemployed.[11] Robert Smith continued the purging when he took office. Among his first acts was to send a terse note to Daniel McNeill informing him that his services were no longer needed under the Peace Establishment Act. Times had apparently grown harder in the interim, as McNeill received nothing but orders to surrender his accounts, as opposed to the four months' severance given Brown.[12]

As Brown's case illustrates, it was not only officers, but also ships that disappeared from American service. The administration sold several vessels to generate revenue while reducing expenses. Since most of these were hastily converted merchant ships purchased for the Quasi War, their loss was fairly painless for the Navy. Even so, enough ships were disposed of or put in ordinary that the new secretary often had more junior officers than he could use, despite the drastic cuts to the officer corps. Smith liberally granted, and at times ordered, furloughs for young officers to spend time in the merchant service, honing their nautical abilities and saving their government the expense of training them.[13]

Although bitterly condemned by the outgoing Federalists (and more than a few subsequent historians), the reduction under the Peace Establishment Act ultimately proved beneficial to the service. A number of officers ill-suited to military subordination were excised from the ranks, leaving behind a small corps who understood and embraced the civilian control. Numerous good officers had to go, a fact that the administration readily acknowledged, but those cut from the corps also included many guilty of frequent drunkenness, defiance, and simple failure to do their duty. While Stoddert's successors still had to face difficulties with insubordination, it was on a much lower scale than might otherwise have been the case. Despite the claims of its critics, the Peace Establishment Act proved to be "the true foundation of the fully professional officer corps that the United States developed between 1801 and 1812."[14]

One reason this reduction proved so beneficial to the service was the staunchly apolitical character of the selection process. While there is evidence that Jefferson and Dearborn zeroed in on Army officers' party affiliation during this period, Samuel Smith angrily rejected any suggestion that the Navy did so. "I have attended much to character, nothing to the political caste" of officers being considered for removal, he informed one correspondent, and proved it by citing a lengthy list of known Federalists retained under the act.[15] Jefferson paid close attention to the politics of virtually everyone in public life, and indeed made a point of lumping Truxtun in with "Federal zealots" during the former captain's ongoing campaign for reinstatement,[16] but the new president drew a distinction between extreme, and therefore dangerous, Federalists and those of a more reasonable variety. Indeed, more than one adequate but unimpressive Republican found himself unemployed, while Federalists like William Bainbridge and Edward Preble not only stayed in the service but enjoyed the favor of the administration. Given that much of the officer corps was drawn from the strongly Federalist world of merchant shipping and coastal areas, this was probably somewhat unavoidable. But there is no indication the administration made any effort to filter officers by politics, relying instead on their performance, while also striving for some measure of geographical balance.[17]

Jefferson's thorough commitment to republican principles meant that he believed in civilian control with absolute certainty, and Robert Smith shared that mindset. The new secretary had no qualms about reminding his captains of their subordinate status when the occasion required. When one purser complained of his assignment, Smith informed him that, as Secretary of the Navy, he was under no obligation to "consult the conveniences or wishes" of his officers, nor should they "expect never to be ordered upon service that may be irksome or disagreeable."[18] Still, if he could be abrupt and imperious in his communications, he also displayed a warm and even pleasant side when he had no grounds for complaint with an officer. For the most part he enjoyed loyalty and support from the officer corps. He also knew when to rely on naval officers' knowledge of their profession. He delegated the task of writing new naval regulations to Thomas Tingey, then circulated them to several other captains for comment before approving them.[19] He also abandoned his plans to commission experienced merchant captains for gunboat commands after Edward Preble voiced objections to the idea.[20] And, of course, he looked to selected naval leaders for guidance and confirmation in his decision not to allow Truxtun back in the service. Smith also systematized promotion; rather than relying solely on individual captains to recommend their own midshipmen for lieutenancies, he ordered that impartial officers examine candidates for promotion, a move that coupled with the Peace Establishment Act to ensure a more competent and professional officer corps.[21]

While the corps grew in professionalism, it also encountered its share of tensions with the civilian population in the years following the Tripolitan War. In the immediate aftermath of the war, many returning officers who were hailed as American heroes came ashore to cheering crowds and celebratory dinners. Governors and prominent citizens were eager to host events honoring Edward Preble on his return, while the war was still in progress; it was not unusual for there to be more than thirty toasts in his honor at these dinners. Stephen Decatur came home to similar acclaim, with one banquet hailing him as a symbol of national unity between the Federalist and the Republican parties.[22] Yet Robert Smith's tenure also saw some incidents of friction between the Navy and civilians. He removed at least one officer after accounts of the offender's "misconduct" appeared in local newspapers.[23] Smith was also willing to stay out of the way and let trusted captains settle disputes on their own. When one New York newspaper libeled the naval officers on the station, Lieutenant James Lawrence wrote back to the paper threatening that a group of gunboat commanders planned to come and cut off the ears of anyone who doubted their courage. The commander of the New York Navy Yard, John Rodgers, sympathized entirely with his subordinates, but he also realized a bloody clash between young officers and angry New Yorkers would be a disaster for the service. He showed impressive skill at diplomacy in calming what could have been an ugly situation.[24]

While the reduction of the Navy was the most far-reaching naval policy of the Jefferson administration, the gunboat program is likely the most famous—or infamous, if the Federalists were asked. Jefferson's plan was to put most of the fleet of frigates in drydock and transition the Navy toward a more defensive, more economical mindset. One of Jefferson's greatest fears when it came to seagoing frigates was antagonizing the British. He was well aware of the recent example made of the Danes. When the Danish government proposed armed neutrality in the Anglo-French war, refusing to participate but repelling attempts by either to interfere with its shipping, Britain sent a squadron to Copenhagen in 1801 and utterly destroyed or seized the entire Danish navy. Jefferson had no desire to watch his country suffer a similar fate.[25]

The key to preventing the U.S. fleet from becoming the center of another Copenhagen was the transition from seagoing, offensive frigates to coastal, defensive gunboats. Gunboats were small, shallow-draft vessels limited in their ability to go far beyond the coastline, but they were rowed independent of the wind, and could cripple larger ships in enclosed waters, especially when the water was becalmed.[26] Since Jefferson wisely decided to spread construction across the country, ensuring economic benefit to numerous cities, there was no single design, but all ranged from forty-five to seventy feet in length and mounted one or two guns in the bow.[27] They were never intended to remove the need for frigates, although Albert Gallatin presciently warned Jefferson that his opponents would cast them as such.[28] In his comments on the president's 1804 annual message, the Treasury Secretary lamented that "the efforts made in the federal papers to impress the idea that this establishment is intended as a substitute for the navy have so far succeeded that some distortion of the President's recommendations will take place."[29] William Plumer, a prominent Federalist senator, blasted the vessels as being completely useless.[30] Meanwhile, the *Washington Federalist* printed a letter referring to Jefferson's program as a "wasteful imbecility."[31]

They were not Jefferson's invention, nor were they particularly novel when he began the program. European powers had been using them in the Baltic and Mediterranean for over a century by this point. The shallow coastal waters in the Mediterranean were ill suited to large frigates, and as early as 1794 Thomas Truxtun had urged the creation of a fleet of gunboats for use against the Barbary Powers.[32] His ideas were vindicated after he left the Navy, when gunboats proved valuable in the Tripolitan War. Preble used them in an offensive capacity in shallow waters, and commanders in the region contracted with Italian states to build more. Meanwhile, tensions with Spain over the Mississippi River basin at New Orleans demonstrated the need for riverine vessels at home.[33]

The Navy itself supported the gunboat program. While Robert Smith apparently felt some qualms about the force, he kept them to himself.[34] Samuel Smith, after returning from his short stint at the Navy Department, was one of the main figures shepherding the gunboat legislation through Congress.[35]

Naval officers generally accepted the new fleet as well. They expressed concern that shore-based small vessels would be inadequate for training young officers but managed to work around this difficulty by sending promising lieutenants and even midshipmen on short cruises in local bays and rivers.[36] Their personal views on the gunboats as a fighting force were mixed but muted. Early in his assignment to supervise construction of several gunboats, Stephen Decatur privately grumbled to Bainbridge that it would not be any great loss if the whole fleet of them sank, and during the war scare with Great Britain in 1807 he urged the secretary to assign him to a frigate, believing that such a post offered more prestige. But he otherwise energetically performed his duty to make sure the gunboats he was assigned to construct were of the highest quality and largely kept his personal feelings to himself.[37] When Jefferson consulted Samuel Barron and Thomas Tingey for their views, both strongly encouraged the use of gunboats to defend rivers and shallow coastal waters. Tingey even acknowledged that the Royal Navy made substantial use of gunboats. Neither in any way implied that gunboats could replace frigates, or that they believed that was the president's intention. Rather, they acknowledged the defensive value of gunboats on coastal waters and rivers.[38] William Bainbridge likewise campaigned for the construction of gunboats and later supervised building them without voicing any objection.[39] Having used gunboats against Tripoli, Preble became a fairly enthusiastic proponent of their value, and threw himself into the task of overseeing their design and construction.[40] Isaac Hull likewise drifted toward Republicanism at this time, and engaged wholeheartedly in the president's gunboat program without complaint. After accusations from a naval agent by the name of Constant Taber that Hull's Federalist leanings were impacting his performance, Robert Smith vetted his politics and found Hull and his family to be strong supporters of Jefferson and the captain's gunboats to be in excellent condition.[41]

The worst civil-military tensions of the Jefferson administration did not come from the gunboat program, but from squabbling over money. Numerous officers objected to their low pay throughout Smith's tenure, with limited success.[42] When Thomas Tingey retired from the Navy as a captain in 1801, he continued on at his last assignment as superintendent of the Washington Navy Yard. Although not on the rolls as an officer any longer, Tingey's position was something of a hybrid, as he continued to oversee the maintenance of the nation's warships and held on to the honorary title of captain; his salary was also set at the same pay a captain in command of a 32-gun frigate received.[43] Therein lay a sticking point for Tingey who, with a young family to support, believed he needed more money. He wrote to ask Smith for a salary of $2,500 per year, and that if he could not have that then he would "reluctantly" have no choice but to resign.[44] Jefferson firmly backed his secretary on the matter. "I am sorry for the resolution Captain Tingey has taken, because I think him a good officer," Jefferson wrote back to Smith. Nevertheless, "our course is a plain one." If Tingey refused Smith's proposed salary "then the office does not suit him."[45]

Belatedly realizing that Jefferson and Smith planned to call his bluff, Tingey took the best deal he could get. Although he lost his post as superintendent of the Washington Navy Yard, Tingey remained on as financial agent while an active-duty officer, Master Commandant John Cassin, took over command of the facility. Tingey would have been only human if it grated on him to report to an officer junior to his last naval rank, but he apparently made the best of the situation, later referring to his demotion as only a "temporary suspension of my power."[46] And indeed, after a year of reporting to Cassin, Congress authorized the creation of the post of commandant of the Washington Navy Yard, and Tingey received a new commission as captain and was restored to command of the yard, where he remained until his death in 1829. He opted not to raise the issue of relative rank upon his return, accepting the new commission dated 1804 that put him behind officers whom he had previously outranked but had remained in the service during his hiatus.[47] Tingey and Smith soon developed a harmonious working relationship, and Smith even let Tingey draft regulations for the Washington Navy Yard that substantially increased the commandant's authority over personnel. While accepting Tingey's draft, Smith did, however, sternly warn him (again) to rein in his expenditures, which became a recurring theme in his letters to Tingey.[48]

David Porter never developed a harmonious working relationship with Smith, or any other Secretary of the Navy for that matter. Smith ordered Porter to New Orleans, where his primary job became chasing smugglers entering the port.[49] While in New Orleans, Porter grew increasingly infuriated at Smith, believing the secretary's parsimony was making his situation unlivable. His troubles began on the journey down the Mississippi. Porter claimed that the gunboats he was authorized to use for the trip were not seaworthy, and on his own authority he purchased a galley for himself, his officers, and his family. Unfortunately, when he notified Smith of the unauthorized purchase, he used the same letter to also ask for a higher salary.[50] Infuriated, Smith rejected Porter's request and refused to refund him for the cost of the galley. He later informed Porter that he would not be accepting *any* expenses sent from New Orleans unless the Navy Department had authorized them beforehand, and further rebuked the captain saying, "The constant enormous expenditures of the New Orleans Station exceed all calculations . . . and they compel me to press upon your attention the strictest regard for economy in all things."[51]

Porter tried to alleviate his perceived poverty by suggesting that a committee of active naval officers approve expenditures, rather than leave that duty entirely in the hands of the civilian secretary.[52] Smith ignored him. Porter's suggestion did come to fruition a few years later in the form of the Board of Navy Commissioners, but at the time the Jefferson administration was determined to maintain its authority over spending and to keep use of federal dollars as frugal as possible.

Porter grew increasingly frustrated with his civilian superiors during his time in New Orleans, with his son later commenting that he became so "disgusted with the management of naval affairs," that he possessed "no confidence in its justice."[53] Even after he returned from the Gulf coast, he continued to fight for funds he felt he was entitled to. The Navy Department only settled in his favor in 1846, when the commodore had been dead for three years. It seems Porter's complaints reflected real poverty. The distraught captain sent a desperate note to his friend Samuel Hambleton one night, pleading that he found himself "destitute" and feared he would be unable to buy food the next morning. Would Hambleton "have the goodness to keep him from *starving*," by loaning him whatever money he had in his house? (emphasis in original)[54]

Porter was the loudest complainer, but he was not the only officer whose accounting practices annoyed the secretary. About this time Smith sent out two separate circulars to all his captains ordering them to keep more careful records.[55] One reason Preble was among his favorite officers is that he was the most scrupulous at keeping expenses to a minimum wherever he was stationed.[56]

In general, questions of Navy Department budgets and spending played out in conversations between officers and the Secretary of the Navy, who acted as an intermediary with the president. On occasion, however, officers appealed directly to Congress on issues affecting their service. During the Quasi War, Congress had made appropriations for two 74-gun ships, significantly larger vessels than anything the U.S. Navy could boast, but the war ended and Jefferson took office determined to cut expenditures before construction could even begin. In 1805, however, Robert Smith pressed Congress to authorize the construction of as many as twelve of these vessels, including the necessary increased appropriations. It is unclear how supportive Jefferson was of this endeavor, but the reasons were sound: the U.S. was engaged in tense negotiations with Spain, particularly over territorial boundaries in Louisiana and present-day Florida, and construction of such warships might improve the American bargaining position. The officers of the Navy, of course, enthusiastically supported this idea, and Edward Preble, William Bainbridge, and James Barron made plans to travel to the nation's capital and lobby on behalf of the 74s. When the time came, only Preble and Bainbridge showed up, with Barron apparently deciding (correctly) that the mission was hopeless. Undeterred, the two officers met personally with members of Congress and made the case for the larger vessels as essential to defending the nation's shipping and, more importantly in their minds, its honor. Civilian and military representatives of the Navy Department had the same measure of success in influencing the legislature—Congress overwhelmingly rejected the 74s.[57]

Naval officers likewise continued to find nothing but frustration whenever they appealed directly to Congress for their own financial well-being. In 1808, a group of officers placed on half-pay until they were needed again sent a desperate plea to Congress, asking for money for rations while out of service, pensions for widows (such as Army officers received), and better pay for midshipmen and masters commandant.[58] Despite the officers' emotional appeals, the Republican-controlled Congress balked. Although the petition was twice referred to the House Committee on Naval Affairs, it never received congressional favor. The summary rejection particularly rankled Isaac Hull, who wrote later to David Daggett, a friend in the Senate, complaining that "our memorandum . . . was treated with so much indelicacy, I may say indecency that every officer has determined never to ask for anything again." Years later, Hull still seethed at how the legislature had treated the country's naval officers. Upon reading the debates on the subject, Hull told Daggett, "I am sure you will blush" for some of your fellow Congressmen; he wondered how "men of feeling could bear such treatment, when the world will and must acknowledge what they have asked was asked respectfully and ought to have been granted?"[59]

Jefferson's first term was a remarkably successful one, in no small measure because he presided over a nation at peace with the world's major powers. This blessing did not carry over into his second term, however, and a war scare with Great Britain—and his own politically disastrous response—marred his final year in office. Determined to hold on to the hard-won gains of the recent war with Tripoli, Jefferson placed all but one of the frigates in ordinary, but planned to keep a frigate in the Mediterranean at all times to enforce existing treaties. By the summer of 1807, it was time to relieve Rodgers, who had returned to the Mediterranean. For this mission, Robert Smith dispatched a vessel soon to acquire a reputation as a cursed ship, the *Chesapeake*, captained by Rodgers' recent nemesis, James Barron.

Barron sailed on June 22 with his ship in a condition that made it clear he did not expect an eventful voyage. Baggage from his civilian passengers lay strewn across the deck, while most of the ship was decidedly not ready for combat. The United States was, at the time, at peace with all the world, and Barron apparently believed there was no chance he and his crew would see combat. He was wrong.[60]

Although America was technically at peace with Great Britain and France, neither nation showed the young republic much respect, and Britain in particular was annoyed with America's laxity in preventing British deserters from finding employment on American vessels. Upon learning that British deserters were not only aboard the *Chesapeake* but openly (and foolishly) flaunting the fact to British officers they encountered on shore in Norfolk, Vice Admiral of the White, Sir George Cranfield Berkeley, commander in chief of the British North American Station, sent out a circular to all captains in the area alerting them about these men, and giving orders for the *Chesapeake* to be stopped and its crew mustered and searched. This was a shocking order, even by the standards of British practice at the time. While British officers had attempted to take men off American naval vessels during the Quasi War, as Isaac Phillips could so painfully attest, these had been actions of individual captains on their own authority. A British admiral was now ordering all ships under his command to violate the sovereignty of a man-of-war in the service of a nation that even Berkeley admitted to being "in terms of peace and Amity" with his own.[61] Oblivious to Berkeley's order, Barron casually sailed his vessel toward an international incident and a career-ruining disaster.

At about 3:30 on the afternoon of June 22, 1807, Captain Salusbury Pryce Humphreys of the British 54-gun ship *Leopard* hailed Barron. It was fairly common at the time for nations at peace to carry mail and other communications for one another, and Barron probably assumed this was all Humphreys wanted. He welcomed Humphreys' lieutenant, John Meade, on board. Only after Meade entered his quarters to speak with him privately did Barron realize that the British meant to seize four Royal Navy deserters from the *Chesapeake*. Meade presented Barron with a copy of Berkeley's circular and another letter from Humphreys expressing his duty to comply with the orders of his commander and also his hope that the entire affair could be settled amicably.[62] Barron responded that he was not aware of any such men among his crew, stretching the truth as he did know of at least a few British deserters aboard, but also that these did not come from Berkeley's squadron.[63] He nonetheless indicated to Meade that his crew was wholly American and promptly returned him to his own ship with a message that the *Chesapeake*'s crew could only be mustered by American officers. Barron was emphatic that it was impossible for him to comply with Humphrey's desire.

Years later, Humphrey claimed that he was grieved by what came next, but that "as an officer and a gentleman," he could only obey and try his best to minimize the damage.[64] Interpreting his orders in the broadest possible terms, he prepared to open fire on the *Chesapeake*. When a warning shot was ignored, he gave orders for a general engagement.[65] The *Leopard* unleashed a broadside on the American ship. The assault took Barron completely by surprise, and the scrambling efforts of the American crew to resist the attack produced something akin to a comic opera. Men stumbled over civilian baggage amid enemy fire, but even without the extraneous items crowding the decks, the crew displayed shocking ineptitude at the most basic tasks of a man-of-war. Many of the seamen failed to report to their proper battle stations throughout the fight, whether from cowardice or, more likely, because the untrained crews did not know where to go or could not find their way in the confusion.[66] Under the oppressive fire of repeated broadsides from the *Leopard*, men scrambled to load guns with improperly fitted cartridges, only to find it impossible to light them. "For God's sake gentlemen, will nobody do his duty?" Barron screamed amid the chaos, then piteously added, "Is it possible we can't get even one of the guns to fire?" Barron himself suffered a serious laceration to his leg in the midst of the onslaught, but bravely pressed on, trying to direct his befuddled crew to accomplish *something* before the inevitable surrender. After firing a lone token shot back at the British, Barron lowered his flag.[67]

Once Humphreys boarded, Barron immediately offered up his ship as a prize, which the British captain declined. His orders were only to seize the four deserters and the two nations were, after all, technically at peace. He even expressed willingness to provide assistance to his American counterpart, though Barron predictably ignored this offer. Once the *Leopard* had sailed away, the *Chesapeake*'s officers surveyed the damage. Three men were dead, sixteen wounded. Three feet of water stood in the hold, and the general state of the vessel was hopeless. Barron and his officers concluded that the ship was far too damaged to go on, and limped back to Norfolk, Virginia.[68]

For the rest of his life, Barron genuinely believed that he had done the best that could be expected of him under the circumstances.[69] He was very decidedly alone in this belief. His fellow officers blamed him for humiliating the service, and they immediately set to work placing the entirety of the guilt for the debacle on him to preserve their own careers. The very next day, six officers present at the attack wrote to Secretary Smith, pinning the disaster entirely on Barron and asking for his arrest.[70] In an ill omen for the commodore, Smith uncharacteristically ignored their blatant violation of the chain of command and wrote them back with praise for calling his attention to Barron's failures.[71]

Barron was summoned before a court-martial and charged with four separate counts of failure to perform his duty—failing to have his ship ready for action, failing to take the likelihood of an attack from the *Leopard* seriously, failing to encourage his men to fight, and failing to make an adequate effort to defeat the *Leopard*.[72] The composition of the court was not likely to reassure him of a fair hearing. The senior officer was John Rodgers, the man Barron almost fought a duel with less than a year before. Stephen Decatur, who assumed command of the *Chesapeake* after the disaster, had also already made up his mind that Barron had acted shamefully. Decatur made no effort to conceal his biases from Robert Smith, telling him that he had "formed and expressed an opinion, that Commodore Barron had not done his duty," and after witnessing the court of inquiry and reading its findings against Barron, he concluded that they were "rather lenient." He bluntly informed Smith, "I am prejudiced against Commodore Barron," and he did not believe he was capable of rendering impartial justice in the case. He therefore asked to be excused from sitting on the court.[73] Smith denied his request, citing a shortage of officers. While it was true enough that finding officers of equal rank with Barron was difficult, the truth is that Smith and Jefferson had already settled in their minds that Barron was guilty of gross negligence, and the composition of the court shows that at the very least they were unworried about the fairness of the trial, if indeed they were not tilting the scales against the defendant deliberately.[74]

The court convicted Barron of neglecting his duty and sentenced him to a five-year suspension without pay. Smith and Jefferson readily accepted the court's findings and sentence. While there is no reason to doubt that all involved sincerely believed Barron deserved his fate, it was also a convenient outcome for everyone (except Barron, of course). The officer corps salvaged its own honor by ruling that the fault for the debacle lay entirely with one man. According to the court's findings, widespread laxity in enforcing regulations and failure to adequately equip junior officers for their duty had nothing to do with the disaster. Likewise, Smith enjoyed indirect justification for his oversight of the Navy Department; only one officer was deficient, not large numbers of the men under his supervision. By purging themselves of Barron—who they rightly judged would face great difficulty returning to duty once his suspension ended—the rest of the officers could continue to look on themselves with collective pride. Barron's fate was also consistent with existing trends in the Navy. While he had not erred as egregiously as Maley or Phillips, who had failed to put up even token resistance, he had still dishonored his profession in the heat of combat. His one ball fired, while he might have thought it symbolically significant, could not compensate for the fact that an American ship and crew looked amateurish against the British navy. Barron had shamed the service, and it could only begin to restore its image by sending a message to all officers, yet again, that such behavior would never merit compassion or leniency. It now fell to the rest of the Navy to prove that Barron was an aberration as soon as they got the chance.

Jefferson's response to the attack on the *Chesapeake* proved to be one of the most controversial decisions of his presidency. Faced with a series of bad options, Jefferson chose to avoid war even at the expense of the American economy. He worked closely with his party in Congress to pass the Embargo Act of 1807, which confined all American shipping to United States waters and crushed the merchant shipping industry of the nation. The hope, never realized, was that the loss of American trade would be a decisive blow to both Britain and France's economies, and force them to treat the United States with greater respect. In reality, the embargo infuriated virtually all of New England and helped revive the flagging Federalist Party, while also causing a brutal depression. The Embargo Act tainted the final year of Jefferson's presidency, but he acted on the belief that it was the only possible alternative to either a ruinous war or the shame of doing nothing in response to Britain's assault on American sovereignty.[75]

The Navy naturally played a substantial role in enforcing the embargo. Despite the officer corps' drift toward Jeffersonian Republicanism, it must surely have been a bitter assignment. While neither Stoddert nor Smith demanded maritime experience for a commission, in practice many officers hailed from seafaring families, and most of them had spent time on furlough in merchant shipping learning their craft. Besides, the Navy's officers yearned to avenge the honor of their profession by striking at the Royal Navy directly, and enforcing an edict against their own unarmed countrymen fell far short. As with the gunboats, however, there was no overt pushback—the Navy dutifully set to work restricting American ships from foreign commerce. Given the scale of the law they were enforcing and the rampant efforts to evade it, the Navy enjoyed as much success as could be expected, and their effectiveness highlights the measure of their commitment to honoring the policies of the executive branch.[76]

Jefferson gladly followed George Washington's precedent and stepped down from the presidency in 1808. Not surprisingly, the office went to his longtime associate and Secretary of State, James Madison. With the changing of presidential administrations came new leadership to the Navy Department. Robert Smith left to become Madison's Secretary of State, a highly honored position since it was at the time seen as a stepping-stone to the presidency. The post would have been especially satisfying to Smith, since Madison's first choice was his old rival, Albert Gallatin. Congressional pressure forced Madison to leave Gallatin in the Treasury, and Smith assumed the duties of overseeing the State Department.[77] To oversee the Navy, Madison turned to

Paul Hamilton, the former governor of South Carolina and owner of a sizable plantation. A man with no maritime experience, Madison "drew the name out of a hat," per one biographer, and Hamilton's choice for the position was based on nothing more than the fact that he was from South Carolina and Madison needed another Southerner.[78]

His lack of experience aside, Paul Hamilton initially showed promise. Thomas Tingey, commandant of the Washington Navy Yard, regularly interacted with Hamilton and considered him to be "an ardent advocate of the service."[79] Hamilton assumed office with the laudable goal of improving the administrative efficiency and educational apparatus of the Navy Department. Like Smith, he valued economy, and he wrote Goldsborough before leaving the capital for a short time not to exceed appropriations unless specifically authorized to do so by the president.[80] He also displayed concern for the moral character of his officers, which led him to occasionally overstep long-accepted, if unwritten, boundaries by interfering in officers' relations with their junior officers and seamen. When he learned that some midshipmen were frequenting taverns where they spent their free hours playing billiards and getting drunk, he ordered Thomas Tingey to rein them in.[81] Alarmed at what he perceived as Isaac Hull's overly harsh treatment of his crewmen, he wrote to urge the captain to avoid "degrading punishments."[82] Insulted, Hull shot back that "I am aware that every attention ought to be paid to the happiness and comfort of the men that enter public service" and that punishments should be "only in proportion to the offense." This, Hull insisted, had always been his practice, and it left him "extremely unhappy" that Hamilton had "impressions so unfavorable towards me as a man of feeling and humanity."[83] Hamilton's compassionate side also showed in his relations with his officers, however. He reinstated a midshipman who had been removed for repeated displays of temper at the appeal of John Rodgers, believing that yet another second chance would finally make a good officer out of him.[84] Hamilton by no means stripped captains of all autonomy in their dealings with subordinates. Days before writing his aggrieved response to Hamilton, Hull informed the secretary that he had accepted the resignation of an officer under his command, and personally taken possession of the man's warrant, on the assumption the Navy Department would approve. Shortly afterward he shifted midshipmen between ships on his own authority and informed the Navy Department after the fact.[85]

Hamilton later acquired a reputation as an alcoholic, and his alleged constant state of inebriation was cited for virtually everything that ever went wrong with the Navy during his tenure. The evidence is thin. David Porter came to loath the new secretary and wrote to a friend that Hamilton had "no energy" and that while he was in office, there was no chance that "a pint of whiskey can be purchased in the whole District of Columbia, it is shameful."[86] Members of Congress also raised eyebrows at rumors of the secretary's drinking habits, but they seem to have been responding to rumors, not firsthand knowledge. Christopher McKee notes that Hamilton's handwriting remained "beautifully small, clear, and precise" until his ouster, hardly an indication the man was in a drunken haze on the job most days. The truth is that Hamilton's problem was not overindulgence, but simply a lack of administrative ability, and this issue was contained for the most part until the outbreak of the War of 1812.[87]

Hamilton's thinking meshed perfectly with that of his predecessors in one crucial aspect: he had no tolerance for any officer who allowed the American flag to suffer insult. He issued general orders reminding the entire corps of "the injustice and insults heaped on our country" by both Britain and France, and specifically of "the inhumane and dastardly attack on the frigate *Chesapeake*, an outrage which has prostrated the flag of our country and has imposed on the American people cause of ceaseless mourning." How should captains of the U.S. Navy respond to such outrages? In Hamilton's mind, the answer was clear: "it is therefore our duty to be prepared and determined at every hazard to vindicate the injured honor of our navy" and "maintain and support at any risk and cost the dignity of your flag." Hamilton expected that no officer under his command would allow Britain to humiliate the United States again, and he soon had the chance to put this resolve on display.[88]

June 24, 1810, found Lieutenant John Trippe sailing toward the New Orleans Station in command of the brig *Vixen*, intending to replace a few gunboats there that had become unseaworthy. He also had a member of Congress on board, as well as the son of Attorney General Caesar Rodney. Trippe sailed with the full confidence of the Navy Department, having established himself as a promising young officer in the war with Tripoli. Hamilton had been careful to choose from among those "whose experience and character entitled them to confidence" for the mission.[89] The department's confidence was short-lived. Mistaking Trippe's brig for a French privateer, a British ship fired a shot at the

*Vixen*, then after only a moment's pause blasted off a second one. Trippe's ship suffered no small damage, although no men were killed. Trippe ordered the crew to prepare for action, but before a full-blown engagement could begin a British officer rowed over with a letter of apology from his captain, who had realized his error. Trippe accepted the apology, and the two ships went their separate ways without any further incident.[90]

Hamilton was furious at Trippe's conduct. While he acknowledged that the common use of false flags by all nations made the British captain's decision to fire the first shot justifiable, both Paul Hamilton and President Madison regarded the continued firing as a gross violation of established conduct and a further sign of Britain's arrogance.[91] Trippe, therefore, should have returned fire rather than allow his crew and passengers to suffer injury. "I fondly cherished the hope that our officers needed only an opportunity to vindicate the wounded honor of our flag," the secretary blasted to his unfortunate lieutenant. Trippe had let just such an opportunity slip away and Hamilton immediately recalled him to the United States to face a court-martial.[92] Yellow fever ended Trippe's career before the Hamilton could, but the secretary's explosive reaction shows how desperately the U.S. Navy desired vindication of its honor and fighting spirit.[93]

By spring of 1811 the humiliation of Barron's performance against the *Chesapeake* had scarcely abated at all for the Navy's officers. They still yearned for a chance to vindicate the honor of their service, and in May the British were kind enough to oblige. Upon learning that a British ship had seized and impressed an American sailor off the coast of New York, Secretary Hamilton ordered John Rodgers and the *President* to sail to the area and protect American vessels. Spying a strange ship in a dense fog, Rodgers called for identification. He would later insist, to the satisfaction of a court-martial, that the vessel had responded to his inquiry with a shot across the bow. The British report, however, claimed the *President*'s attack was totally unprovoked. Whatever the case, Rodgers, knowing his opposite was a British vessel, ordered a full broadside, unleashing the full firepower of the *President*, and killing or wounding thirty-two men from the other ship. He later discovered that he had opened fire from his 44-gun frigate on a British corvette armed with a mere twenty guns.[94]

Rodgers apologized for his error to Captain Arthur Bingham of the now-mangled *Little Belt*, but he did so in such a way that Bingham found it "evident, that had he fallen in with a British frigate, he would certainly have brought her to action." It seems beyond question that Rodgers sailed out spoiling for a fight. Certainly, attacking a vessel of equal size would have brought more honor to his profession, and we may believe his insistence that he was not fully aware of the other ship's size in the dense fog. However, his inclination apparently was to open fire on any pretext, regardless of the possible ramifications. Hamilton expressed no dismay at his commodore's trigger-happy display. The "chastisement" Rodgers had delivered was "very properly inflicted," the secretary gushed, and he promised Rodgers whatever he needed to repair the slight damages to his own ship immediately. "You must want nothing," he pledged. The lone "wounded boy" from Rodgers' ship deserved reward, and Hamilton inquired if he was appropriate material for a midshipman's warrant. "I would hug him to my bosom . . . while I made him an officer," if only he had character to match his gallantry, promised the secretary. As for Rodgers, "I declare that my sentiments towards, and estimation of you, go beyond what may be expressed."[95]

While Hamilton's effusive praise for the commodore's destruction of a ship less than half the size of his own may seem excessive, there was great symbolic significance of Rodgers' actions. He was not only willing to fight but sought out a clash with the Royal Navy at a time when the Navy's last two encounters with British vessels had produced nothing but disgrace and humiliation. More importantly, his ship had been fully prepared for action. In his orders to Rodgers to rendezvous with Decatur, he urged him to ensure that Decatur's crew was "equally prepared" to his own.[96] Although much had changed in the transition from Adams and Stoddert to the Jeffersonians, one thing remained constant: captains who went to sea unready to face any threat could expect shame and chastisement; those who evinced a fighting spirit that credited the service could count on the department's highest praise.

One year later the officers of the U.S. Navy had ample opportunity to prove their fighting spirit. The war with Britain that Jefferson desperately sought to avoid finally came, and it painfully exposed the shortcomings of the gunboat program. Yet the conflict became a watershed moment for the Navy; its popularity soared after a series of celebrated single-ship engagements, and the difficulties of the war laid the groundwork for improved naval administration. The unprepared condition of the United States for war, on land and sea, has justly been laid at the feet of Jefferson and Madison, yet it was in their administrations that much of the preparation for the Navy's successes was also made. The Peace Establishment Act, and the administration's apolitical execution of it, forged a far more professional officer corps than had existed before. The gunboat program, while it proved misguided, highlighted a strong sense of subordination to civilian control among the officer corps, who demonstrated a willingness to work closely with the administration even if most of them did not share its politics. Robert Smith and William Hamilton also continued Stoddert's tradition of cultivating officers who were bold, courageous, and unwilling to countenance any injury to their nation's honor, and these traits brought great victories for the Navy, even as they continued to create very real headaches for the Navy Department.

# –6–

# "The Precious Germ of Our National Glory"

## *The Navy and the War of 1812*

**OCTOBER 25, 1812.** Fourteen-year-old Samuel Leech stood "in motionless suspense" as he drifted toward the first naval battle of his life. A lookout had spied an enemy frigate closing with his ship, and the crew efficiently made preparations to engage. "The guns were shotted, the matches lighted," a lieutenant passed out "pikes, cutlasses, and pistols" in case of a boarding action, while the captain "exhorted the men to fidelity and courage." That done, Leech and his shipmates could only stand at the ready and wait for the two vessels to come within each other's range. When the captain bellowed the command to open fire, the tense silence gave way to "the most hideous noise" of roaring cannon, while the stillness at every station as the enemy approached was blasted away into a scene "indescribably confused and horrible." Though the brutality of war was new to him, he managed to keep to his duty, scrambling back and forth amid the carnage to supply first one gun with powder, then two, and then at least three as his fellow powder-boys were cut down by enemy fire. That enemy was a new one for him and his shipmates. His ship, the British frigate *Macedonian*, had been at sea combatting the French, but had only days before learned that Great Britain was at war with the United States. Leech and the rest of the men of the *Macedonian* believed—incorrectly as it turned out—that they were engaged in the first battle of what came to be called the War of 1812. The horrors that came with fighting at sea in the era, however, left no room for reflection on the enemy's country. Amid the "torrents of blood which dyed our decks" and the "deafening roar . . . like some awfully tremendous thunder storm" of gunfire, Leech witnessed limbs blown off, bowels split open, and wounded men who were judged beyond hope thrown overboard alive. After two hellish hours, it was suddenly over. With the ship reduced to "a complete wreck," the officers concluded that further resistance was pointless, and struck their colors. Samuel Leech was a prisoner of the frigate *United States*.[1]

Leech took the occasion of his captivity to desert on American soil, where he caught a glimpse of the euphoric reaction of the American government and citizens at the news of the *Macedonian*'s capture. Upon reaching New York, Leech witnessed—then began partaking in—the celebratory atmosphere and jubilant crowds.[2] The glee was occasioned not only by the capture of the *Macedonian*, but also the earlier defeat of the *Guerriere* by the U.S. frigate *Constitution*. Later, the *Constitution* notched another victory, capturing the British ship *Java*. These victories over the vaunted, seemingly invincible Royal Navy ensured the U.S. Navy's fame among the American public and paved the way for unprecedented Congressional support in the aftermath of the war. While the War of 1812 on land went badly—far worse than anyone had imagined—in the early days of the war, unexpected naval victories bolstered public morale and infuriated those in Britain who were accustomed to an unbroken record of success at sea.

The glow of victory, however, caused Americans in and out of the Navy to overlook unpleasant strategic realities. Britain had no shortage of ships. Even though it was fighting a two-front war, the Royal Navy's numeric superiority to the Americans was staggering, and single-ship actions such as the *United States–Macedonian* fight risked a huge percentage of America's naval force against a completely disposable British weapon. James Madison and Paul Hamilton never confronted this reality, having given little thought to naval strategy in the months leading up to the war and largely neglecting the maritime element once it began. In 1813, however, William Jones replaced Hamilton at the head of the Navy Department; he brought clear strategic thinking and the force of personality to enforce it, and that changed how the U.S. Navy operated. Jones shied away from the "honor at all costs" mentality that his

John Barry was one of the heroes of the Revolutionary War at sea, and later became the first captain of the U.S. Navy. *Naval History and Heritage Command, NH 51521*

Joshua Barney resigned from being one of the first captains in the Navy over a dispute involving relative rank, but he later became one of the heroes of the War of 1812. *Naval History and Heritage Command, NH 56818*

A contemporary drawing of the USS *President*, one of the original six frigates of the U.S. Navy. The pen and ink illustration was created in 1802 by Antoine Roux. *Naval History and Heritage Command, 76-327-A*

Benjamin Stoddert, first Secretary of the Navy. Portrait by E. F. Andrews. *Naval History and Heritage Command, NH 54797-KN*

“A representation of the medal presented by the United States to Thomas Truxtun esquire, and a copy of the resolution of Congress,” approved March 29, 1800, in honor of the action between USS *Constellation* and the French ship *La Vengeance* on February 1, 1800. Engraving shows both sides of the medal, depicting Truxtun and the battle. *Naval History and Heritage Command, NH 43170*

Thomas Truxtun, one of the new nation's first naval heroes and a frequent source of frustration for the first two men to serve as Secretary of the Navy. *Naval History and Heritage Command, 119313*

Oil on canvas by Orlando Lagman depicting the aftermath of the engagement between the *Enterprise* and the *Tripoli*. Lieutenant Andrew Sterrett is preparing to board the just-surrendered Tripolitan vessel. *Naval History and Heritage Command, NH 54386-KN*

*Burning of the Frigate Philadelphia in the Harbor of Tripoli*, by Edward Moran, 1897. *Naval History and Heritage Command, KN 10849*

Engraving of Commodore John Rodgers, whose decades-long naval career included serving as the first chairman of the Board of Navy Commissioners. *Naval History and Heritage Command, 2008-058-1102*

Small gunboats were a key part of Jefferson's plans for the Navy, though they never lived up to his hopes. *Naval History and Heritage Command, NH 109625*

Robert Smith served as Secretary of the Navy for almost the entirety of Thomas Jefferson's administration. Portrait by Freeman Thorpe. *Naval History and Heritage Command, NH 77361-KN*

This contemporary engraving depicts the American frigate *United States* clashing with the Royal Navy's *Macedonian* on October 25, 1812. *Naval History and Heritage Command, 84-166-B*

Secretary of the Navy William Jones. Portrait by Gilbert Stuart. *Naval History and Heritage Command, 54764-KN*

Lithograph of HMS *Shannon* bringing the captured *Chesapeake* into Halifax. Inscription reads, "To Captain Philip Bowes Vere Broke Bert. K. C. B. This Representation of HMS Shannon Leading Her Prize the American Frigate Chesapeake into Halifax Harbour on the 6th of June 1813, Is Dedicated By His Obliged and Most Grateful Servant R. H. King." *Naval History and Heritage Command, 2019-082-01*

David Porter served in the Quasi War, Tripolitan War, and War of 1812 before becoming one of the first members of the Board of Navy Commissioners. Painting by Orlando S. Lagman. *Naval History and Heritage Command, 66-335-T*

predecessors had so zealously ingrained in the officer corps. He avoided direct combat with the British navy and instead sought to engage in attacks on enemy commerce that would damage the British economy and force Parliament to grant concessions. As shown by James Lawrence's death and the loss of the *Chesapeake*, the officers under Jones' direction proved reluctant in implementing this change, but the course of the war vindicated Jones's judgment.

Meanwhile, the War of 1812 also marked the first major interaction between naval officers and the American public. It did not go particularly well. Naval officers had to deal with recalcitrant and sometimes openly hostile civilians, both in the general public and local officials—particularly in New England, where opposition to the war ran strongest. Their authority in cities fell short of martial law, even when their jurisdiction was facing almost certain invasion by the British. Underfunded and undersupplied, they lacked the resources to enforce their will on populations that were in some cases openly siding with the enemy.

Despite the civil-military strains, the War of 1812 demonstrated a marked degree of professionalism among the Navy's officer corps. There was less-than-enthusiastic enforcement of some of the more unpalatable policies handed down from Washington, but nothing like outright defiance. Although their commitment to the honor of their brotherhood of officers was as strong as ever, naval officers also (mostly) implemented the Navy Department's policies and showed restraint in their interactions with hostile civilians. The standards of professionalism had made substantial advances since the creation of the Navy Department, and the war confirmed and solidified those standards, laying the groundwork for a postwar division of responsibilities that strongly affirmed civilian control of the military while leaving a significant space for the officer corps to manage naval affairs.

The entire nation was woefully unprepared to engage Great Britain, and the Navy was no exception. Jeffersonian Republicans harbored deep mistrust and outright hatred of the British, but they feared the threat posed by large military forces and the taxes required to sustain them far more. Since coming to power, they had limited the country's ability to wage war. This trend continued even as Madison moved ever closer to a declaration of war against the world's mightiest military power. Madison abandoned his predecessor's embargo when he became president, but even as hostilities became increasingly certain during his first term, he failed to rally his party in Congress to provide anything remotely approaching an adequate buildup of the armed forces on land or sea. Congress increased the army only slightly, but just months before declaring war overwhelmingly voted against increasing the Navy.[3] Paul Hamilton faced a host of manpower and materiel shortages at the outset of the conflict. Most of the men, munitions, and supplies the Navy had available went to the frigates, leaving the navy yards that would play a crucial role in combating smuggling and repelling British invasions with deficient materials or none at all.[4] To his credit, Hamilton appealed to Congress for greater appropriations to address these problems, but he met with limited success.[5]

The Great Lakes were in even worse condition, a problem all the more inexcusable since American strategy hinged on seizing Canadian territory. Believing that defeating the Royal Navy was impossible, Madison and his cabinet concluded, not unreasonably, that the best strategy was to seize all or part of Canada and then barter it for concessions on impressments and neutral commerce.[6] Controlling Canada, however, hinged on controlling the Great Lakes. Yet naval officers in charge of gaining and holding these waters had to build fleets from scratch with minimal support from Washington. Although congressional parsimony contributed to these problems, Hamilton bears part of the blame, having sorely neglected in the Lakes in favor of the Atlantic. Because of the great distances and unreliable mail service, commanders in the Great Lakes theater were far more cut off from their civilian superiors than those on the Eastern Seaboard.[7] Hamilton's seeming disregard for the situation on the Canadian border vexed his officers considerably. Lieutenant Melancthon Woolsey, who sent far more letters to the department than he received, begged Hamilton at one point to simply provide him enough officers to man the few ships he did have. "I am now about to sail without a single officer that has seen any service in the Navy," he complained, adding that "not one of my midshipmen have ever been at sea." He continued to supply Hamilton with regular reports of his efforts and plight, still without a response. "It is much to be lamented, sir, that we have not sufficient means of defense," he pleaded a few days later. He finally received a perfunctory response from Hamilton that assured him a few more cannon were on their way. The promise of marginally greater firepower was a help, but did nothing to ease his fear that the secretary was oblivious to his desperate straits.[8]

Hamilton's leadership during wartime was unquestionably lacking, but he did not differ from the president in this regard. Madison was almost no help.[9] As a member of the House of Representatives, he initially opposed the creation of the Navy, and as president he shared his cabinet's conviction that Britain would annihilate the force in short order. While he hoped privateers would harass British commerce and possibly help hasten John Bull to the negotiating table, he assumed American frigates would play no role in the conflict and did not factor them into his strategy. There is evidence that Madison and Hamilton (the instigator of the idea is unclear) at least considered confining the Navy to port once hostilities began, on the assumption that Britain would wipe America's fleet out if it went to sea. The main source for this, Charles Stewart, developed a reputation later in life for exaggerating his own exploits, and he of course took most of the credit for changing the president's mind. William Bainbridge joined with him in traveling to Washington to protest the suggestion. While the accuracy of the story is debatable, it was widely accepted in the years after the war because it fit plausibly with Madison and Hamilton's prewar views. Stewart's occasional looseness with the truth aside, it is certainly the case that neither Madison nor his cabinet expected much from the Navy once the war began.[10]

Hamilton turned to two of his senior officers to provide him with a strategy. Early in the summer of 1812, with war looming, Hamilton asked John Rodgers and Stephen Decatur for their recommendations for using the nation's limited naval forces.[11] Both of them offered sound advice, although, conveniently, each man's recommendations worked out to his own personal benefit. They agreed that it would be a serious mistake to keep the entire Navy in one location, where America might have "the whole of our marine crushed at one blow"—a view that was not far removed from Madison's.[12] Rodgers recognized this reality, but was less worried about grouping ships together. He argued instead for small squadrons to harass British shipping and threaten British colonies. He further argued that one squadron should travel to the coast of England itself, to terrify the population and maximize damage to British commerce. Finally, if an opportune moment presented itself, the entire Navy could form a single fleet and strike at one of the bountiful East India convoys.[13]

Such an ambitious plan was possible, Rodgers argued, because the British sent all their vessels out at the onset of a war to attack the enemy's forces in their own harbors, leaving Britain and its colonies undefended. His judgment was later vindicated, when American privateers wreaked havoc on British shipping, even on the very coast of England.[14] Nevertheless, Rodgers also enjoyed immense personal benefit from his plan. As the senior officer, he would be in command of the largest squadron and thus would be the most likely to win laurels for himself, while Decatur and other ambitious officers would serve under him.[15] If the American Navy was divided up, other officers might win great victories apart from him. Moreover, as squadron commander over Decatur, Rodgers would stand to receive a share of all prizes, whereas if Decatur sailed alone, any prizes the younger officer's ships captured would be of no financial benefit to Rodgers.

Although he recognized the numerical disparity between the American and British navies, when considering the prospect of facing off with the British, Rodgers showed the kind of spirit and national pride the nation expected of its naval officers. With his thrashing of the *Little Belt* still fresh in his mind, Rodgers swept aside any hint of concern about challenging the undefeated might of the Royal Navy. "[The British] have already . . . honored me with the title of *Buccaneer*," he chortled to Hamilton, "and nothing on this side of the grave would afford me with more satisfaction, than . . . affording them a more bitter subject for their still more bitter and illiberal animadversions." He was not only zealous for his own reputation, however. Rodgers' goal for the U.S. Navy was nothing less than to "astonish all Europe." While Britain had enjoyed a string of unbroken success against other European powers, let them challenge Americans, he said, and "they will soon find that we are neither Frenchmen, or Spaniards, Hollanders, or Danes."[16]

Decatur was less verbose in his response, but agreed that concentrating the Navy posed too great a risk. It would be best, he suggested, to send American ships out individually or at most in pairs, thereby ensuring that the British could not destroy nearly the entire Navy in one battle. As to what should be done with these ships, he encouraged the secretary to send them out loaded with ample provisions for long cruises, and "without giving them any specific instructions, as to the place of cruising, but to rely on the enterprise of the officers." His advice was sound, and probably more realistic than Rodgers, but he did not miss the opportunity to call for greater autonomy for himself and his fellow officers from Washington's control, as well as removing himself from Rodgers's command and ensuring that he received full credit—and prize money—from any victories he might win.[17]

Hamilton did not act on either captain's advice right away. He and the entire cabinet continued to waffle on the best use of the Navy even after the declaration of war in June. Gallatin hoped to use what forces America had for commerce protection.[18] Given the vulnerability of American merchant shipping, this was an understandable perspective, but using the Navy in a purely defensive role also stripped it of any chance to force concessions from Britain. In any case, it flew in the face of the Navy's culture. The officer corps had been molded since its creation to favor aggressive action against the enemy. They thirsted for glory, and taking ships from the greatest naval power of the age was their ultimate prize. To spend the war merely safeguarding commercial ships would have been the most frustrating outcome imaginable, and indeed it is impossible to envision America's glory-hungry corps complying with such a strategy. In any case, Hamilton continued to dither in making a decision. In the process, he also avoided definitively siding with either Rodgers or Decatur on whether American ships should cruise in squadrons or separately. On June 21, he sent orders to his captains informing them that they were "entitled to every belligerent right to attack and capture and defend," and urging them to act aggressively against the enemy, without offering any specifics beyond that.[19] Meanwhile, Albert Gallatin argued forcefully for confining the Navy to commerce protection, and Hamilton apparently caved in to his demands; less than a week later, he sent orders to Rodgers informing him that "it has been judged expedient to employ our public armed vessels as to afford our returning commerce all possible protection." He ordered Rodgers and Decatur to cruise separately, but to stay in constant contact in case they determined it would be best to link up into a single squadron. The likelihood that Decatur would ever judge it best for him to leave independent command and subordinate himself to Rodgers was quite remote, of course, but on paper that door was left open. Hamilton thus managed to concur with both Rodgers' and Decatur's suggestions, another example of the secretary's inability to make a decision. Even what he did "decide"—that the foremost purpose of the Navy was to protect American commerce, and striking at the enemy was of decidedly secondary importance—came when he yielded to the desires of the strong-willed Gallatin.[20]

But by this time Rodgers was already at sea. Interpreting Hamilton's initial orders as giving him the right to sail immediately against the Royal Navy, he rushed his men to sea within minutes of receiving word from the secretary that the two nations were at war. Hamilton was unable to communicate with him for the next four months, and essentially lost control of the senior officer of the U.S. Navy.[21] As for Rodgers, his cruise failed to bring him the glory he craved. He managed to bring the British frigate *Belvedera* to action, but when the winds died down, he was unable to draw close enough for his guns to do any serious damage, and the enemy escaped. Throughout the remainder of his cruise, he captured a mere seven small merchant vessels. Although he found it "a truly unpleasant task to be obliged to make a communication thus barren of benefit to our country," he did console himself with the fact that his very presence in the Atlantic occupied the Royal Navy's attention and allowed American merchants to reach home unscathed.[22] This gave Rodgers little consolation though—he had failed to land the spectacular blow against British pride that he so craved; his brash letter to Hamilton recommending a strategy had said nothing about merely distracting the Royal Navy. Nevertheless, Rodgers' cruise hinted at the strategic vision Jones would soon bring to the Navy.

Meanwhile, other officers were enjoying much better luck against their adversaries. Even before Decatur captured Samuel Leech and the *Macedonian*, the frigate *Guerriere* had become the first British ship to strike to an (approximately) equal adversary since John Paul Jones defeated the *Serapis* in 1778. Shortly after that, the long-suffering William Bainbridge finally vindicated his honor in a brutal three-hour battle that ended in the surrender of the British 38-gun *Java*. These victories sparked euphoric celebrations across the country. Britain's naval dominance had been so thoroughly unquestioned since Horatio Nelson wiped out the combined Franco-Spanish fleet at Trafalgar in 1805 that the idea of ships of the Royal Navy striking their colors one after another with no consoling victories seemed unthinkable. Certainly, British observers found it disheartening. From faraway Portugal, the Duke of Wellington groused that the war would end quickly "if we could take one or two of these damned frigates." Although the American ships were technically all larger than the British vessels they captured, that gave little consolation to a naval force that was not used to losing *any* ships, regardless of circumstances.

The Admiralty ordered John Borlase Warren, theater commander in North America, to impress on his officers the need to "[vindicate] the honor of His Majesty's Arms." Sir Philip Broke, among the most tenacious officers in the Royal Navy, lamented to his wife that "honor is a jewel of more value than whole fleets and armies and public prejudice waits not to enquire into the particulars of a defeat where the result is so mortifying."[23] British newspapers were equally distraught. The *Naval Chronicle* announced the *Java*'s loss but refused to print any further details, as "the subject is too painful for us to dwell on." The *London Pilot* managed to comment at greater length. "Anyone who had predicted such a result of an American war this time last year would have been treated as a madman or a traitor," it opened, further reminding its readers that British public opinion (and Madison and his cabinet, it might have added) had assumed it would take only a few months to annihilate the American Navy. Instead, "not a single American frigate has struck her flag." American captains "insult and laugh at our want of enterprise and vigor," while sailing where they please from the West Indies to South America to even Europe itself.[24]

Ecstasy from the American public, dismay from the British Admiralty, and elation from officers whose honor and reputation were exalted in victory could not hide the fact that these frigate victories had limited strategic value. Britain had an abundance of ships; losing three hardly made a dent in the Royal Navy's force, even when fighting a two-front war. In the emotional aftermath of victory, Americans reading accounts of the battles might be forgiven for forgetting this fact, but Paul Hamilton cannot be excused so easily. His duty was to come up with a plan for victory, focusing on what would give his country the best chance to force concessions from Great Britain and achieve the nation's stated war aims. The single-ship actions had little hope of accomplishing that, so long as Britain had an ample supply to draw from. Yet Hamilton was as caught up in the euphoria of the moment as anyone. "In this action, we know not which most to applaud, your gallantry or your skill," he gushed to Hull.[25] In the thrill of victory, the secretary and president were not inclined to lessen the moment by questioning any detail from a heroic captain's account of battle. Thus, Decatur was allowed to insist that the ship he captured was superior to his own in size and firepower, despite the fact that the British ship was clearly smaller. Indeed, in all three of the most celebrated engagements, the American frigate had been slightly larger and boasted more guns than its capture. Later British writers exaggerated the significance of this fact—the ships were roughly equal—but it mattered a great deal for American captains because they took home a larger share of the prize money for capturing or sinking a superior enemy vessel. Delighted as they were with unexpected success, Madison and Hamilton were not about to quibble on this point.[26]

Throughout the early victories of 1812, Secretary Hamilton continued to look primarily to his officers for how to manage the United States' limited naval forces.[27] He did finally make a decision on how to organize his ships, dividing his forces into three squadrons under the command of Rodgers, Decatur, and Bainbridge. But beyond that, the commodores were on their own. He ordered each squadron to "pursue the course, which to the commanding officer may, under all circumstances, appear the most expedient to afford protection to our trade and annoy the enemy." The only caveat was that they were to write the department "at all proper opportunities."[28] Hamilton's deference to his captains only increased with victories. One historian concludes that, by the end of his tenure, his relationship with Rodgers, Decatur, and company was "solicitous and at times almost fawning," and that he was completely beholden to their advice to know how to oversee the Navy.[29] The problem may not have been so much Hamilton's attitude toward his officers as that, lacking a coherent strategy himself, he was easily swayed by others. Daniel Dobbins, a merchant captain on the Great Lakes prior to the war, convinced Hamilton that Presque Isle Bay, which just happened to be his home, would be an ideal spot to construct additional vessels for the battle to control the lakes. Oblivious to the situation on the Great Lakes (or their geography), Hamilton accepted Dobbins' pitch at face value and immediately commissioned him as a sailing master and signed the orders to move ship construction facilities to Presque Isle without consulting Jesse Elliot and Isaac Chauncey, his two officers already at work on the lakes. Although the wisdom of using Presque Isle was later vindicated, Hamilton strained his relations with Elliott and Chauncey by his handling of the episode.[30] Upon dispatching Dobbins, Hamilton returned to ignoring the Great Lakes.

Officers in the Atlantic received more attention, but scarcely more direction. What efforts Hamilton did exert to control his officers were limited and confined to a few of the more problematic captains. He sternly rebuked David Porter for standing by and allowing his crew to tar and feather a seaman who claimed to be British. John Irving, a sailor who apparently was born in Britain but had signed on to an American ship before the declaration of war, informed Porter that he would be unable to take an oath of allegiance to the United States now that the two countries were at war. Momentarily abdicating leadership, Porter cheerfully granted the rest of his crew permission to cover Irving in tar and feathers, and cast him off in a strange port where he had no friends or acquaintances to turn to. The police took him into protective custody.[31] Hamilton was infuriated at Porter's report and sharply informed him that "mobs should never be suffered to exist on board a man of war." Instead, "order and discipline and perfect observance of the law should be enforced."[32] Still, Hamilton's relationship with Porter was always tense, dating back to the captain's days at the New Orleans Station. Only in egregious cases did he intervene in a captain's treatment of those under his command. When a group of employees at the Washington Naval Yard sent him a petition complaining of Thomas Tingey's authoritative ways, he sent the petition back to Tingey and promptly forgot about it.[33] This was certainly in keeping with precedent; like Stoddert and Smith before him, Hamilton preferred to leave officers' relations with their subordinates alone, be they seamen or civilian employees.

Hamilton also found himself in trouble with his officers over promotion practices. While he initially tried to make the department more efficient and systematized, he had a tendency to get carried away in the aftermath of victory. Following the precedent set with Stephen Decatur, Hamilton allowed Lieutenant Charles Morris to jump two ranks to captain, skipping that of master commandant, after his heroic conduct in the *Constitution*'s capture of the *Guerriere*. Fellow officers, and especially the long-serving masters commandant Morris leapt over, were disgusted at what they regarded as excessive reward.[34] While all praised Morris, they felt that a promotion of just one rank would have sufficed. Master Commandant Arthur Sinclair pointedly informed the secretary that he had been serving faithfully for fifteen years, his only shortcoming next to Morris being that his career had begun in peacetime. If every lieutenant with the good fortune to fight a battle with a British frigate jumped over all his peers, Sinclair hinted that Hamilton would face a mass exodus from the officer corps. Master Commandant James Lawrence was even more forceful, announcing that he would have no choice but to resign from the service if Morris moved past him in rank.[35]

Hamilton scrambled to contain the crisis. First and foremost, he stared down Lawrence's threat to resign, writing him that, "if (without cause) you leave the service of our country, there will still remain heroes and patriots to support the honor of its flag," essentially warning the disgruntled master commandant that he was free to walk away from the service, and it could survive without him. Calling Lawrence's bluff apparently worked; the aggrieved officer immediately wrote back a less than contrite letter accusing Hamilton of questioning his patriotism, but he at least assured the secretary that he had no thoughts of actually resigning.[36] Hamilton apparently learned from the debacle. When Stephen Decatur tried to secure a similar reward for his first lieutenant, William Allen, after defeating the *Macedonian*, Hamilton declined.[37]

Although Lawrence backed down from his threat to resign, he did not give up entirely. He and Charles Ludlow, another master commandant over whom Morris jumped, wrote a petition to the Senate asking them not to confirm Morris' appointment as a captain. Hamilton also delayed in sending Morris' promotion to the Senate for ratification, perhaps hoping to let the furor die down somewhat. Thus, Morris hung in limbo for the rest of the year, serving as an acting captain, and with his forthcoming promotion publicized across the nation in the celebration of the *Guerriere*'s capture, but with the Senate unable to either approve or deny a formal commission.[38] In the meantime, Hamilton's general ineptitude in managing the Navy Department came to a head, and Madison asked for his resignation late in 1812. His successor, William Jones, considered the matter with Madison almost as soon as he took office. While Lawrence had walked back his resignation threat, the fact remained that there were eight very angry masters commandant who might still opt to leave once Morris assumed his captaincy. Jones decided not to press his luck. He did send Morris's promotion to the Senate for confirmation, but also recommended three masters commandant whose excellent service, he believed, entitled them to promotion as well. Among those Jones put forward for promotion was James Lawrence, who thus retained his seniority over Morris. Charles Ludlow, however, remained a master commandant, moving Morris ahead of him in rank. He made good on his threat to resign, and Madison and Jones let him go.[39]

William Jones' replacement of Hamilton came as a surprise to no one. Although an adequate secretary over a tiny navy in peacetime, Hamilton simply lacked the ability to manage a service at war. His problem was not only that he was overly deferential to his officer corps. That was certainly true most of the time, but he also occasionally overruled them or gave explicit orders, and his forceful handling of Lawrence's resignation threat shows that he was capable of standing up to his officers if forced to do so. The major issue in his directives and relations with those under his authority was his inconsistency, and the fact that he proved too easily convinced to follow anyone else's advice on virtually any issue. At his core, Hamilton had no coherent strategy, no concrete idea of how to put his means toward a definite end, and thus he was willing to defer to anyone who appeared to know what they were doing. The rumors of his alcoholism were largely inaccurate, but his inept management of the department allowed claims that he did his job in a drunken haze to flourish. Under pressure from Congress and belatedly realizing that the Navy would have to play a major role if America was to achieve anything approaching a victory, Madison extracted a resignation from Hamilton.[40]

Although Congress, and much of the nation, saw the war at sea as a stark contrast between spectacular victories in the theater and equally spectacular mismanagement from the capital, the truth was that the frigate victories masked serious problems. Early on, the United States had enjoyed the advantage of Britain's neglect of the war, focused as the Royal Navy was on the seemingly never-ending struggle to topple Napoleon. With most of the British fleet dedicated to European waters, it was impossible to mount a truly effective blockade or to provide adequate protection to British commerce. Both the U.S. Navy and America's fleets of privateers could run wild in the early months of the war, but once Britain began channeling adequate resources into the fight, America's fortunes at sea declined considerably. Beginning early in 1813 and increasing as the year went on, privateers and frigates found it progressively more difficult to escape from the British blockade, while Britain could launch lightning amphibious raids on American coastal cities with near-impunity. Hamilton's replacement thus faced a very different strategic situation from his predecessor.[41]

The man who confronted these challenges was William Jones. Jones' connection to the Navy dated almost from its creation. In 1798, an aspirant to the officer corps begged Jones to "use your interest with the Secretary of the Navy on my behalf."[42] Jones' familiarity with the sea stretched back before that, having served on Thomas Truxtun's privateer during the American Revolution after service in the Continental army under Washington. Since then, he had enjoyed a thriving career as a ship captain and merchant. He was recognized as a strong candidate for Secretary of the Navy early on, with Jefferson offering him the post before turning to Robert Smith. With the country at war, Jones found it more difficult to say no to Madison. While Jones weighed the possibility of taking the post, Congressman Jonathan Roberts of Pennsylvania appealed to him that the country was "in a state of public suffering to be relieved only under your saving hand."[43] Moreover, the public outpouring of support for the Navy meant that instead of overseeing downsizing as he would have for Jefferson, Jones could now head a growing maritime force.[44] On the other hand, Jones' business was suffering from the embargo and the war, and accepting the post would only cause his personal finances to deteriorate further. He came very close to declining the position on those grounds, but he concluded that "we are engaged in a war *more just and inevitable* than our glorious revolution," and "the same indignant feelings which impelled me, not to the 'tented field,' but to the frozen *untented* heights of Princeton, Pluckamin, and Morristown" (emphasis in original) now compelled him to abandon his private affairs for the sake of his country.[45] Laying aside personal considerations, Jones accepted the post.

Jones threw himself into the task of managing a wartime navy with vigor. He was up every morning at seven and at his desk until midnight, he wrote to his wife, Eleanor. He fortified himself each day with four glasses of wine at dinner but, no doubt mindful of his predecessor's scandals, he did not allow himself "a drop of any kind of spirit since I have been here."[46] Although he considered his new role "a Herculean task," and appreciated the commiseration of friends, he was still upbeat about the labors he faced. "Having accepted the trust with reluctance, but with the purest motives and most ardent zeal for the cause of our country, why should I despair?"[47]

His most frustrating task, even more than grappling with the Royal Navy, was removing those he considered corrupt or inept from the administrative posts. He complained of the "excessively disordered and confused state of which I have found every branch of the department," and the "corruption of self-interested men who have taken root in the establishment and, like the voracious poplar, nothing can survive in their shade."[48] He promptly fired all department employees but one. Even Chief Clerk Charles Goldsborough was not immune from his purging. Although he had contributed a great deal to the department in its early days, even briefly serving as acting secretary prior to Hamilton's arrival, Goldsborough had apparently followed his boss's example a bit too much early in the war, doing little to salvage the department from Hamilton's mismanagement. Jones might have been inclined to remove a long-serving and powerful subordinate from a prior administration anyway, but Goldsborough did himself no favors when he began trading increasingly vicious public broadsides with Dr. Thomas Ewell, a former naval surgeon. Ewell referred to Goldsborough as "one of the most cunning scoundrels with whom I have ever come in contact," and compared him to a rabid dog. Goldsborough gave as good as he got, and the entire affair became a giant embarrassment to the Navy Department.[49] Jones insisted on Goldsborough's resignation, though he did feel some compassion for the man, and allowed him to remain in the department a few days and purchase some of its furniture to at least give the appearance of a mutual and amicable parting.[50] Benjamin Homans, a staunch Republican and former merchant captain who had the endorsement of Vice President Elbridge Gerry and Secretary of State James Monroe, had the unenviable task of replacing Goldsborough as clerk and trying to restore some semblance of order to the department.[51]

His relationship with his officers got off to a good start. Decatur no doubt spoke for many of his brethren when he wrote Jones to express his happiness with the change in leadership. "I in common with all my brother officers feel now that the establishment in which our feelings and interest are involved will have nothing to struggle against, but such things as ought fairly to be charged against it," he wrote, apparently believing that the Navy would be free to achieve new heights of success against the Royal Navy, now that its incompetent civilian head was out of the way. Decatur added that "whatever may have been the talents of the gentleman filling that office, his deficiency in practical nautical knowledge was such as to increase the expense of our establishment infinitely beyond what it ought to have been," and he hoped "the enormous unnecessary expenses our establishment has been taxed with" would cease under Jones' direction.[52] Bainbridge likewise rejoiced at Jones' appointment, and commiserated with his old friend—and now superior—about "the unorganized state of your department. . . . I can say that there never was any system in it, and for the want of which great abuses have crept in."[53]

Though no doubt gratified to receive Bainbridge and Decatur's endorsement, Jones came into office determined to make sure every officer knew who was in charge in the Navy Department. "The latitude and discretion you have been in the habit of exercising is altogether inadmissible, and must not be repeated," he wrote to one officer early in his tenure.[54] As with Smith and Hamilton, spending habits proved the biggest source of conflict between Jones and his officers. He fired another officer for making an unauthorized purchase (the man had been tried once before for conduct unbecoming an officer). More common were his sharp reprimands to officers who consistently exceeded what Jones thought were acceptable expenditures. "I have great concern that the expenses on the New Orleans [Station] are extravagant beyond all reasonable bounds," he charged one captain, before threatening not to reimburse him. Throughout his tenure, he waged an ongoing battle to "check the great and astonishing extravagance" of his officers' spending.[55] "The expenditure at your station has been very extravagant and must be corrected," he ordered another captain, otherwise "for every expense not authorized by law or the sanction of this department . . . you will be held accountable."[56]

Still, Jones followed the precedent of giving limited attention to disputes between officers and trusting officers to manage affairs on their stations without his interference. Indeed, Jones waited months to weigh in on a chain-of-command clash in Norfolk, even after both officers appealed to him for clarification. Captain Charles Gordon commanded the *Constellation*, based at the Norfolk Navy Yard, while Captain Joseph Tarbell commanded the flotilla there. In December of 1813, Tarbell angered Gordon by taking a small number of gunboats out on a raid against British forces, which terrified the local residents that the bulk of the city's defenses would be captured. They complained to Gordon, who complained to Jones, who did nothing. Tarbell for his part later protested to the secretary about Gordon ordering the flotilla to pour time and resources into helping the *Constellation* escape the British blockade.[57] Under repeated appeals from both men, Jones clarified the chain of command, but initially tried to do so without stripping either officer of his authority. The flotilla, Jones wrote, was under Tarbell's command, and while the department wished him to use the flotilla to aid the *Constellation*'s escape, "the extent and nature of cooperation" was entirely at Tarbell's discretion. Only later, when the blockade had become so severe that Gordon's escape was utterly hopeless, did Jones finally establish Gordon as the commander over all naval forces at Norfolk.[58] Jones also rejected a request from William Bainbridge to put the Marine guards at navy yards under his authority. Under the laws of the time, Marines were under the authority of the captain and naval regulations when at sea, but they came under the Army's jurisdiction on land. This meant that the Marines at the Charlestown Navy Yard were free from the threat of corporal punishment, a method of discipline that Bainbridge was known to dole out liberally. Jones rejected Bainbridge's request on the grounds that he had no legal authority to change the rules, and also took the chance to issue a rare commentary on a naval officer's treatment of subordinates. While he never tried to stop flogging in the Navy, Jones did warn Bainbridge that such punishments "may brutalize but cannot reform," and urged the captain to adopt more "mild and humane leadership."[59]

Jones displayed similar trust in naval officers to manage joint operations. While he found it necessary to order his captains, at times, to coordinate with land forces, he sympathized with their frustrations at joint command and granted them considerable leeway to clash with their Army counterparts. "In all cases where your cooperation with the military shall be required, you are to be the exclusive judge of the nature, extent, time, and circumstances of the required cooperation," he wrote to Arthur Sinclair, adding only that he should put forth a genuine effort to give any aid that he could "with propriety."[60]

While Jones sought to maintain the prerogatives officers were used to, he emphatically affirmed the Navy Department's right to determine when to defer to officers' wishes, and when to assert its own authority. When one captain wrote to complain that the first lieutenant on his ship was not satisfactory, Jones took the opportunity to lecture him on the department's determination over officer assignments. While in principle Jones wished all captains to command only subordinates in whom they placed complete confidence, that principle "must have its limits, and those limits must be determined by this Department. . . . The judgment and opinion of commanders will always have, with me, their due weight," but the Navy Department was ultimately responsible for officer assignments.[61]

On the Great Lakes, Jones showed a similar preference for trusting officers with most of the oversight of their stations, while also strongly affirming the department's authority whenever it was called into question. Isaac Chauncey commanded the entire Great Lakes theater from his bases on Lake Ontario, while Oliver Hazard Perry commanded the forces on Lake Erie. Initially, Chauncey had asked for Perry, but any goodwill between the two quickly vanished in a competition for scarce men and resources. Perry complained that Chauncey was withholding desperately needed seamen, and the men he did send were the worst of what was available. Chauncey, for his part, was annoyed at Perry's complaining, and more annoyed at his subordinate writing directly to the Secretary of the Navy rather than going through the chain of command. In addition to complaining directly to Jones, copies of the nasty letters between the two men ended up on the secretary's desk as well. Jones tried to stay out of the conflict, intervening only when he found it unavoidable.[62]

Jones, did, however, assert the department's authority when Perry tried to use his quarrel with Chauncey to escape the Great Lakes theater altogether. "I cannot serve longer under an officer who has been so totally regardless of my feelings," Perry complained. "I beg most respectfully and most earnestly that I may be speedily removed from this station." In his response, Jones tried to butter up Perry first, commiserating with his frustrations and praising his devotion to country and duty, but in the end he rejected Perry's request emphatically. "It is the duty of an Officer . . . to sacrifice all personal motives & feelings when in collision with the public good," he wrote to Perry, before ordering him to remain on his current station.[63] This proved enormously fortunate for Perry, who only two months later won lasting fame at the Battle of Lake Erie, where he seized control of the lake from the British. This, combined with Thomas Macdonough's victory on Lake Champlain the following year, played a far greater role in forcing Britain to abandon the war than any frigate victories, and helped maintain national morale after the string of naval victories on the high seas ceased.[64]

As with all his predecessors, Jones came into office understanding that naval officers represented the nation by their conduct, and if one of them behaved in a shameful manner he shamed the entire country. "The moment an officer becomes a commander," he wrote to one lieutenant thirsting for promotion, "the honor and reputation of the nation is committed to his single judgment, discretion, and valor."[65] However, Jones took a more limited view of officers' duty to national honor than any man who had overseen the Navy Department to that point. He regarded "impetuosity" or "dashing" as signs of desperation, and commented to one officer that "certainty of superiority" mattered more than plunging recklessly into a fight.[66] Jones wanted officers to exercise restraint, not risk battle with the Royal Navy needlessly. When he learned one of the service's most promising young officers had been killed in combat, he lamented to Madison that the "excessive ardour and prowess of our officers will not be restrained until we sustain a few losses."[67]

Unlike Hamilton, Jones came into office with a clear idea of how he planned to match America's naval means with its stated goals of forcing British concessions. His new strategy, however, marked a radical departure from earlier attitudes in the Navy Department. No longer would officers be pressed to hazard everything in the pursuit of national honor. Instead, Jones instituted a cautious policy that praised officers who shrunk from needless combat. The purpose of sending out the U.S. Navy against Britain was not primarily to achieve glory, earn prize money, or boost public morale (though that was a welcome bonus), and it was certainly not to cripple the Royal Navy. Jones sought to damage British commerce enough to affect her economy and force concessions regarding impressment and neutral rights.[68] While Stoddert had opened his career as Secretary of the Navy by informing his most senior officer that "a spirit of enterprise and adventure cannot be too much encouraged in the officers under your command," Jones took a different tack, advising his officers, "Our great inferiority [to the British] in naval strength does not permit us to meet them . . . without hazarding the precious germ of our national glory."[69] Where Hamilton had told his officers it was their duty to "be prepared and determined at every hazard to vindicate the injured honor of our navy" and "maintain and support at any risk and cost the dignity of your flag," Jones instructed that they were "strictly prohibited from giving or receiving a challenge to or from an enemy vessel . . . *the character of the American Navy does not require those feats of chivalry*" (emphasis added).[70]

Jones based his change of outlook and tactics on simple math. Britain could replace the ships it lost, while America could not. Rather, naval vessels should cruise individually and target "rich and exposed commercial fleets," which would force Britain to pull valuable ships away from the blockade, thus achieving "the two-fold object of increasing the pressure upon the enemy and relieving ourselves."[71] In this, the new secretary had the president's wholehearted backing. Madison encouraged Jones to order captains "never to fight when they can avoid it, and employ themselves entirely in destroying the commerce of the Enemy."[72]

Jones also forbade his officers from bringing prizes into port for adjudication. Not only was it virtually impossible to get a prize all the way back to the United States without it being retaken by the British, but by diminishing his own crew to man the prize a captain made his ship vulnerable—any enemy ships taken should be promptly destroyed. Burning prizes was frustrating enough, but Jones' instructions to avoid engaging Royal Navy ships were even more repugnant to his officer corps. By and large, naval officers complied—with Lawrence and the *Chesapeake* being the notable exception. By the summer of 1813 their main problem was simply getting to sea through the British blockade, not what to do once they got there.[73]

Rodgers managed to slip through the blockade in the *President*, and his cruise perfectly illustrates the disconnect between Jones' strategy and the mentality of naval officers. Rodgers sailed out in the spring of 1813 and began seizing and burning British merchant vessels, forcing the Royal Navy to divert valuable ships to track him down. The American captain led the British on a merry chase across the Atlantic for five months. Still, at the end of it, he had only a dozen destroyed merchant ships to show for his efforts. While not a bad record for a cruise of that length, Rodgers still felt less than elated with his performance. A hundred merchantmen probably would not have satisfied him. Rodgers wanted his name added alongside Hull, Decatur, and Bainbridge; he wanted to capture a prize from the Royal Navy. After all the hardships at sea suffered by himself and his crew, he still returned feeling that he had failed to "add any additional luster to the character of our little navy."[74]

Jones had no such reservations. He did not want Rodgers to capture a single British vessel. Given the disparity of numbers, the loss of one would not restrict the enemy's ability to blockade the coast. Far better to keep an entire squadron in pursuit, while also showing British insurers that the Royal Navy was helpless to protect its merchant vessels.[75] If Rodgers struggled to accept the concept, it was not lost on the British public. "How gratifying it must be to him," reported the *Morning Chronicle*, "to learn that not single ships but squadrons were dispatched after him, one under the command of *an admiral*" (emphasis in original).[76] Of course, part of Rodgers' ability to draw such a significant force away from blockade duty to give chase stemmed from the earlier frigate victories. Britain dared not send "single ships" after the *President* specifically because they feared a repeat of their earlier embarrassments. But this only serves as further evidence that the American Navy did not need any more engagements with the British. Their earlier victories were sufficient to prompt an overreaction whenever a U.S. ship slipped through the blockade.[77]

Meanwhile, the British finally achieved a measure of redemption for their debacle at sea during the first year of the war when Broke captured the *Chesapeake*. When it became obvious that the ship was lost, the dying Lawrence urged his men to blow it up rather than allow it to fall into British hands. Fortunately for all aboard, the remaining officers ignored him, loath though they were to strike the flag.[78] Lawrence's seemingly outrageous order was not entirely an American phenomenon. A British lieutenant urged Captain John S. Carden to sink the *Macedonian* with all hands rather than surrender to Decatur, though he too was overruled.[79] For many in this generation of naval officers, death seemed preferable to disgrace. Of course, some of this was more empty talk than genuine attitudes; no one ever actually blew up their ship rather than surrender in the War of 1812, nor did any captain fight to the last man, despite multiple captures by both navies. Such conduct would have violated international norms of warfare, but the fact that such outlandish suggestions appear in multiple battles speaks to how much officers of the period hated the thought of admitting defeat. Falling honorably was better than craven surrender or submission, but it was still a loss.

Certainly the American reaction to the loss of the *Chesapeake* found no consolation in honorable defeat. The U.S. Navy had nothing to be ashamed of in the aftermath of the battle, all things considered. Broke was among the best officers in the Royal Navy, and he sailed to North America carrying an almost pathological obsession to capture an American frigate. The two ships were roughly equal in size, weight of metal, and crews, and Broke had enjoyed his share of luck as well. Yet the American officer corps was not the least bit interested in admitting defeat in a fair fight. They immediately began a quest to look for scapegoats and excuses, disregarding the fact that Lawrence and his men had fought with honor and a large portion of the men aboard had given their lives before the ship finally fell.[80] Had this battle opened the war, the American reaction would surely have been very different. Lawrence had fulfilled the expectations laid down for naval officers by Stoddert, Smith, and Hamilton, and enthusiastically accepted by the leaders of the officer corps. He had not shrunk from battle, he had stood courageously on deck throughout the engagement at the cost of his own life (in the mold of Nelson), and he had earned the approbation of his enemies. That glorious defeats were no longer good enough speaks to the growing confidence of the officer corps, as well as the heightened expectations created by the war's initial successes. Victory and victory alone was an acceptable outcome now, and the quest for excuses for the *Chesapeake*'s loss began as soon as word of the defeat spread throughout the country.

The court of inquiry heaped blame on the *Chesapeake*'s bugler, William Brown, claiming that in his terror he had failed to sound the men to quarters fast enough, and had subsequently sounded the bugle with inadequate zeal. He was sentenced to three hundred lashes, though Madison reduced that to one hundred. Still not satisfied, the Navy also charged Acting Third Lieutenant William Cox with negligence. Cox had helped carry the dying Lawrence below, then struggled to get back on deck through a crowd of fleeing seamen. For this, the court had him cashiered, and Madison readily signed off on the verdict. Cox served as a private in the Army for the remainder of the war, then spent the rest of his life fighting to clear his name. It was not until 1952 that the verdict was finally repudiated, a century after his death.[81]

In addition to fixating the blame on two men, a host of other excuses for the *Chesapeake*'s performance began to circulate. A large contingent of Portuguese seamen supposedly diminished the fighting ability of the crew, according to one rumor. Many also claimed, not unreasonably, that the crew was exceptionally green, with most of the men having never experienced combat before and the crew so new as to be unfamiliar with the ship. Improbably—and in a mirror image of British claims made about American victories earlier in the war—naval officers even insisted that the *Shannon* was significantly larger than the *Chesapeake*.

Jones, however, responded not with dubious excuses but with fury that his orders had been ignored and one of his most valuable ships was lost in a needless battle. He reiterated, even more forcefully, that officers should not engage with Royal Navy vessels. "Should any attempt be made to allure you by a challenge to single combat, I am directed by the President to prohibit strictly your acceptance," he wrote to Charles Stewart. Reiterating his earlier exhortation that America's honor was not worth the loss of irreplaceable frigates, he bluntly told Stewart that "[Madison's] confidence in your skill and gallantry is entire, and no apprehensions are maintained for the honor of the flag." The first priority for captains was no longer proving American mettle, but "the safety of the precious ship entrusted to your care."[82]

If their ability to fight the British was diminished, naval officers continued to clash with each other too. As usual, the issues of relative rank and prize money drove a wedge between many fellow captains. Stephen Decatur took one of his subordinates to court over the prize money for a capture made thousands of miles from his location. On January 13, 1813, while operating off the coast of Africa, the *Chesapeake*—nominally part of Decatur's squadron, although Decatur was in New York at the time—encountered a British merchant vessel that had foolishly strayed from its naval convoy. Captain Samuel Evans of the *Chesapeake* easily seized it, and the ship and cargo were condemned (in maritime legal parlance) in New Hampshire for almost $200,000. Initially, the prize money was awarded only to Evans and his crew, but Decatur immediately pounced. Suffering from failing eyesight and ill health, Evans permanently shifted to shore assignments as soon as he returned to port, passing power of attorney and prize money disbursal duties to his purser, Thomas Chew. Although he was considerably inferior to Decatur in rank, Chew was unwilling to disburse prize money to him or anyone else until the legality of Decatur's claim was settled. In theory, Decatur could have made trouble for Chew, given his rank and immense popularity, but he apparently agreed without complaint to hand the matter over to the courts. He no doubt realized that this would set precedent, but also that he had the overwhelming weight of English common law practice behind him. His calculations proved correct—the court awarded him the squadron commander's share of one-third of the captain's earnings.[83] The incident was settled amicably, by all accounts. Jones, for his part, kept out of it. He apparently regarded it as a matter for the courts and made no effort to intervene in a personal squabble.

In addition to their occasional clashes with each other, officers had to deal with tense relations with the American people whom they were sworn to defend. Prior to the War of 1812, civilians' interaction with naval officers had been fairly limited and, not unrelated, generally harmonious. The exception, of course, was when naval officers were called on to enforce Jefferson's embargo, seriously damaging their standing with civilians. But the thrilling victories over the Royal Navy made captains popular with Americans again, and they enjoyed a brief moment of celebrity as the country's most gallant heroes. Unfortunately, these heroes had a less inspiring perception of Americans. They complained constantly to Hamilton and Jones about civilian trade with the enemy, legal and otherwise, and rampant smuggling.[84] In the Northwest, Thomas Macdonough even had to send one of his men away to avoid prosecution after he was attacked by a tavern keeper and his men killed the assailant in the scuffle.[85] In Portsmouth—part of present-day Maine—Isaac Hull tried to get a Marine sentinel who shot and killed a civilian tried by a military tribunal, believing there was no chance of him getting a fair trial from the state of Massachusetts. Jones and Attorney General Richard Rush initially supported Hull in refusing to hand the man over to the Massachusetts authorities, but when the courts determined that the Marine had fired from Massachusetts' soil, Hull promptly handed him over. Fortunately for the young man, he did receive an impartial hearing and was found not guilty.[86]

Direct clashes between civilians and naval officers became especially frequent when the Navy Department appointed captains to oversee defensive preparations for British invasions. The war seemed to confirm the worst fears of standing militaries raised by Americans since before the Revolution. But naval officers' authority in shore stations, even when the threat of British invasion was imminent, never approached absolute. Although a poor wartime president in many ways, Madison deserves high marks for his scrupulous adherence to civil liberties. The restraint displayed by the Navy Department was part of this larger policy.[87] Although laudable from a constitutional perspective, Madison's regard for civil liberties meant that naval officers and their Army counterparts quarreled with one another and civilian officials in a murky civil-military division of authority that usually produced little in the way of effectiveness.

Few faced as much hostility from the civilian population as Joshua Barney. His naval career had seemingly ended after his stint in the French navy before the Quasi War, and accusations of deficient patriotism or even treason had dogged him ever since. Even when the United States declared war on Great

Britain and was desperate for officers, Hamilton refused to grant Barney a commission, and instead he sailed out as a privateer. A reasonably successful run against British shipping, and no small measure of desperation on the part of the Navy Department, finally enabled him to return to service, and Jones assigned him to lead the defense of the Chesapeake.[88] Although he threw himself into the task, he was less enthusiastic about protecting the inhabitants of the region, many of whom seemed to favor the British. Barney grew increasingly disgusted with the Federalists who dominated local politics, and they seemed to confirm his dim view at every turn. One man openly encouraged his fellow citizens not to resist a British invasion; he tried to obtain information from Barney that he planned to pass on to the enemy. Barney tried to have the man arrested as a spy, but was apparently prevented from doing so. Meanwhile, a militia unit not only abandoned Barney, but absconded with vital provisions, while other civilians openly wished both Barney and the president were condemned to hell.[89]

Barney did finally lash out against at least one Baltimorean. Lemuel Taylor wrote to the department and accused the captain of being a "most abandoned rascal as to politics and morals," and claimed that "he is despised by nine-tenths of those who have taken part in the defense of Baltimore." Jones rallied to Barney's defense, publishing a lengthy letter in the same paper strongly endorsing the captain's character and career. The secretary called Taylor's accusations "flatigious [*sic*] libel," and taunted him that his accusations "[have] at length been read by the scavengers . . . of the common sewer." Taylor responded by calling Jones "an unprincipled villain and a base coward."[90] Given the exchange, it is probably not surprising that Jones followed precedent and looked the other way while Barney fought a duel with Taylor, slightly wounding him.[91]

Jones' support for Barney in his clashes with civilians only went so far, however. Opposed to the war and even more opposed to anything that impaired their ability to make money, local merchants adamantly refused to provide Barney with the supplies he desperately needed to fend off a British invasion. Jones and Madison alike apparently never even considered the idea of allowing Barney or his counterparts in other Federalist cities to requisition supplies; the prospect of even limited martial law was likewise not up for discussion.[92] The resistance of the merchant community to helping Barney extended to his efforts to acquire men as well as materiel. Barney tried to recruit seamen from the city, but with limited success. Even at the height of the British blockade, many preferred to take their chances trying to get to sea on merchant ships or privateers rather than defending against an invasion. "The cupidity of our merchants is such that they care not how much the city is threatened [as long as] they can get a vessel to sea," Barney groused to Jones.[93]

By the time the war ended, the situation became so intolerable that Barney once again quit the Navy in protest. He and his men had performed heroically at the Battle of Bladensburg, a single bright spot in an otherwise humiliating defeat, yet their contribution failed to earn them anything but callous disregard from their country.[94] Barney then watched in disgust while for months after the battle the government failed to pay his men, until many of them were gaunt with hunger and their wives reduced to begging in the streets. Under the circumstances, he evaded and then defied orders to put them to work raising sunken merchant vessels so that civilians (many of whom had infuriated Barney by their lack of patriotism) could resume making money while the war continued. Shortly thereafter, he resigned in a rage, citing the government's dreadful treatment of himself and his men, and fears that, badly undermanned and undersupplied, "much will be expected from us, and we must disappoint public expectation to our discredit."[95]

William Jones had stepped down as Secretary of the Navy by this point, and either interim Secretary Benjamin Homans or Jones' replacement, Benjamin Crowninshield, convinced Barney to withdraw his resignation.[96] The reasoning behind the decision to hold on to Barney harkens back to Truxtun's treatment in the Quasi War. Barney had mounted a laudable defense at a time when the British were launching amphibious coastal raids with impunity. Whoever enticed him to come back probably felt sympathy for his reasons for resigning, which in this case had more to do with the care of those entrusted to his authority, rather than his own honor. But the main issue was that the Navy badly needed his services in a war that was going very decidedly in Britain's favor by that point.

Meanwhile, William Bainbridge also struggled to maintain a healthy relationship with the people he was supposed to protect. After capturing the *Java*, Bainbridge was stationed in Boston to supervise construction of America's first 74-gun battleship, the *Independence*. He surely knew he would face a less than enthusiastic response from the local population. Massachusetts was a hotbed of Federalism, and its citizens' opposition to the war culminated in

December 1814 with the island of Nantucket formally declaring neutrality.[97] The rest of the state was little better; the governor of Massachusetts, Caleb Strong, had declared a day of fasting and prayer in June 1812 to seek God's forgiveness for declaring war on "the nation from whom we descended, and which for many generations has been the bulwark of the religion we profess." British blockading ships actually entertained prominent Federalist citizens at the height of the war. A few of those prominent citizens even requested that Bainbridge hand the almost-complete ship over to the British in hopes they would relent from attacking the city.[98]

A fair number of Bostonians eventually came around and contributed to the war effort, but only when the threat of invasion became dire. Even when the local government agreed to take measures against a probable invasion, there was civil-military conflict. The citizens hoped to sink hulks in the harbor, making it impossible for British ships to get in. Bainbridge countered that it would also make it impossible for U.S. naval vessels to get out, and he opposed the measure. When the local citizens pressed for their plan, Bainbridge referred to Secretary Jones, who agreed with the captain that the matter was "a question of some delicacy." Jones concluded that a state government had no right to blockade the American Navy, and he authorized Bainbridge to oppose the plan for sinking hulks. Jones still stopped short of completely overruling the citizens of Boston though. He told Bainbridge that "the President trusts the committee [Boston's marine committee] will ultimately see the superior advantages" of not blocking the harbor, but it fell to Bainbridge to persuade them with Madison's apparent backing; the captain was not given authority to forbid the blockading scheme in the president's name.[99] Inevitably, the matter came up again, this time with Bostonians pressing for permission to sink the hulks in the event a British invasion was imminent. Whether because he realized further naval operations out of Boston were unlikely or because he saw there was no stopping the plan, Bainbridge wrote back to Jones saying he now supported the idea, and Jones deferred to his judgment.[100] As with Barney, Jones—with Madison's backing—refused to assert too much authority over the local government, and the naval commander in Boston was left to negotiate with sometimes-hostile citizens as best he could.

Isaac Hull found himself fighting a two-front war from the Portsmouth Navy Yard, located on an island between the Federalist strongholds of Massachusetts and New Hampshire. As Hull prepared to fend off British raiding parties, he also kept a watchful eye on the Federalist populations that he was tasked with protecting. Republican William Plumer had recently served as governor of New Hampshire, and he had taken a few steps toward defending the coasts and islands from the British, but the elections of 1812 ousted Plumer in favor of Federalist John Taylor Gilman, who made his own views of the war clear by promptly revoking orders to supply rations to militiamen assigned to defend the state. "I see no disposition on the part of the people to secure their harbor," Hull lamented to Jones; "we must therefore endeavor to defend ourselves."[101] Hull became convinced that he was without support among the population, later writing to Jones that even in the event of an actual British invasion of the island, the locals would do nothing to help. He pleaded with Gilman for munitions for the forts on the island, and asked the War Department to further impress upon the recalcitrant governor the urgency of his requests, but to no avail.[102] Gilman budged a little when British vessels appeared within eyesight of the coast, but even then Hull's difficulties continued. While Hull lived in, and was responsible for defending, New Hampshire, the island that housed the Portsmouth yard was technically part of Massachusetts, then under the control of Bainbridge's nemesis, Caleb Strong. Strong consistently refused to grant Hull any materials that he could keep under state control.[103] Meanwhile, the enthusiasm of the populations of both New Hampshire and Massachusetts fluctuated based on their perceived likelihood of a British attack, and Hull lived under constant strain until he received word of the end of the war.[104]

Jones and Madison were certainly aware of their officers' troubles. In addition to their frequent complaints, they also received regular updates from pro-war citizens on trade with the enemy and near-treason from Federalists.[105] In every instance, naval officers assigned to protect citizens from British coastal raids depended on their own ability to inspire—or beg for—support to rally civilians to their own defense. Despite the dire nature of the war effort by 1814, the government only allowed very limited imposition of federal will. Full martial law, Reginald Stuart argues, was "politically impossible to propose, let alone apply and enforce."[106] The results were predictable. In Baltimore, where the people of the city voluntarily rallied around John Rodgers, the British failed in their attack on the city. Elsewhere, British raiding parties were able to land on the American coast at will, inflicting dreadful damage, culminating in the burning of the capital on August 24, 1814.[107]

Jones' career in the Navy Department was influential but brief. Like Hamilton, his personal finances suffered greatly during his tenure in government, and he too became worn down by the staggering administrative responsibilities. He tendered his resignation in the spring of 1814, although he remained on another eight months until Madison found a replacement.[108] By the time he left Washington in December of 1814, the war was essentially over. American and British negotiators formally agreed on the Treaty of Ghent less than a month later. Jones' successes had been limited. His commerce-raiding strategy had frustrated the British, but the strength of the blockade by the end of the war meant that few warships were getting to sea, and those that did inflicted little damage thanks to the Royal Navy's convoys. Moreover, throughout Jones' tenure, the Navy proved totally incapable of preventing British coastal raids. He took over a badly undersupplied department overseeing an undermanned navy, and the situation only deteriorated under his watch. All of this, it should be added, was largely beyond his control. Given the tools at Jones' disposal, it is remarkable what the Navy did accomplish during his tenure as secretary, including two major victories in the vitally important—if often ignored—Great Lakes.

Moreover, his career included a maturation of the U.S. Navy. For the first two decades of its existence, the Navy had been a tiny force, starkly limited in its ability to project power or intimidate rivals. Given the Navy Department's small size and the overall weakness of the infant nation, successive secretaries sought officers with ambition, zeal, and even recklessness to compensate for a deficiency of force. Cautious or even lazy officers were publicly shamed and ejected from the service. This zealous mindset showed in the beginning of the War of 1812, as captains sailed with one goal: find and defeat a Royal Navy vessel of equal size (or what they could claim was equal size with a reasonably straight face). Jones' demand for a less aggressive strategy therefore called for a dramatic shift in military culture.

Naval officers generally complied with the policies of the government, yielding to Jones' new strategy for the war, if somewhat reluctantly, and working within the administration's restraints in dealing with frustrating state governments and civilian populations. The vexations of the final months of the war could not obscure the fact that the Navy emerged from the conflict with unprecedented popularity and support from Congress that surpassed even the height of the Quasi War. Civilian and military leaders alike now turned from combating the British to building an administrative apparatus to oversee this newly expanded service. The question of the Secretary of the Navy's role became an issue of very real contention under this new paradigm, but what ultimately emerged proved to be a lasting settlement in the division of responsibility between civilian and military leadership.

# –7–

# "A Radical Change of System"

## *The Navy Board and Professionalism, 1815–1824*

**NOVEMBER 29, 1814.** William Jones' eagerness to get out of Washington could wait no longer. While he was proud of the services he had rendered as Secretary of the Navy, his personal finances had already been strained when he accepted the position, and now they demanded immediate attention. It was time to leave. In his search for a new secretary, Madison initially made an unprecedented choice. Looking within the officer corps, he asked John Rodgers to resign his commission and assume the Navy's top civilian post. Rodgers had been one of the most respected and influential naval leaders for years, so the choice made sense. It was an appealing offer for the captain as well. He could count on the support of the officer corps, who would no doubt be pleased to have one of their own heading the department. For all that, Rodgers said no. He explained to Madison that "my abilities are not of a kind to justify my acceptance" of the post, as "neither my habits, temper, nor education are such (as in my own estimation) to sanction" assuming the job of civilian head of the Navy. His stated reasons are, to put it mildly, questionable. As we shall see, when he served as chairman of the Board of Navy Commissioners he never acted like a man with no confidence in his own administrative abilities. In fact, Rodgers hinted at his real reason for declining when he said he would be willing to serve as an interim secretary, but only if he could do so while retaining his commission.[1] He could not bring himself to resign from a job he had performed his entire adult life and come to love. Then, of course, there was the reality that he could remain a commissioned officer for life, while a cabinet appointment was a political office with an uncertain tenure (Robert Smith's eight years were by far the record at this point).

All of this might not have been enough to induce Rodgers to reject Madison's offer if the Secretary of the Navy wielded total control of naval affairs. But Rodgers' recent career made it obvious that remaining a naval officer would not deprive him of the chance to play a role in shaping the future of the service. He already enjoyed a healthy influence within the Navy Department, having been consulted on strategy in the War of 1812, and before that he had played a principle role in the Navy's decision to reject Robert Fulton's torpedo experiments and had demonstrated laudable tact and diplomacy in resolving a conflict between several of his subordinates and a group of angry citizens during his tenure at the New York Navy Yard.[2] Rodgers knew from firsthand experience that remaining in the Navy would not leave him entirely divorced from decision-making. And the ability to shape naval policy without resigning his commission promised to grow even more in the coming months. It was obvious by the time Jones left that the Navy's reputation with the American public was secure, and that the fleet would expand significantly after the war. It was equally obvious that oversight had become too big a job for just the secretary, and that the officer corps, or at least picked men within it, would soon enjoy official status as overseers and administrators of a growing American Navy. Even as Rodgers weighed and then declined the secretary's office, Congress moved to create a formal body of naval officers to assume responsibility for managing naval affairs. Although he opted out of becoming secretary, Rodgers soon took the next highest post: senior officer of the newly created Board of Navy Commissioners.

The War of 1812 changed the status of the U.S. Navy. True, the conflict had its share of disasters—including the burning of the capital—but the Navy's thrilling victories helped force a stalemate and bolstered the infant republic's international prestige. No longer would partisans debate the usefulness of a seagoing navy. Jefferson's gunboat program was quietly scrapped in favor of ships of the line, and the Navy's permanence was assured. Along with improving fortunes came meaningful changes within the Navy. With the nation no longer feeling the need to carry a chip on its shoulder into interactions with other global powers, the emphasis on defending their country's honor at all costs became more subdued. A growing sense of professionalism combined with wider cultural shifts called for greater restraint on questions of personal honor. The ideal of civilian control of the military remained firmly entrenched, and when the new Navy Board tried to subvert this ideal in its opening days, Madison sharply reaffirmed the primacy of the Secretary of the Navy. Such was the official reality. In practice, however, the influence of the officer corps over naval affairs grew significantly in the years following the War of 1812. Although the messy turf war in its opening days ended in a definite assertion of civilian control, the Board of Navy Commissioners still brought about a diminution of the Secretary of the Navy's power. Its early history marks the formal recognition by the government of naval officers' professional expertise, and of the officer corps' congressionally sanctioned role in governing naval affairs.

After Rodgers declined to become Secretary of the Navy, Madison turned to New Englander Benjamin Crowninshield. In terms of experience, Crowninshield was eminently qualified. He, like most of his predecessors, came into the office with extensive knowledge of maritime affairs. His father, also named Benjamin, was among the most respected and successful merchants of New England. The elder Crowninshield served as a midshipman in the Royal Navy, but left to join the American militia at the outbreak of the Revolution, and was wounded at Bunker Hill.[3] Following the Revolution, he spent several years as a merchant captain, before founding an East Indies trading company, which proved tremendously successful and soon accumulated substantial wealth for the family.[4] The younger Crowninshield had grown up in the heart of America's maritime commercial industry. He also had political experience, boasting a term in the Massachusetts House of Representatives and later in the state senate; and after his career in the Navy Department he went on to serve in the U.S. House of Representatives.[5]

His qualifications on paper did not, however, guarantee the respect of seasoned sailors in the naval officer corps. Warm and friendly, Crowninshield was temperamentally quite different from Benjamin Stoddert, Robert Smith, or William Jones. In contrast to his war hero father, known as "Sailor Ben" in the maritime community, the younger Crowninshield was dubbed "Philosopher

Ben." A bookish young man, it is unclear if Crowninshield Jr. ever captained a vessel.[6] He preferred intellectual and philosophical pursuits, commenting that "no American [should] dare to think lightly of philosophy and science, and if my countrymen wish to acquire power, influence, and respect among nations, and convenience and perfection in society, let learned men be honored and a spirit of enquiry be encouraged."[7] He was in his element conducting scientific experiments and debating points of philosophy, but he apparently lacked his father's hardheaded business sense or love of the sea.[8]

Moreover, he could be indecisive and directionless. He dithered for months over whether to accept the post, leaving Chief Clerk Benjamin Homans the de facto secretary for a time.[9] Even in his intellectual pursuits he occasionally showed a lack of commitment and drive. He filled numerous notebooks with chapters for his ambitious project, "A General History of Mankind from the beginning of the world to the present time," though he never came close to finishing it.[10] Samuel Flagg Bemis, the great historian of American diplomacy, regards Crowninshield as "irresolute and vacillating," and "barely competent to handle the navy." Crowninshield's biographer, Reginald Hall, agrees. Although crediting his subject with some measure of effective leadership early in his tenure, he criticizes him for a "lack of initiative," and concludes that he was "in general content to let [others] do his work for him."[11]

Crowninshield's waffling caused trouble early on. As soon as the War of 1812 began, Algiers declared war on the United States as well, banking on the British navy to crush the tiny American fleet and leave the defeated country in a pitifully weak bargaining position.[12] This miscalculation proved costly. With hostilities against Britain resolved, the Madison administration now turned its Navy—a much larger and more powerful Navy than the one Jefferson had at his disposal in the Tripolitan War—against Algiers. Crowninshield tapped William Bainbridge to lead the expedition, offering him a golden opportunity to avenge the humiliation of losing the *Philadelphia*. Stephen Decatur, however, also thirsted for glory. He had lost the frigate *President* to the British late in the war, and feared his status as a heroic icon for the American people would be tarnished. Actually, Decatur had been in a damaged ship and badly outnumbered; the only person who seemed to think the defeat might taint his reputation was Decatur himself. Nevertheless, he asked for a court-martial, which not only absolved him of guilt but piled on

rather gratuitously in praise of his performance, including a claim—based on somewhat dubious logic—that although "the British had gained a ship, the victory was ours."[13] Nevertheless, Decatur craved further victories to enhance his status and silence those in Britain gloating over his most recent defeat. Nothing Crowninshield offered him measured up. The secretary gave him the choice of commanding the Charleston Navy Yard, going on Bainbridge's expedition as second-in-command (Bainbridge's captain's commission predated Decatur's) and assuming command of the Mediterranean squadron on Bainbridge's return, or following Bainbridge in one of the Navy's new 74s and assuming command of the Mediterranean squadron upon arrival.

Decatur wanted more. He easily talked Crowninshield into letting him leave ahead of Bainbridge in a division of the fleet and commencing action against Algiers early while Bainbridge finished fitting out the new 74-gun *Independence*. Of course, Bainbridge's preparations suffered even more delays once supplies were diverted to Decatur's ships, and Decatur began offering higher bounties to get men to sign on to his crew. True to form, Decatur won his great victory, negotiating at the mouth of a cannon and imposing terms on Algiers at will. He finally achieved Jefferson's dream of peace without tribute. Algiers released its American prisoners without ransom, paid compensation for the American property it had seized, and abandoned any expectation of tribute from the United States. It got nothing in return. Decatur capped off his Mediterranean adventures by resolving differences with Tunis and Tripoli, again negotiating from the deck of his flagship and extracting everything the United States could possibly ask. By the time Bainbridge reached what was to be the site of his own triumph, there was nothing left for him to do but seethe with frustration.[14]

Upon Decatur's return, there was rejoicing in the Navy Department and the nation as a whole over finally achieving honorable peace with the Barbary Powers far beyond what even Britain demanded. It was indeed a historic occasion and a truly impressive performance, but Crowninshield's decision to let Decatur write his own orders poisoned Decatur's relationship with Bainbridge. It may also have contributed to the idea among senior officers that naval oversight was shifting from the province of the Secretary of the Navy to the officer corps itself. Whatever its sources, this line of thinking certainly became apparent in the coming months with the creation of the Board of Navy Commissioners.

Crowinshield's deficiencies aside, the task of administering the Navy had simply grown too large for even the most energetic secretary. William Jones understood this. "It has been affirmed, and cannot be denied, that imperfections exist in the civil administration of the naval establishment," Jones reported to Congress near the end of his tenure, asserting that "a radical change of system alone can remedy the evils." Jones called for expanding the size of the Navy Department, allowing the secretary to delegate substantial responsibilities thereby reducing the workload on himself and his successors. He recommended a Board of Inspectors, consisting of three naval officers and two civilians, all chosen by the president and approved by the Senate, assume a significant share of the workload in administering the Navy.[15] His proposal had ample precedent. Stoddert had also recommended such a body before his retirement.[16] In 1805, James Barron and Thomas Tingey campaigned strongly in favor of the creation of such a board to establish uniformity in ship design, examine candidates for promotion, and advise the Secretary of the Navy.[17] Shades of the board can also be seen in Porter's proposal for a group of officers to oversee expenditures (which Paul Hamilton rejected). All these proposals, however, came at a time when there was simply far too little interest in Congress for expanding the naval establishment. In the heady aftermath of the war with Great Britain, the Navy Board was an idea whose time had finally come.

With Jones' proposals before them, Congress sought the input of the officer corps for what such a board should look like. Their recommendations had a significant impact on the final composition of the Navy Board. Jones had suggested a five-man body consisting of three officers and two civilians. Not surprisingly, the captains consulted by Congress preferred a board consisting solely of active-duty officers, and this change was implemented. Stephen Decatur and John Shaw went even further, however, suggesting that the Secretary of the Navy be part of the board, serving as its presiding officer, and thus putting him on much more equal footing with the officer corps.[18]

Decatur and Shaw's recommendation was entirely out of touch with what many in Congress intended for the Navy Board. Even Jones offered the board more authority than Congress was willing to grant. Although Jones' proposal called on the board to report to the Secretary of the Navy, he clearly envisioned it administering all aspects of naval affairs, assigning the body "general superintendence and direction of the affairs of the navy, under the instructions from, and powers delegated by, the President of the United States, and authority over all the officers, agents, and persons, employed under the Navy Department."[19] The final bill passed by Congress, however, explicitly stated that "nothing in this act shall be construed to take from the Secretary of the Navy his control of the naval forces of the United States." Rather than receiving "authority over all officers, agents, and persons" in the Navy, and "general superintendence" over the service, as Jones had proposed, the board was quite explicitly designated as "attached to the office of the Secretary of the Navy and under his superintendence." With its relations to the secretary established, the board was assigned "all the ministerial duties of said office, relative to the procurement of naval stores and materials, and the construction, armament, equipment and employment of vessels of war, as well as all other matters connected with the naval establishment of the United States."[20]

Historians have criticized the board's congressional mandate as being far too vague, a recipe for a clash with the Secretary of the Navy.[21] True, the commissioners' list of responsibilities, while clearly focused on the construction and outfitting of ships, ended with an open-ended "all other matters" clause that seemed to lift any restrictions on their authority (although it was the reference to "employment of vessels of war" that ultimately triggered a confrontation). Actually, Congress stated quite clearly and explicitly that the board served under the Secretary of the Navy, and that any actions it took must be approved by the Navy's civilian head. Even matters relating to ships of war that Congress specifically mentioned the board overseeing were not removed from the chain of command; in the second clause of the act creating the board, commissioners were tasked with drafting rules to establish uniformity in ship construction, outfitting, and repair. These rules, however, were to be drafted "by and with the consent of the Secretary of the Navy." The only authorization given the commissioners that did not specifically mention the Secretary of the Navy was to appoint their own secretary and set rules for their own meetings. Finally, lest there be any remaining confusion about the chain of command, Congress ended with the clause noted above that "nothing in this act shall be construed to take from the Secretary of the Navy his control and direction of the naval forces of the United States."[22] Any vagueness about the board's relationship to the Secretary of the Navy existed only in the minds of the first three commissioners.

With the new board authorized, Madison and Crowninshield assumed responsibility for assembling it. Rather than install the three highest-ranking officers to the board, Congress gave the executive branch discretion as to who would serve, and Crowninshield immediately sought out Rodgers' help. Rodgers returned a thoroughly candid assessment of his fellow officers. He informed the secretary that he regarded Isaac Chauncey as "better qualified for command at sea" and readily admitted that Perry and Macdonough, two heroes of the recent war, had never "paid so much attention to the naval service as to qualify . . . for such a situation." In the end, Rodgers recommended that Bainbridge, Hull, and Morris be appointed, and failing one of those, he also strongly endorsed Porter. Bainbridge was, at the time, preparing for his Mediterranean cruise, but Crowninshield obviously took Rodgers's advice to heart otherwise. The first three commissioners were Rodgers, Hull, and Porter.[23]

The commissioners wasted no time trying to establish themselves as coequal with the Secretary of the Navy. On April 25, the day of the board's first meeting, someone signing himself "D" wrote a lengthy letter to the Washington *National Intelligencer* to drum up public support for the commissioners' autonomy. "D" was almost certainly David Porter, and it is equally probable that he wrote his argument in consultation with his two fellow board members. They claimed nothing less than that the Navy board served alongside, equal to, and free of interference from the Secretary of the Navy. "From an accurate and legitimate construction of the act by which this Board was constituted, it must follow conclusively," Porter insisted, "that its members are not subject to the orders, nor under the control of the Secretary of the Navy." Of course, Congress had quite explicitly said exactly the opposite in its legislation creating the board, so the commissioners had to use rather creative legal reasoning to support their claim. In a masterpiece of hairsplitting, Porter argued that "superintendence" and "control" are two different things. He went on to insist that, if the board were not independent of the Secretary of the Navy, any vindictive secretary could simply bar them from meeting. The board members also tried to dismantle the "by and with the consent of the Secretary of the Navy" clause in their orders to issue regulations for naval construction. They argued that they only needed to secure Crowninshield's consent for the final draft, but once written the new regulations would be approved by the president; from this they insisted that from that point on the board would report directly to the president, without going through the Secretary of the Navy. In short—and mirroring the commissioners' later case to Madison—they argued that it was both necessary and implied in the act of Congress that the Navy Board function as a co-Secretary of the Navy, in the process marginalizing the actual secretary and putting a trio of officers in control.[24]

In official communications, however, the commissioners were not nearly so bold. On their first day, they assumed no responsibility for themselves other than writing Crowninshield that they were "ready to receive communications from the Secretary of the Navy" and promptly adjourned until such messages were received. Two days later, the board again convened, but, since they had not heard from the secretary, they again adjourned without conducting any business. In the interim, they established their own internal rules and regulations, which specified their hours, who could open their mail, and when members could leave the District of Columbia. They agreed that "while the Board is in session, no business of a nature not closely connected with the duties of them is to be introduced by any member." However, there is no indication in their minutes as to what exactly they believed those duties consisted of.[25] There was a hint, even here, that they were bent on weakening the Secretary of the Navy's office. Finding that the lone clerk allotted them was not enough for their duties, they asked that two be taken out of Crowninshield's office and sent over to them. Crowninshield declined.[26]

Crowninshield's first substantive communication with the commissioners went out on April 27, two days after the board's first meeting, and related exclusively to the "kind and proportion of Guns, Shot, Stores, Powder, Provisions, and Spars" for the *Independence* and the *Washington*, then under construction. Crowninshield would obviously have seen the letter in the *Intelligencer*, and he went out of his way to express his desire for a congenial working relationship, promising them that "you may, at all times, rely upon every aid and accommodation, which it is personally or officially in my power to bestow." He also expressed confidence in the commissioners' abilities and sense of duty, while using the compliment as a chance to subtly remind them that they worked for him; Crowninshield assured them that his faith in their talents gave him "the happiness to know, that, besides a vigilant and able discharge of the ministerial duties, which, under the superintendence of the Secretary, the Law assigns to [the board], I shall enjoy upon every occasion, the benefits of the friendly and confidential co-operation of all its Members." Kindly expressions aside, Crowninshield still gave the board a very explicit list of the projects he intended them to fulfill, asking for a report of the "actual state" of the Navy's ships, materials, ordnance, and the like, and for rules and regulations to impose uniformity on ship construction and repair.[27]

In addition, it was clear by the end of the first week that both parties expected the board would have considerable responsibility for the appointment and promotion of officers. Crowninshield looked to the commissioners to order the relative rank of officers promoted on the same day, based on their merits. They also wrote a circular asking each commander for a list of his subordinate officers, as well as a record of "remarkable conduct, whether good or bad," by any junior officer. "[That] the character and qualifications of each member of our navy should be intimately known to the commissioners is obvious," they urged their fellow captains, and assured them that it should be equally obvious "that we are highly interested in cherishing merit, and in removing from the service those who do it no honor."[28] A few days later, Crowninshield sought the board's opinion on whether a purser should be discharged from the service based on "the suspicions attached to his character as respects to his intentions of going over to the enemy during the late war—and facts of his having disobeyed orders and overrun his furlough, as well as his being in arrears to the government for a large amount." Not surprisingly, the commissioners agreed that he should be dismissed.[29]

Any harmony was certain to be short-lived, however, as Crowninshield and the commissioners held fundamentally different views about the board's purpose and role within the Navy Department. On May 16, the board wrote to Crowninshield complaining about the "want of necessary information as to the disposition made by the Department of the naval forces of the United States." Specifically, they wanted Crowninshield to tell them exactly where and when he intended to send naval ships. They believed themselves fully entitled to this information, and wrote with more than a hint of accusation that even "the appearance of reserve" from the department as to how naval forces were to be used "does not comport with the law authorizing the establishment of the Board." Crowninshield's first impulse was to be diplomatic, writing a placating letter that reiterated at length on his confidence in them and desire for harmony, but nonetheless insisted that their understanding of the board's role was "erroneous"; "control and direction of the Naval Forces of the United States, belong to the Secretary of the Navy, acting under the authority of the President of the United States, and the Secretary of the Navy is a member of the Administration confidentially consulted by the President upon affairs of State."[30]

Mutual efforts to be diplomatic lasted all of two days. Immediately upon receiving Crowninshield's reply, the board wrote back laying out a detailed case for their coequal status with the secretary, and therefore their need to be fully informed in *all* matters relating to United States naval forces. Now heated, Crowninshield replied that their arguments were weak and unconvincing, and that the board "was created only to assist in the performance of ministerial duties."

> The tone and character of your correspondence with this Department are as unexpected as they appear to me extraordinary. I am not conscious, that, in my Official or personal conduct towards the Members of your Board, there exists any foundation for a course of proceeding [which] carries with it an air of hostility; but as I believe I know my duty, and as I mean to perform it, with all the responsibility attached to it, I shall still abstain from entering into any altercation upon the topics of your letter, and submit it, with the rest of our correspondence to the President of the United States for his consideration.

The commissioners likewise wrote to Madison, laying out their own views of their congressional mandate and asking him to settle the matter.[31] For the next three weeks, the board met daily and, after noting in its minutes that it had received no reply from the president, promptly adjourned.[32] That the three commissioners were not the only officers hoping to see the Navy Board supplant the Secretary of the Navy is obvious from a letter Bainbridge wrote Porter lamenting that if the president ruled in Crowninshield's favor, the board members would find themselves "in the honorable status of Clerks to the Secretary's Clerks."[33] Madison felt otherwise, however, ruling that the Secretary of the Navy is an extension of the president, and as such "he is understood to speak and act with Executive sanction, or, in other words, the Executive is presumed to speak and act through him." Rejecting Porter's claim that the board's appointment by the president and referral of regulations to the president made it separate from the Secretary of the Navy, Madison insisted that the secretary was the president's arm in dealings with the board. "According to the terms of the law," Madison concluded, "the Board is attached to the office of the Secretary of the Navy, and shall discharge all its ministerial duties under his superintendence."[34] Madison firmly and emphatically came down on the side of civilian control, insisting that the creation of the Board of Navy Commissioners had done nothing to change that principle.

Upon receiving Madison's reply, the commissioners seemed to accept defeat gracefully. Or at least two of them did; Isaac Hull resigned from the board and assumed command of the Charleston Navy Yard.[35] In the meantime, they wrote the Secretary of the Navy "asking a conference to settle certain points of etiquette," though the meeting was obviously meant to clear the air and return to a harmonious working relationship. They agreed that the board should oversee matters of ship construction, procuring supplies, and other administrative matters, while the secretary would have control over ship movements and officer assignments. However, the commissioners do seem to have used this meeting as a bargaining session as well. Somewhat incongruously with the division of labor they agreed to, the minutes of the meeting note that it was "generally understood that the Secretary should consult this Board in the appointment of officers." Even with Madison's backing, Crowninshield agreed to give the board a central role in appointing and promoting officers, albeit with the secretary holding final decision-making power.[36]

Although no doubt disappointed with their reduced role, and despite having wrung some minor concessions from Crowninshield, there is no evidence the commissioners surreptitiously sought to seize power for themselves. When Joseph Bainbridge wrote the board about matters they believed more properly Crowninshield's responsibility, they immediately wrote that Bainbridge's problems, "being a subject . . . on which alone the Secretary of the Navy has the power of deciding they do not feel themselves at liberty to express any opinion relative to your claims without an official notice from him that such expression is desired."[37] They also yielded on questions of "pay and subsistence of officers," and immediately referred inquiries on this subject to the secretary.[38]

There are, however, hints that the members of the board were frustrated by Madison's ruling, and maintained their resentment for several months. The first signs of this come through in somewhat testy letters sent to officers who communicated directly with the secretary on issues that were specifically delegated to the board. "The Secretary of the Navy has communicated an extract of your letter of the 12th, which ought, as you will perceive by this reference of the Department, to have been addressed to this Board," they wrote to one officer when he failed to go through them to determine how much beef, bread, and pork he could take for a cruise. They made sure to protect their (now smaller) sphere of authority, sharply reminding another captain that any letters relating to supplies for the use of the Navy "must be addressed to the Commissioners of the Navy."[39] Although Madison issued his ruling in June, by November the members of the board were still rankled enough to begin their official report with a reference to the difficulties they struggled to work under stemming from "the reserve that unavoidably attends an exercise of powers which are doubted," and contended that their murky legal status made it impossible to "extend as far as is desirable, their knowledge of matters connected with the naval establishment of the United States."[40]

The genial Crowninshield, however, was not one to hold a grudge and worked hard to build a healthy relationship with the commissioners. By March of 1817, the board had even developed a fondness for him and wrote in concern when it was rumored that he planned to step down from his post as secretary. Crowninshield was quick with an equally generous reply, assuring them that the recent spat "never did give me any unpleasant feeling of a personal nature."[41]

A major factor in the mutual mending of fences between the secretary and the commissioners was that there were a host of matters which Crowninshield was only too happy to let the board handle. Rodgers, Porter, and Decatur—the latter having replaced Hull—threw themselves into their official duties. The November report, which began with a pointed reference to the clash between the board and Crowninshield, went on to cover a wide variety of subjects and made sweeping recommendations to Congress. It recommended shutting down several navy yards, dramatically expanding others, removing unsatisfactory officers promoted during the war, and setting up a more efficient educational apparatus for incoming officers.[42]

The Navy commissioners took the public trust they held seriously. One of Decatur's earliest biographers recounts an episode in which a man approached the captain and proposed his invention of a new type of gun. When Decatur appeared uninterested, the man offered him a bribe. An infuriated Decatur assaulted the would-be inventor, and he had to be forcibly restrained by Rodgers as he threatened to kill the offender.[43] Most of the work was far more mundane. The commissioners' primary focus was on maintaining and overseeing the various navy yards, which successive secretaries delegated entirely to them.[44] The board also assumed near-complete control of ship maintenance and outfitting squadrons for cruises, again with the consent of the Navy Department.[45] Naval hospitals and the overall health of seamen also came under their purview, with generally positive results.[46] The board also grew in its influence over personnel matters; it was the board, and not the secretary, who wrote the new rules and regulations for the Navy in 1818. The proper conduct of officers, the consequences of deviation from that conduct, standards for discipline of seamen, and matters of dress and ceremony were all spelled out for officers by officers themselves.[47]

Another hint of the growing influence of the Navy commissioners is Rodgers' ongoing refusal to become Secretary of the Navy. When Crowninshield did resign in 1818, James Monroe again offered the post to Rodgers. When he declined the first time, Rodgers had foreseen the creation of some sort of Navy Board, and he had good reason to assume that he would enjoy substantial influence within the Navy without resigning his commission. Given how quickly the board moved to place itself on equal footing with Crowninshield, Rodgers might even have turned down the post of secretary in 1814 believing he could get much the same job by serving on the Navy Board. By the end of Crowninshield's tenure, however, the board's subordination to the Secretary of the Navy was firmly established, and Rodgers could have no illusions that chairing the board made him anything other than a subordinate of the Secretary of the Navy. This time, the officer corps seemingly had good reason to place one of their own in the secretary's office. Yet Rodgers again refused. "Whatever attractions the secretaryship might have held for him, they paled in comparison to the prestige, prerogatives, and financial security" that came with his commission as a naval officer, asserts Rodgers' biographer.[48] That is accurate enough, but if Rodgers' position on the board had truly reduced him to the status of a "clerk to the secretary's clerks," it is difficult to believe any degree of permanent financial security could have kept him from seizing the promotion immediately. Rodgers declined to become secretary a second time because the Navy Board wielded sufficient power over naval affairs to satisfy his desire for influence. His decision to reject Monroe's offer shows that the officer corps had come to believe it had a meaningful voice in the Navy Department.

Indeed, the existence of the board, and its competent performance, freed presidents from having to worry about a potential secretary's knowledge of the sea and sailing. Crowninshield was the last in a series of Navy Department heads to come into the job with experience in maritime affairs. He was succeeded by a series of secretaries that Charles Oscar Paullin dubs "legal and juridical" in background rather than experienced seafarers, observing that after Crowninshield, "politics, and not a practical knowledge of the marine" became "the controlling factor in choosing naval secretaries." This new line of naval administrators' ignorance of maritime affairs naturally served to increase the influence of senior officers.[49] Smith Thompson, who succeeded Crowninshield as Secretary of the Navy in 1819, had no experience whatsoever in maritime matters. That is not to say he was unsuited for a government post. He had helped write the New York state constitution and served as chief justice of the New York Supreme Court for four years prior to joining the cabinet. Following his tenure in the Navy Department, he served on the U.S. Supreme Court for almost two decades.[50] Still, having no prior maritime experience, it would have been easy for him to feel overwhelmed by the new responsibility. It does not appear he expended much energy stressing over the role, however. Referring to Thompson, Secretary of State John Quincy Adams noted that "the office sits easy upon his shoulders." Thompson and Crowninshield both made a practice of spending a limited amount of time in the nation's capital, and the younger Adams was not entirely disapproving of their behavior, conceding that the "navy commissioners make the duties of that department comparatively light."[51]

Among the reasons Thompson's duties were "comparatively light" was that the board continued to assume responsibility, with the secretary's consent, for issues relating to officer disputes and duty assignments. In all cases, the secretary held final authority to approve the board's decisions, but Crowninshield and Thompson never overruled the board on any matter of consequence. Within a year of their clash with Crowninshield, the board wrote him unapologetically that Joseph Bainbridge had approached them, and not the secretary, about a duty assignment, and on their own authority they had informed him that there was no work for him to do at that time.[52] Crowninshield did not object, and the following year, he requested a detailed report and recommendations from the board on the "merit and qualifications . . . of candidates for promotion."[53] The commissioners later corresponded with Crowninshield regarding "not worthy officers to retire to private life." When Oliver Hazard Perry clashed with the commandant of a navy yard over authority, the matter was referred to the board, which ruled in Perry's favor.[54] Likewise, when Thomas Macdonough, the hero of the Battle of Plattsburg, clashed with Isaac Chauncey, the secretary consulted the board on the matter, and they recommended in favor of Macdonough.[55] Later, Macdonough again came to the board's attention, when he was serving under Commodore Charles Stewart in the Mediterranean. Their feud became so intense that Stewart relieved Macdonough of command and sent him home. Thompson and President Monroe made the final decision to restore Macdonough to duty, but the board advised the secretary in settling the matter, and John Rodgers especially played an influential role in the controversy's outcome.[56]

The growing influence of the Navy Board—and concurrent deference by the Secretary of the Navy—also contributed to one of the most infamous events of the early Navy. On March 22, 1820, James Barron shot and killed Stephen Decatur in a duel. The tragedy rocked Washington, where Decatur was one of the nation's most celebrated war heroes and, according to more than a few rumors, a potential rising star in the political realm. The road to the duel began with Barron's court-martial. The suspension had been devastating. Unable to find work in the United States, thanks largely to the Jefferson embargo's crippling effect on merchant shipping, he traveled to Europe to try and support his family. His stay abroad proved of little value financially, and he appears to have been miserable the entire time. London was "a detestable place" and its people insufferable.[57] The separation from his family added greatly to Barron's misery. Barron, by all evidence an extremely devoted husband and father, regularly sent affectionate letters back to his wife and daughters, and his pain intensified when he was forced to miss his eldest daughter's wedding.[58] Commerce was stunted in Europe as much or more than across the Atlantic thanks to Britain's epic struggle with Napoleon, and Barron had to subsist off the limited income he received from various inventions, with most of this going back to his family.[59] Repeated efforts to return home during the course of the war proved futile.

Barron finally reached his native shore in 1818 and Crowninshield, concluding that the disgraced captain had served his suspension, readmitted him to the service. However, Barron was indefinitely placed on half-pay since he was not on active duty. Technically, it was for the Secretary of the Navy to determine whether to assign him a command. But by the agreement reached in the aftermath of Madison's ruling and subsequent practice, the board also held substantial power over assignments. It could only hurt Barron's chances that Crowninshield and Thompson were in the capital infrequently, placing him even more at the mercy of the board for a duty assignment. For Barron, the expanded power of the board turned out to be devastating. Stephen Decatur had never abandoned his dim view of Barron as an officer that he formed following the *Chesapeake-Leopard* episode, and he vigorously opposed allowing Barron any responsibility.[60]

A feud soon developed between the two, with a nasty exchange of letters drifting inexorably toward a challenge. Barron cast himself as a man whose honor had been slandered, claiming Decatur bragged that he could insult Barron with impunity. Decatur denied this and consistently maintained that he bore Barron no personal grudge, only that he did not consider him deserving of an assignment to active duty when plenty of other officers—who had never been convicted by a court-martial and who had been present in the country during a time of war—were available. Barron did take it personally, and it was clear very early in their exchange he wanted a duel. Upon receiving a belligerent missive from Decatur, Barron lashed back: "I consider you as having given an invitation, which I accept," and then boldly claimed to have the choice of weapons for the forthcoming duel.[61] But Decatur had obviously issued no challenge, and he said so in his response. In the ensuing correspondence, this would become a frequent theme, with Barron interpreting challenges where there were none, yet unwilling to take the step of issuing a challenge himself. "I have not challenged, nor do I intend to challenge you," Decatur finally asserted in exasperation. "It will not be lost sight of, that your jeopardizing your life depends upon yourself, not upon me." Decatur then spoke directly to the real issue, Barron's desire for a duel was done "with a view of fighting your own character up." Finally forced to make the call to the field himself, Barron responded that "whenever you will consent to meet me on fair and equal grounds . . . you are at liberty to view this as that call."[62]

There was a slight delay while Decatur sought a second. Both Rodgers and Porter refused, warning Decatur that there was no doubt in the officer corps' mind of his honor. Their attempts to convince him that the duel was foolish were wasted; Decatur was determined to proceed. Yet their refusal to act as his second did slow things down, as Decatur soon learned that no one of equal social standing was willing to help him meet Barron on the field of honor. This difficulty was resolved when William Bainbridge conveniently reentered Decatur's life after having refused to speak to him for the last five years, ever since Decatur beat him to the Mediterranean and glory. Having abruptly reconciled, Bainbridge readily agreed to act as Decatur's second for the duel. The convenient timing has left a cloud of suspicion around Bainbridge ever since.[63] This is especially so considering the two seconds negotiated the pistol exchange at a near-suicidal distance of eight yards to account for Barron's poor eyesight. The two duelists seemed to come close to reconciliation in the moments before exchanging fire, but the rules of the code duello forced the affair to its bloody conclusion. Barron aimed to wound Decatur, hitting him in the hip, but the bullet sliced through his groin into vital organs, and the hero of two wars knew even before he fell to the ground that he was dying.

The Barron-Decatur duel created a sensation at the time, and it has been well-trodden ground by historians ever since. However, most of the many historians who have studied the affair treat it as a personality clash between two proud men or as an example of the honor culture of the time. It was indisputably both of these. Nevertheless, it is impossible to overlook the fact that, despite having killed a national hero and prominent member of the naval establishment, Barron's career turned around dramatically with Decatur's death. Decatur had been unwilling even to grant him a hearing, but within months of the duel he appeared before a court of inquiry. Shortly thereafter, Thompson agreed to grant Barron command of the Philadelphia Navy Yard.[64] He retired in 1838 as the second-highest ranking officer in his country's Navy. Even Barron's highly sympathetic biographer concedes that "the death of Decatur removed the chief stumbling block that Barron had always encountered in his efforts to be employed again."[65] Secretary of the Navy Thompson and President Monroe had no qualms about Barron returning to service, as plainly evinced by their actions, but their inaction prior to the duel also shows Decatur's—and by extension the Navy Board's—tremendous influence over officer assignments; the fact that eliminating a key board member could dramatically change an officer's prospects highlights the board's enormous power.

That the board's reach extended well beyond the division of labor originally intended by Congress can be seen in less dramatic ways. By 1820, the euphoria over the War of 1812 had subsided, and many in Congress began to doubt the huge annual appropriation for naval construction authorized in 1816. Tunstall Quarles of Kentucky proposed suspending the construction program. The House Naval Affairs Committee sought Smith Thompson's input on Quarles' motion. Thompson promptly referred the matter to the board. Rodgers, as chairman, wrote back with a stout defense of the construction program, arguing that to stop work on ships that were already in progress would cause the incomplete vessels to go to ruin and make all the labor (and money) invested in them wasted. Smith dutifully acted as a go-between, but nothing more, passing Rodgers' response on to the House.[66]

Congress acquiesced, but the truth was that some measure of retrenchment on naval spending was inevitable. Internationally, America was at peace with all the world, and after the War of 1812 the need to show off its legitimacy as a real nation had abated. At home, the Panic of 1819 meant that money was harder to come by, and Congress registered its concern.[67] The House again pressed Thompson on whether the appropriations listed in the 1816 law could be amended, and Thompson again turned to the commissioners for direction. By now it was obvious that Congress intended to find ways to trim the budget, and they would do so with or without the Navy Board's cooperation. Yielding to reality, the commissioners agreed that it was feasible to stretch out the time remaining in the law by an additional three years, thereby halving the annual budget. They also offered a detailed plan for constructing a system of sheds to house newly built ships, so that they could be brought out with relative ease once the need arose.[68] The members of the Board of Navy Commissioners understood how politics worked, and though the secretary served as the intermediary, it was the board that negotiated with Congress over the reduction in naval expenditures. Initially, these negotiations failed—Congress voted to cease construction on all ships of the line and refused to even allocate the funds for Rodgers' protective sheds over the new warships. In 1823, however, appropriations finally did come through for adequate housing for the vessels not immediately in use.[69]

Although they had limited (at best) success in advancing their objectives with Congress, the role of the Navy commissioners in the debate should not be overlooked. They were the primary source of information and advice on naval appropriations. Whatever his status vis-à-vis the board on paper, Smith Thompson took a decidedly secondary role in practice. At the head of the naval officer corps were seasoned bureaucrats, and the management of naval affairs was now very heavily entrusted to the officers themselves. Their clout fluctuated over time, depending on the secretary—Andrew Jackson's short-lived initial Secretary of the Navy, John Branch, strongly asserted himself in office, for example—but no secretary could operate independently of the Navy Board.[70] While the principle of civilian supremacy remained firmly entrenched in American ideology, managing naval affairs without the expertise of naval officers was impossible. In part, this was a function of the complexity of naval science and the growth of the naval establishment, but it was also an achievement of officers themselves. The officer corps had succeeded in maintaining a sphere of authority for itself within the growing naval bureaucracy; it did so without subverting the principle of civilian control of the military. They accomplished this through their own professionalism, guided along the way by strong assertions of the department's authority from the Secretary of the Navy.

# Conclusion

**NOVEMBER 14, 1824.** David Porter was already frustrated with the Navy Department when he sailed for his third cruise to the West Indies in two years, and the feeling was mutual.[1] He had come down with the dreaded yellow fever on his previous voyage and was lucky to still be alive. Almost as vexing as the disease-ridden environment were the ostensibly friendly Spanish officials Porter had to contend with. Overwhelmed with their own wars against colonial rebellions—or the Latin American Wars of Independence, as they would later be called—the Spanish had limited ability or interest in checking the rampant piracy Porter was sent to quash, and both Porter and his predecessor seethed in anger when they pursued pirates all the way to a Spanish shore, only to be denied permission to continue the chase on land.[2]

Secretary of the Navy Samuel Southard realized the delicacy of the situation, where American commercial interests demanded an end to piracy in the area, but relations with Spain were already fraught with tension. America had only recently endorsed Andrew Jackson's decision to enter the Spanish territory of Florida in pursuit of Native Americans, then later pressed Spain to surrender the territory to the United States. Furthermore, to Spain's annoyance, American policy generally favored Latin American independence. The situation required that any commodore sent to the region must be skilled in the art of diplomacy—something no one would ever think of attributing to Porter.[3] Southard's instructions to the commodore were therefore extremely vague. Porter was to use every exertion against the pirates, while making equally great efforts to avoid offending the Spanish. What exactly would constitute inadequate measures against the former or unacceptably belligerent behavior toward the latter went unspecified.[4]

After two frustrating and largely ineffective cruises in the West Indies, one of which had almost killed him, Porter reacted badly upon being ordered on a third. He sent a belligerent and nearly insubordinate letter of protest to Southard. The secretary ignored it, but relations between the two men were further soured. When Porter arrived in the West Indies again in 1824, he was in no mood to exercise the careful diplomacy the geopolitical situation called for. The Spanish, for their part, soon added deliberate insult to their carelessness and lack of cooperation. When a U.S. Navy lieutenant, Charles Platt, went to the city of Fajardo seeking stolen property, he was jailed by Spanish officials who refused to believe his identity and forced him to send his clerk back to the ship, twice, to bring evidence of his affiliation with the United States. Platt and his party languished in a Fajardo jail throughout the ordeal, and even when he was finally released the Spanish "heaped upon them the most outrageous abuse" before allowing them to return to the *John Adams*.[5]

Porter exploded when he heard Platt's report. Gathering a force of two hundred of his men, the commodore rowed back to Fajardo, scattered the Spanish soldiers guarding a small battery, and spiked the guns. He then sent word ahead that if he did not receive an apology for the shameful treatment of his subordinate, he would march into town, seize those responsible, and burn the city to the ground at the slightest resistance. Spanish officials immediately offered profuse apologies, which Lieutenant Platt summarily accepted, and the matter seemed closed. Porter and his men returned to the *John Adams*. Porter's biographer speculates that Porter "then settled down to await the commendation he expected the government to extend."[6] If Porter did anticipate applause from the Navy Department, he had ample historical evidence to justify his expectations. After all, he had come of age in a Navy that heaped praise on officers whose zeal for the honor of their service and their country forbade them from accepting even the slightest insult. He had entered the Navy as a lieutenant under Thomas Truxtun on the *Constellation*, one of the young men of "zeal and spirit" that Stoddert so prized.[7] His actions were in keeping with Preble's bold defiance of a British frigate and Rodgers' destruction of the *Little Belt* to avenge the *Chesapeake*. Even the Spanish seemed to have felt he was within his rights, as they never formally protested.[8]

Times had changed, though. For one thing, Porter had made a thorough enemy of Secretary of the Navy Samuel Southard by this point (a recurring theme in Porter's career); Southard considered him insubordinate and quarrelsome. While Stoddert and Smith had put up with insubordinate and quarrelsome officers who vigorously defended the nation's honor, America's geopolitical situation had changed by the time Southard took over the Navy. While the War of 1812 had essentially ended in a draw, victories over the Royal Navy and Andrew Jackson's spectacular defeat of a British invasion at New Orleans had permanently proven the United States was not a power to be trifled with. The current administration instead looked to avoid picking fights. This was especially true since President James Monroe had only recently issued his famous doctrine against European meddling in New World affairs. For all the confidence the United States seemed to project with the Monroe Doctrine, the country was in no hurry to be compelled to enforce it, and the president looked askance at one of his officers giving Britain or France a pretext to insert themselves into U.S.-Spanish relations. The Spanish, meanwhile, already had ample reason for hostility toward the United States, as Andrew Jackson had only recently invaded their territory in Florida.[9]

Porter did himself no favors either, responding to questions about his handling of the situation with his usual complete disregard for tact. His letters to the department and the president were combative, even getting him an additional charge of insubordination. He angrily stormed out of the court of inquiry, skipping the proceedings and forfeiting his chance to cross-examine witnesses. He then threw the proverbial match in the powder magazine to whatever goodwill he had left in the administration by publishing his defense in pamphlet form *before* the court-martial even met. His pamphlet excoriated the president (to whom it was also dedicated), and self-righteously denied even the slightest wrongdoing on his part.[10]

Southard was actually concerned that a court-martial composed of Porter's naval brethren would side with one of their own and vindicate him with an acquittal. He need not have worried. The court-martial ruled that Porter had indeed acted improperly and suspended him from the service, albeit with pay, for six months. He responded by resigning, believing he could never again serve in the Navy with any dignity. He went on to a stint in the Mexican navy, and later represented the United States to the Ottoman Empire as a civilian ambassador. It was while in Turkey that Porter compared a naval ship to a "petty kingdom," and its captain to a "petty despot."[11] A deeply embittered man by this point, he made an oblique reference to Truxtun, his first commanding officer, in the text, mentioning the "proud and tyrannical, though gallant" naval officer he first served under. Truxtun was long dead by this time, and had been out of the Navy for even longer. However fair one might regard Porter's characterization of his first commanding officer, it is clear that the U.S. Navy very quickly moved beyond captains in Truxtun's mold to a generation of officers who took their subordination to the civilian government more seriously than Truxtun ever had. As Porter himself painfully learned, the relationship between the Navy Department and the officer corps was quite different by the end of his naval career than when he had first been assigned to the *Constellation*.

Of course, there was a great deal of continuity in the culture of the Navy and how it shaped civil-military relations. Officers still cared about their honor in deep and profound ways, and they still lashed out when they felt disrespected, including to the point of killing one another in duels. And officers certainly still butted heads with the Secretary of the Navy.[12] While dueling is, of course, no longer a problem, civil-military tensions have always existed, and because of the Navy's unique culture that grew out of captains being separated from Washington and wielding massive authority on board ship, these tensions have been, at times, particularly pronounced.

Such continuity should not blind us to the significant changes in naval civil-military relations that occurred between the Revolution and the years after the War of 1812. By the early 1820s, the relationship between the civilian government and the naval officer corps, if still occasionally contentious, was at least much more stable. Over the first two decades of the nineteenth century, ideas about personal honor gave way to a more modern sensibility that expected men of honor to put the national or institutional good ahead of their own quest for status. While Truxtun and Sterrett, among others, had been quick to resign over disagreements with the Navy Department, protest resignations ceased almost entirely after 1815. This marked the beginnings of a military culture that abhors the thought of protest resignations.[13] Dueling remained an issue, but it declined markedly among senior officers and even lieutenants after 1820, becoming primarily a problem for hotheaded and status-conscious midshipmen. Meanwhile, officers worked closely with the Secretary of the Navy to try and curb the practice.[14] More broadly, changing attitudes had imposed new, severe limits on how much open hostility a captain could display toward the government.

A clearer division of responsibility enhanced civil-military harmony. The president and Secretary of the Navy now claimed the exclusive right to direct ship movements and naval strategy, though of course wise civilian leaders still sought the input of naval officers over these matters. The officer corps, primarily through the Board of Navy Commissioners, dominated issues best handled by naval professionals—ship design, construction, and outfitting; selection and training of junior officers; and even disciplinary problems within the officer corps. Indeed, in 1843 Captain Alexander Slidell Mackenzie provided an extreme example of this when he hanged three men aboard his ship that he suspected of plotting a mutiny. He was later vindicated by a court-martial, whose proceedings were promptly accepted by President John Tyler.[15] Tyler insisted that his approval of the court's findings was based entirely on his deference to the Navy to police itself in such matters. "If [the court] had ordered Mackenzie shot, I would not have interposed to save him," he explained afterward.[16] Petty despotism had been tamed, but by no means eradicated.

The U.S. Navy rightly celebrates the years covered in this book. This was the period when it enjoyed spectacular triumphs, and when it forever earned a place in American lore through stirring actions by men like Truxtun, Decatur, and Preble, names still revered in the service today.[17] Behind all these triumphs, another process was taking place—the institutional culture of the Navy was being formed, and many of the precedents set during this period carry over into the twenty-first century. The first five Secretaries of the Navy, and the first generation of naval officers that served under them, bequeathed the nation an officer corps that was fiercely committed to the nation's honor, but that also prized duty and a strong commitment to civilian supremacy. It also produced an officer corps that downgraded early modern attitudes about personal fame and reputation in favor of celebrating professionalism and a commitment to subordinate personal considerations to the good of the service. This, alongside the stirring victories over French, Tripolitan, and British vessels, ranks among their greatest contributions to their country.

# Notes

## Introduction

1. The account of the *Chesapeake-Shannon* engagement is taken from Philip Broke, "An account of the *Chesapeake-Shannon Action,*" June 6, 1813; Lieutenant George Budd to Secretary of the Navy William Jones, June 13, 1813, *The Naval War of 1812: A Documentary History*, 4 vols. (Washington, DC: Naval Historical Center, 1985–), II:129–34; and George C. Daughan, *1812: The Navy's War* (New York: Basic Books, 2011), 187–95.
2. Broke to Lawrence, undated, 1813, *Naval War of 1812*, II:126–29.
3. Daughan, *1812*, 192–94; Ian W. Toll, *Six Frigates: The Epic History of the Founding of the U.S. Navy* (New York: Norton, 2006), 412–13.
4. It was almost a century before Alfred Thayer Mahan became one of the first Americans to criticize Lawrence for his decision to engage the *Shannon* and for his decision-making in the battle. Mahan, *Sea Power in Its Relations to the War of 1812*, 2 vols. (New York: Dodo Press, 1905), II:119–36.
5. Daughan, *1812*, 195; Mahan, *Sea Power*, 118–19.
6. Jones Circular to Officers, February 22, 1813, *Naval War of 1812*, II:48
7. Daughan, *1812*, 190–91.
8. Christopher McKee, *A Gentlemanly and Honorable Profession: The Creation of the U.S. Naval Officer Corps, 1794–1815* (Annapolis, MD: Naval Institute Press, 1991), 258–61; Paul A. Gilje, *Liberty on the Waterfront: American Maritime Culture in the Age of Revolution* (Philadelphia: University of Pennsylvania Press, 2004), 69–78, 83; Matthew Taylor Raffety, *The Republic Afloat: Law, Honor, and Citizenship in Maritime America* (Chicago: University of Chicago Press, 2013), 75–80.
9. David Porter, *Constantinople and Its Environs in a Series of Letters, Exhibiting the Actual State of the Manners, Customs and Habits of the Turks, Armenians, Jews and Greeks as Modified by the Policy of Sultan Mahmoud by an American Long Resident at Constantinople*, 2 vols. (New York: Harper and Brothers, 1835), 10–11.
10. Porter to Samuel Hambleton, February 28, 1812, reprinted in David Dixon Porter, *Memoir of Commodore David Porter of the United States Navy* (Albany, NY: J. Munsell Publisher, 1875), 100.

11. Captain George Smith, *An Universal Military Dictionary, A Copious Explanation of the Technical Terms & c. Used in the Equipment, Machinery, Movements, and Military Operations of an Army* (London: J. Millan, 1779).
12. William Duane, *A Military Dictionary* (Philadelphia: Printed and Published by William Duane, 1810), 270.
13. Robert Donkin, *Military Collections and Remarks* (New York: H. Gaine, 1777), 202. Donkin was actually not the first to draw comparisons between honor and the human eye. A century prior, Sir William Waller also compared his public reputation and his eye, saying "Nature bids me defend one, Honour the other." Wayne Lee, *Barbarians and Brothers: Anglo-American Warfare, 1500–1865* (New York: Oxford University Press, 2011), 78.
14. Joanne Freeman, *Affairs of Honor: National Politics in the New Republic* (New Haven, CT: Yale University Press, 2001); Bertram Wyatt-Brown, *Southern Honor: Ethics and Behavior in the Old South* (New York: Oxford University Press, 1982); Douglas Adair, "Fame and the Founding Fathers," in *Fame and the Founding Fathers: Essays by Douglas Adair*, edited by Trevor Colbourn (New York: W. W. Norton, published for the Institute of Early American History and Culture, 1974).
15. Wyatt-Brown, *Southern Honor*, 4.
16. Duane, *Military Dictionary*, 270.
17. Christopher Duffy, *The Military Experience in the Age of Reason* (London: Routledge and Kegan Paul, 1987), 77.
18. Adair, "Fame and the Founding Fathers," 9–13.
19. McKee, *Gentlemanly and Honorable Profession*, 47.
20. Jones to Minister of Marine Antoine de Sartine, September 13, 1778, James Bradford, ed., The Papers of John Paul Jones, Library of Congress (LOC), Washington, DC, 10 reels, reel 2.
21. N. A. M. Rodger, *The Command of the Ocean: A Naval History of Britain, 1649–1815* (New York: Norton, 2004), 391.
22. N. A. M. Rodger, "Honour and Duty at Sea, 1660–1815," *Historical Research* 75, no. 190 (2002): 425–47, see page 437 for the question of refusing certain orders. Michael W. McCahill, "Peerage Creations and the Changing Character of British Nobility, 1750–1830," *English Historical Review* 96 no. 379 (1981): 259–84. See page 272 for nobility declining diplomatic postings.
23. Thomas Truxtun, "Reply of Commodore Thomas Truxtun to an Attack made on him by the *National Intelligencer* in June 1806," Thomas Truxtun Papers, Historical Society of Pennsylvania, Philadelphia, PA.
24. Kohn, *Eagle and Sword*, 18–39; John Ferling, *Almost A Miracle: The American Victory in the War of Independence* (New York: Oxford University Press, 2007), 554–56.

25. William B. Skelton, *An American Profession of Arms: The Army Officer Corps, 1784–1861* (Lawrence: University Press of Kansas, 1992), 51, 53.
26. Frederick C. Leiner, "Decatur and Naval Leadership," *Naval History* 15, no. 5 (2001): 30–34.
27. Richard Dale to Secretary of the Navy Benjamin Stoddert, September 28, 1800, *Naval Documents related to the Quasi-War between the United States and France* (hereafter referred to as *NDQW*), 7 vols. (Washington, DC: U.S. Government Printing Office, 1935–38), VI:389–90.
28. In the 1820s, this situation started to change somewhat. While during the years this book covers promotion was fairly rapid and opportunities to distinguish oneself readily available, with the conclusion of the War of 1812 promotion stagnated, and many officers remained stuck in a lieutenancy for many years. Tensions between junior and senior officers naturally emerged, and both groups occasionally appealed to the Secretary of the Navy or the president for support, though civilian leaders still generally sided with the ranking officer. See: Linda Maloney, *The Captain from Connecticut: The Life and Naval Times of Isaac Hull* (Annapolis, MD: Naval Institute Press, 1986), 449–68, esp. 457; Claude Berube and John Rodgaard, *A Call to the Sea: Captain Charles Stewart of the USS* Constitution (Dulles, VA: Potomac Books, 2006), 126–32; David Curtis Skaggs, *Thomas Macdonough: Master of Command in the Early U.S. Navy* (Annapolis, MD: Naval Institute Press, 2003), 174–85.
29. Rodger, "Honour and Duty at Sea," 444.
30. Wilson, *British Naval Officers*, 201. The discussion of the shift from honor to duty is found on pages 196–203.
31. Samuel Watson, *Jackson's Sword: The Army Officer Corps on the American Frontier, 1810–1821* (Lawrence, KS: University of Kansas Press, 2012), x, 255–56, 282–85; Skelton, *American Profession of Arms*, xv, 87, 109–30.
32. Portions of my article "There Will Still Remain Heroes and Patriots: The Politics of Resignation in the Early American Navy, 1775–1815," *Journal of Military History*, 84, no. 2 (April 2020): 369–94, are reprinted throughout this book, with each instance cited in the notes. My thanks to the *Journal* for permission to reprint.

### Chapter 1. "To Be Obeyed It Is Necessary to Be Esteemed"

1. Tim McGrath, *Get Me a Fast Ship: The Continental Navy and America's Revolution at Sea* (New York: NAL Caliber, 2014), 273–82; William M. Fowler Jr., *Rebels under Sail: The American Navy during the Revolution* (New York: Charles Scribner's Sons, 1976), 104–9.
2. McGrath, *Get Me a Fast Ship*, 281–82; Fowler, *Rebels under Sail*, 109.
3. James M. Volo, *Blue Water Patriots: The American Revolution Afloat* (Lantham, MD: Rowman and Littlefield, 2006), 38–43.

4. Sheldon S. Cohen, *Commodore Abraham Whipple of the Continental Navy: Privateer, Patriot, Pioneer* (Gainesville, FL: University Press of Florida, 2010), 31–35.
5. Instructions to Captain Abraham Whipple of the Armed Sloop *Katy*, *Naval Documents of the American Revolution*, 13 vols. (Washington, DC: U.S. Government Printing Office, 1964–), I:670, hereafter *Naval Documents*. Cohen, *Abraham Whipple*, 45–46; George C. Daughan, *If By Sea: The Forging of the American Navy from the Revolution to the War of 1812* (New York: Basic Books, 2008), 27–28.
6. Gardner Allen, *A Naval History of the American Revolution* (Williamstown, MA: Corner House Publishers, 1970, first published 1913), I:4–20; Fowler, *Rebels under Sail*, 17–21; Volo, *Blue Water Patriots*, 37–43; Daughan, *If By Sea*, 22–26.
7. "George Washington's Instructions to Captain Nicholson Broughton," September 2, 1775, *Naval Documents*, I:1287–88. See also Chester Hearn, *George Washington's Schooners: The First American Navy* (Annapolis, MD: Naval Institute Press, 2005), 5–7.
8. According to the Appendix in Hearn, *George Washington's Schooners*, the vessels took fifty-five prizes. However, that includes ships captured after Congress assumed control of Washington's vessels.
9. George Washington to Lieutenant Colonel Joseph Reed, November 20, 1775, Abbot, *The Papers of George Washington*, II:409.
10. George Washington to John Hancock, December 4, 1775, Abbot, *The Papers of George Washington*, II:485.
11. Major General Artemis Ward to George Washington, May 3, 1776, Clark, *Naval Documents*, IV: 1391. Manley was later placated and went on to one of the more successful careers at sea of the Revolutionary War. Louis Arthur Norton, *Captains Contentious: The Dysfunctional Sons of the Brine* (Columbia, SC: University of South Carolina Press, 2009), 33–45.
12. Fowler, *Rebels under Sail*, 55.
13. Journal of the Rhode Island General Assembly, August 26, 1775, *Naval Documents*, I:1236.
14. Evan Thomas, *John Paul Jones: Sailor, Hero, Father of the American Navy* (New York: Simon and Schuster, 2003), 42–43.
15. Fowler, *Rebels under Sail*, 206–17; Volo, *Blue Water Patriots*, 131–34.
16. Daughan, *If By Sea*, 27, 49–50, 97–98.
17. Allen, *Naval History of the American Revolution*, 35–36.
18. McGrath, *Give Me a Fast Ship*, 273.
19. For naval administration during the Revolutionary War, see Fowler, *Rebels under Sail*, 39–86; Charles Oscar Paullin, *The Navy of the American Revolution: Its Administration, its Policy, and its Achievements* (New York: Haskell House Publishers, 1906), 31–60, 79–103; Volo, *Blue Water Patriots*, 51–67.

20. Fowler, *Rebels Under Sail*, 67.
21. Washington's vexations with the failure of Congress to keep his men supplied with money, food, or much of anything else is well attested in virtually any book on his command in the Revolution. See, for example, Robert Middlekauff, *Washington's Revolution: The Making of America's First Leader* (New York: Alfred A. Knopf, 2015), 170, 223–24, 287–88; Edward G. Lengel, *General George Washington: A Military Life* (New York: Random House, 2005), 269–70, 326.
22. Paullin, *Navy of the American Revolution*, 104–5.
23. Volo, *Blue Water Patriots*, 57.
24. Marine Committee to Captain Isaiah Robinson, April 18, 1777, Charles Oscar Paullin, ed., *Out-Letters of the Continental Marine Committee and Board of Admiralty* (New York: Naval History Society, 1914), I:98–100; Marine Committee to John Barry, November 20, 1778, Paullin, *Out-Letters*, II:31–32.
25. Ferling, *Almost a Miracle*, 364; Fowler, *Rebels under Sail*, 225.
26. Fowler, *Rebels under Sail*, 225–28.
27. Louis A. Norton, *Captains Contentious: The Dysfunctional Sons of the Brine* (Columbia, SC: University of South Carolina Press, 2009), 137–43.
28. Gilje, *Liberty on the Waterfront*, 69–78, 83.
29. Jones to Joseph Hewes, April 14, 1776, *Naval Documents*, IV:815–18.
30. Fowler, *Rebels under Sail*, 234–35.
31. Ferling, *Almost a Miracle*, 523–28.
32. Marine Committee to Eastern Navy Board, May 30, 1778, Paullin, *Out-Letters*, I:250–51.
33. Samuel Adams to James Warren, July 27, 1778, Edmund C. Burnett, *Letters of the Members of the Continental Congress*, 8 vols. (Washington, DC: Carnegie Institution, 1921), III:353
34. James Warren to John Adams, March 23, 1777, *Naval Documents*, VIII:184.
35. Gilje, *Liberty on the Waterfront*, 84–85; Morison, *John Paul Jones*, 171.
36. Thomas, *John Paul Jones*, 72–73, 114–26; Morison, *John Paul Jones*, 80, 143–47.
37. Nathan Miller, *Sea of Glory: A Naval History of the American Revolution* (Annapolis, MD: Naval Institute Press, 1992, originally published 1974), 299–300.
38. Board of Admiralty to Benjamin Franklin, May 12, 1780, Paullin, *Out-letters*, 193–94.
39. For soldiers in the Continental army, see Caroline Cox, *A Proper Sense of Honor: Service and Sacrifice in George Washington's Army* (Chapel Hill, NC: University of North Carolina Press, 2004). Of course, the Continental army also had problems with desertion and even mutinies. Ferling, *Almost a Miracle*, 334–38, 466–69.
40. McGrath, *Give Me a Fast Ship*, 398–99.
41. Gilje, *Liberty on the Waterfront*, 106–12.
42. McGrath, *Give Me a Fast Ship*, 220.

43. McGrath, *Give Me a Fast Ship*, 128–29.
44. McGrath, *John Barry: An American Hero in the Age of Sail* (Yardley, PA: Westhome, 2012), 240–42.
45. Fowler, *Rebels under Sail*, 239–40.
46. Journal of the Continental Congress, December 22, 1775, *Naval Documents*, III:207.
47. Miller, *Sea of Glory*, 56.
48. McGrath, *Give Me a Fast Ship*, 31–32.
49. Naval Committee to Hopkins, January 5, 1776, *Naval Documents*, III:637–38.
50. McGrath, *Give Me a Fast Ship*, 60–68; Volo, *Blue Water Patriots*, 107–8.
51. Miller, *Sea of Glory*, 214–17.
52. Officers of the Continental frigate *Warren* to Robert Treate Paine Taunton, February 11, 1777, *Naval Documents* VII: 1,166–67; *Warren* Officers to Continental Marine Committee, February 19, 1777, *Naval Documents*, VII:1,234–35.
53. Miller, *Sea of Glory*, 216–17; Morison, *John Paul Jones*, 96–97; Fowler, *Rebels under Sail*, 241; McGrath, *Give Me a Fast Ship*, 118.
54. Journal of the Continental Congress, April 17, 1776, *Naval Documents*, IV:867.
55. William Bell Clark, *Lambert Wickes: Sea Raider and Diplomat, The Story of a Naval Captain of the Revolution* (New Haven, CT: Yale University Press, 1932), 80–81.
56. The list can be found in "Journal of the Continental Congress," October 10, 1776, *Naval Documents*, VI:1,200–1,201.
57. *Journals of the Continental Congress, 1774–1789*, 34 vols. (Washington, DC: U.S. Government Printing Office, 1904–37), XX:710–11; Morison, *John Paul Jones*, 87–90; McGrath, *John Barry*, 102–4.
58. Fowler, *Rebels under Sail*, 228–29; Volo, *Blue Water Patriots*, 89–91.
59. Journal of the Continental Congress, November 6, 1776, *Naval Documents*, VII:66.
60. Journal of the Continental Congress, April 19, 1777, *Naval Documents*, VIII:379.
61. Allen, *Naval History of the American Revolution*, I:33–34.
62. Continental Marine Committee to the Navy Board of the Eastern Department, July 10, 1777, *Naval Documents*, IX:256–57.
63. Paullin, *Navy of the American Revolution*, 106.
64. Marine Committee to Navy Board of the Middle Department, November 5, 1777, Paullin, *Out-Letters*, I:166–67; Board of Admiralty to President of Congress, August 14, 1780, Paullin, *Out-Letters*, II:243–44.
65. George Everett Hastings, *The Life and Works of Francis Hopkinson* (Chicago: University of Chicago Press, 1926), 212–20.
66. Central Navy Board to the Pennsylvania Council of Public Safety, April 9, 1777, *Naval Documents*, VIII:306.

67. Washington to Hazelwood, September 23, 1777, *The Papers of George Washington*, XI:303–304; McGrath, *John Barry*, 121.
68. McGrath, *John Barry*, 125
69. William B. Clark, *Gallant John Barry: The Story of a Naval Hero of Two Wars* (New York: The Macmillan Company, 1938), 122.
70. Numerous works recount the loss of Philadelphia to the British. A few examples include Ferling, *Almost a Miracle*, 242–58; and Robert Middlekauf, *The Glorious Cause: The American Revolution, 1763–1789* (New York: Oxford University Press, 2005), 396–401.
71. Washington to Navy Board, October 25, 1777, *The Papers of George Washington*, XI:610.
72. Paullin, *The Navy of the American Revolution*, 96–97.
73. Navy Board to Washington, October 26, 1777, *The Papers of George Washington*, XII:8–9.
74. Washington to Navy Board, October 27, 1777, *The Papers of George Washington*, XII:31–32.
75. Washington to Navy Board, October 27, 1777, *The Papers of George Washington*, XII:32.
76. See Clark, *Gallant John Barry*, 127; Congress to Washington, "Commission of the Continental Congress," in Abbot, ed., *The Papers of George Washington*, I:6–7.
77. Navy Board to Barry, November 2, 1777, *Naval Documents*, X:377.
78. Barry related his version of this conversation in his defense to Congress of his conduct. See Captain John Barry to the Continental Congress, January 10, 1778, *Naval Documents*, XI:85–88.
79. McGrath, *John Barry*, 129.
80. John Barry to the Continental Congress, January 10, 1778, in Clark, *Naval Documents*, XI:85–88.
81. Clark, *Gallant John Barry*, 130; McGrath, *John Barry*, 130–31.
82. Navy Board to George Washington, November 10, 1777, Clark, *Naval Documents*, 453–54.
83. Hastings, *Francis Hopkinson*, 223.
84. Captain John Barry to the Continental Congress, January 10, 1778, Clark, *Naval Documents*, XI: 85–88.
85. Journal of the Continental Congress, February 21, 1778, Clark, *Naval Documents*, XI:397.
86. Joseph Gurn, *Commodore John Barry: The Father of the American Navy* (New York: P. J. Kennedy & Sons, 1933), 69.
87. Paullin, *Navy of the American Revolution*, 255; McGrath, *Give Me a Fast Ship*, 122–23.
88. Morison, *John Paul Jones*, 177–78.

89. Paullin, *Navy of the American Revolution*, 265.
90. Franklin to Jones, July 8, 1779, Bradford, Jones Papers, reel 4.
91. McGrath, *Give Me a Fast Ship*, 283–84.
92. Paullin, *Navy of the American Revolution*, 256–57.
93. Morison, *John Paul Jones*, 174, 197–98; McGrath, *Give Me a Fast Ship*, 265.
94. H. W. Brands, *The First American: The Life and Times of Benjamin Franklin* (New York: Doubleday, 2000), 533–34.
95. Petition of Officers of the Continental Ship *Ranger* on Behalf of Lieutenant Thomas Simpson, Continental Navy, May 30, 1778, *Naval Documents*, XII:782–83; Crew of the Continental Ship *Ranger* to the American Commissioners in France, June 3, 1778, *Naval Documents*, XIII:887–89. See Morison, *John Paul Jones*, 167–72 for a detailed account of Jones's clash with Simpson.
96. Commissioners in France to Jones, June 3, 1778, *Naval Documents*, XIII:890–91.
97. Jones to Commissioners, June 1778, *Naval Documents*, XIII:872–74.
98. McGrath, *Give Me a Fast Ship*, 256; Morison, *John Paul Jones*, 190.
99. Diary of John Adams, May 12, 1779, Adams Papers, *Founders Online*, National Archives and Records Administration (NARA).
100. Morison, *John Paul Jones*, 208–12, 234–35.
101. Morison, *John Paul Jones*, 296–97; McGrath, *Give Me a Fast Ship*, 341–42.
102. R. H. Lee and Lovell, Committee of Foreign Affairs, to the Commissioners at Paris, December 2, 1777, Francis Wharton, ed., *The Revolutionary Diplomatic Correspondence of the United States*, 6 vols. (Washington, DC: U.S. Government Printing Office, 1889), II:438–41; A. Lee to Committee of Foreign Affairs, July 29, 1778, Wharton, *Diplomatic Correspondence*, 673–74.
103. Ferguson, *Truxtun of the* Constellation, 46.
104. Jones to Truxtun, October 24, 1780, James C. Bradford, ed., The Papers of John Paul Jones, David Library of the American Revolution, reel 6.
105. Eugene S. Fergusen, *Truxtun of the Constellation: The Life of Commodore Thomas Truxtun, U.S. Navy, 1755–1822* (Baltimore: Johns Hopkins University Press 2000, first published 1956), 39–42.
106. Jones to Truxtun, October 24, 1780, Bradford, John Paul Jones Papers, reel 6.
107. William Ellery to William Vernon, June 5, 1781, "Papers of William Vernon and the Navy Board, 1776–1794, Reprinted from the *Publications of the Rhode Island Historical Society*, Vol. VIII, No. 4, January 1901" (Providence: Snow & Farnham, Printers, 1901), 73–76, quotation on page 76.
108. John Adams to the President of Congress, July 6, 1780, Wharton, *Diplomatic Correspondence*, III:833–34.
109. Adams to President of Congress, July 6, 1780, Wharton, *Revolutionary Correspondence*, III:833–34.
110. Ferguson, *Truxtun of the Constellation*, 39–42.

### Chapter 2. "To This Great National Object"

1. Richard O'Brien to Jefferson, August 24, 1785, Thomas Jefferson, *The Papers of Thomas Jefferson*, ed. Julian P. Boyd, et al. (Princeton, NJ: Princeton University Press, 1950–), VIII:440–41; James Leander Cathcart, *The Captives: Eleven Years a Prisoner in Algiers*, reprinted in Robert J. Allison, ed., *Narratives of Barbary Captivity* (R. R. Donnelley & Sons, 2007), 9–16.
2. Richard B. Parker, *Uncle Sam in Barbary: A Diplomatic History* (Gainesville: University Press of Florida, 2004), 208–9.
3. For the Barbary corsairs, see Frank Lambert, *The Barbary Wars: American Independence in the Atlantic World* (New York: Hill and Wang, 2005); Michael L. S. Kitzen, *Tripoli and the United States at War: A History of American Relations with the Barbary States, 1785–1805* (Jefferson, NC: McFarland, 1993); Joshua London, *Victory in Tripoli: How America's War with Barbary Pirates Established the U.S. Navy and Built a Nation* (Hoboken, NJ: John Wiley & Sons, 2005); and Robert Allison, *The Crescent Obscured: The United States and the Muslim World, 1776–1815* (New York: Oxford University Press, 1995).
4. Ian Toll, *Six Frigates: The Epic History of the Founding of the U.S. Navy* (New York: W. W. Norton, 2006), 18–19.
5. Morrison, *John Paul Jones*, 360–90; Evan Thomas, *John Paul Jones: Sailor, Hero, Father of the American Navy* (New York: Simon and Schuster, 2003), 267–99.
6. For Barry's postwar merchant career, see McGrath, *John Barry*, 359–403. For Truxtun, Eugene Fergusen's 1956 biography remains the sole study of his life. His merchant career can be found in Fergusen, *Truxtun of the* Constellation: *The Life of Commodore Thomas Truxtun, 1755–1822* (Baltimore: Johns Hopkins University Press, 1956), 60–99.
7. Louis Arthur Norton, *Joshua Barney: Hero of the Revolution and 1812* (Annapolis, MD: Naval Institute Press, 2000), 102–4.
8. Charles Biddle, *The Autobiography of Charles Biddle: Vice-President of the Supreme Executive Council of Pennsylvania, 1745–1821* (Philadelphia: E. Claxon, 1883), 217–20.
9. McGrath, *John Barry*, 358–64.
10. Article I, Section 8, and Article II, Section 2, Constitution of the United States, https://constitution.congress.gov/constitution/.
11. Article I, Section 8, Constitution of the United States.
12. Article I, Section 10, Constitution of the United States, https://constitution.congress.gov/constitution/. For the views of the Framers of the Constitution on military matters, see Richard H. Kohn, *Eagle and Sword: The Federalists and the Creation of the Military Establishment in America, 1783–1802* (New York: Free Press, 1975), 73–81. Kohn, "The Constitution and National Security: The Intent of the

Framers," in *The United States Military under the Constitution of the United States, 1789–1989*, ed. Richard Kohn (New York: New York University Press, 1989), 61–87, also addresses the drafting of the Constitution in light of national security concerns, and the strong desire to curtail the states' power over military affairs.

13. Publius [Alexander Hamilton], "The Federalist: No. 11," in *The Federalist: The Gideon Edition*, ed. George Carey and James McClellan (Indianapolis: Liberty Fund, 2001), 49–55. Hamilton also addresses the role of the central government and naval forces in "The Federalist: No. 24," 117–22.
14. The discussion of Antifederalist opposition to the creation of a navy during the debate over ratification comes primarily from Marshall Smelser, *The Congress Founds the Navy, 1787–1798* (Notre Dame, IN: University of Notre Dame Press, 1959), 13–18.
15. James McClellan and M. E. Bradford, eds., *Jonathan Elliot's Debates in the Several State Conventions on the Adoption of the Federal Constitution*, 7 vols. (Richmond, VA: James River Press, 1989), III:430.
16. Smelser, *Congress Founds the Navy*, 13–18; Kohn, *Eagle and Sword*, 81–86.
17. Jeffrey J. Seiken, "American Naval Policy in an Age of Atlantic Warfare: A Consensus Broken and Reforged, 1783–1816" (PhD diss., Ohio State University, 2007), 8–26.
18. Thomas Jefferson to John Adams, July 11, 1786, in *Naval Documents relating to the United States' Wars with the Barbary Powers*, 6 vols. (Washington, DC: United States Government Printing Office, 1939), I:10–11 (hereafter *NDBW*).
19. James Simpson to Secretary of State, November 25, 1793, *NDBW* I:56–57.
20. Toll, *Six Frigates*, 37.
21. Act Pertaining to the Navy, March 27, 1794 in *NDBW*, I:69–70. For the debate over the creation of the Navy, see Craig L. Symonds, *Navalists and Antinavalists: The Naval Policy Debate in the United States, 1785–1827* (Newark: University of Delaware Press, 1980), 17–49; Toll, *Six Frigates*, 40–44.
22. Barry to Samuel Nicholson, June 24, 1794, John Barry Papers, Vol. 5, Naval Historical Society Collection, New York Historical Society. For Barry's role in selecting the first officer corps, see McGrath, *John Barry*, 423; Toll, *Six Frigates*, 56–57.
23. Kohn, *Eagle and Sword*, 294.
24. Washington to Alexander Spotswood, March 15, 1794, *The Papers of George Washington: Presidential Series*, 19 vols. (Charlottesville: University of Virginia Press, 1986–), XV:388–89.
25. Skelton, *American Profession of Arms*, 45–51; N. A. M. Rodger, *The Wooden World: Anatomy of the Georgian Navy* (London: William Collins, 1986), 254; Evan Wilson, *A Social History of British Naval Officers, 1775–1815* (Woodbridge,

Suffolk, UK: Boydell Press, 2017), 17–18. See also, Sheppard, "There Will Still Remain Heroes and Patriots," 381.

26. Barry to Nicholson, June 24, 1794, NYHS.
27. Knox to six captains: Barry, Nicholson, Talbot, Barney, Dale, and Truxtun, June 5, 1794, "Letters Sent by the War Department relating to Naval Matters," Washington, DC.
28. Toll, *Six Frigates*, 57.
29. Toll, *Six Frigates*, 57, contends that Truxtun was in fact an "afterthought," for Washington, Knox, and Barry, which seems unlikely given his contact with Barry in Canton. Toll does go on to note that Truxtun "would do more to shape the culture of the officer corps than any on the roster above him." See also Fergusen, *Truxtun of the* Constellation, for Truxtun's Revolutionary career, 17–50, and lack of patronage, 102–3. Of course, the fact that no letters of recommendation on Truxtun's behalf remain does not necessarily mean none existed, or that Truxtun did not have friends verbally endorsing him to Washington and Knox. Truxtun also owned stock in "The Asylum Company," a venture owned by Revolutionary War financier and former head of the Continental navy Robert Morris (Thomas Truxtun Collection, Box 51, Folder 2, LOC, Washington, DC).
30. Louis Arthur Norton, *Joshua Barney: Hero of the American Revolution and the War of 1812* (Annapolis, MD: Naval Institute Press, 2000), 128–30; Hulbert Footner, *Sailor of Fortune: The Life and Adventures of Commodore Barney, USN* (New York: Harper & Brothers, 1940), 193–94.
31. William M. Fowler Jr., *Jack Tars and Commodores: The American Navy, 1783–1815* (Boston: Houghton-Mifflin, 1984), 23; Louis Arthur Norton, *Joshua Barney: Hero of the Revolution and 1812* (Annapolis, MD: Naval Institute Press, 2000), 128–30.
32. Fowler, *Jack Tars and Commodores*, 30; Toll, *Six Frigates*, 68–70.
33. Act Pertaining to the Navy, United States Statutes at Large, An Act supplementary to an act entitled "An act to provide a Naval Armament," April 20, 1796, *NDBW*, I:150.
34. Toll, *Six Frigates*, 62.
35. War Office to Sever and Talbot, June 4, 1796, Letters Sent by the War Department (Dale's notification is not included); War Office to Sever, January 18, 1797, Letters Sent by the War Department; Gardner Allen, *Our Naval War with France* (1910. Reprint, Hamden, CT: Archon Books, 1967), 49–50.
36. James Fenimore Cooper, *Lives of Distinguished American Naval Officers*, vol. 1 (Philadelphia: Carey and Hart, 1846), 258–59.
37. Fowler, *Silas Talbot*, 117–27.
38. Mark Puls, *Henry Knox: Visionary General of the American Revolution* (New York: Palgrave Macmillan, 2008) is an excellent recent biography of one of Washington's closest friends and political allies.

39. Knox oversaw selecting the locations where the frigates would be constructed and initiated the process, and all three maintained regular communication with him while the ships were under construction. The details of initiating construction of the frigates can be found in Knox's extensive correspondence in Letters Sent by the War Department. It appears Alexander Hamilton, then Secretary of the Treasury, was involved in the process, as Knox sent him a detailed account of estimated costs early on and sent regular updates thereafter: Knox to Hamilton, April 21, 1794, Letters Sent by the War Department. For the delegation of authority, see Knox, "Instructions to the Persons Appointed for Building the Frigates," Letters Sent by the War Department; and Barry, Dale, and Truxtun to the Secretary of War, December 18, 1794, in *American State Papers: Naval Affairs*, I:8. For secondary accounts of the construction of the frigates, see Toll, *Six Frigates*, 44–62; and Charles Oscar Paullin, *Paullin's History of Naval Administration, 1775–1911: A collection of Articles from the U.S. Naval Institute* Proceedings (Annapolis, MD: Naval Institute Press, 2012), 89–96.
40. There is, to date, only one biography of McHenry: Bernard Steiner, *The Life and Correspondence of James McHenry: Secretary of War under Washington and Adams* (Cleveland, OH: Burrows Brothers, 1909). Overly sympathetic to its subject, the work also functions as more of an edited volume of McHenry's writings than a true biography, relying almost exclusively on excerpts and quotations rather than analysis. The definitive study of his life remains to be written.
41. Kohn, *Eagle and Sword*, 241–49.
42. Hamilton to Washington, October 29, 1798, *Papers of Alexander Hamilton*, XXII:221; Hamilton to Washington, July 29-August 1, 1798, *Papers of Alexander Hamilton*, XXII:36–40.
43. Michael Palmer, *Stoddert's War: Naval Operations During the Quasi-War with France, 1798–1801* (1987. Reprint, Annapolis, MD: Naval Institute Press, 2000), 7–9; Ron Chernow, *Alexander Hamilton*, (New York: Penguin Press, 2004), 565–66.
44. John Ferling, *John Adams: A Life* (Knoxville: University of Tennessee Press, 1992), 333.
45. For a concise summary of the so-called "XYZ Affair," see William Stinchcombe, *The XYZ Affair* (Westport, CT: Greenwood Press, 1980); Ferling, *John Adams*, 352–53; and Allen, *Our Naval War with France*, 23–27.
46. The story of the subscription warships is ably recounted in Frederick Leiner, *Millions for Defense: The Subscription Warships of 1798* (Annapolis, MD: Naval Institute Press, 2000).
47. For the debate over the militia and the accompanying dispute over central versus state control, see Kohn, *Eagle and Sword*, 128–38.

48. On merchant influence in officer assignments, see William Gary Anderson, "John Adams and the Creation of the American Navy" (PhD diss., State University of New York at Stony Brook, 1975), 127.
49. Leiner, *Millions for Defense*, 66.

## Chapter 3. "To Rid Our Navy of Such Men"

1. Edward Stevens, US Consul General, St. Domingo to Captain Silas Talbot, January 2, 1800, *Naval Documents related to the Quasi-War between the United States and France* (hereafter referred to as *NDQW*), 7 vols. (Washington, DC: US Government Printing Office, 1935–38), V:1–3; extract from the journal of Lieutenant William Maley, Captain of the *Experiment*, January 1, 1800, *NDQW*, V:4.
2. Secretary of the Navy to Secretary of State, November 25, 1800, *NDQW*, VI:548.
3. David Dixon Porter, *Memoir of Commodore Porter of the United States Navy* (New York: J. Munsell, 1875), 29–32. Porter's version of events is recounted in David Long, *Nothing Too Daring: A Biography of David Porter* (Annapolis, MD: Naval Institute Press, 1970), 12–13; Fowler, *Jack Tars and Commodores*, 51–52.
4. Palmer, *Stoddert's War*, 166–67.
5. Palmer, *Stoddert's War*, 169–70.
6. Stoddert to Barry, December 7, 1798, in *NDQW*, II:70–71.
7. Paullin, *History of Naval Administration*, 109–10.
8. "An act to establish an executive department, to be denominated the Department of the Navy," April 30, 1798, *NDQW*, I:59–60
9. George Cabot to Timothy Pickering, May 11, 1798, Henry Cabot Lodge, *The Life and Letters of George Cabot* (Boston: Little, Brown, 1878), 156–58.
10. David Craft, "The Expedition of Col. Thomas Hartley against the Indians in 1778, to Avenge the Massacre of Wyoming," *Wyoming Historical and Genealogical Society, Proceedings and Collections* 9 (1905): 189–216; Palmer, *Stoddert's War*, 10–14; Paullin, *History of Naval Administration*, 103–4.
11. Stoddert to Stephen Higginson, July 12, 1798, in *NDQW*, I:198–99.
12. Palmer, *Stoddert's War*, 22–23.
13. Stoddert to Captain Johns, October 16, 1784, Benjamin Stoddert Papers, Manuscript Collection, LOC, Washington DC, emphasis in the original.
14. Adams to Stoddert, March 31, 1801, Charles Francis Adams, ed., *The Life and Works of John Adams*, 10 vols. (Boston: Little, Brown, 1856), IX:582–83; Palmer, *Stoddert's War*, 14.
15. Stoddert to Adams, *NQQW* III:234–37; IV:111.
16. Stoddert to Adams, May 25 and June 25, 1799, *NDQW*, III:252–53, 405.

17. Adams to Stoddert, May 31, 1799, *NDQW*, III:285.
18. Stoddert to Adams, April 19, 1799, in *NDQW*, III:66–67.
19. Stoddert to Stephen Higginson, August 28, 1798, in *NDQW*, I:350; Stoddert to Adams, May 28, 1799, *NDQW*, III:264–65.
20. Stoddert to Stephen Higginson, August 28, 1798, in *NDQW*, I:350.
21. Circular to captains of the U.S. Navy from the Secretary of the Navy, June 27, 1799, in *NDQW*, III:420–21.
22. McKee, *A Gentlemanly and Honorable Profession*, 38. The following discussion of the selection, promotion, and purging of officers draws heavily from this monumental work.
23. McKee, *A Gentlemanly and Honorable Profession*, 46.
24. Stoddert to Robert Oliver, October 15, 1798, Miscellaneous Letters Sent by the Secretary of the Navy, M209, NARA, Washington, DC.
25. McKee notes that it would have been difficult for Stoddert to do otherwise, as the speed with which the navy needed to mobilize to meet the immediate threat posed by privateers precluded a lengthy process of sorting through applications. See McKee, *A Gentlemanly and Honorable Profession*, 48–53.
26. Stoddert to Christopher Perry, September 28, 1798, in *NDQW*, I:463.
27. Stoddert to Nicholson, July 6, 1798, *NDQW*, I:172.
28. Stoddert to Silas Talbot, May 29, 1799, in *NDQW*, III:274–75.
29. Stoddert to Henry Knox, Nathaniel Bosworth & Others, Midshipmen U.S. Navy on board the U.S. Frigate *Constitution*, May 29, 1799, in *NDQW*, III:275; Alexander Murray to Lieutenant Jeremiah Barton, May 5, 1800, *NDQW*, V:479–80; also note Murray to Barton, March 17, 1800, *NDQW*, V:316.
30. Stoddert to Lieutenant Blake Cordis, September 17, 1799, *NDQW*, IV:198–99.
31. Stoddert to John Rodgers, July 29, 1799, Rodgers Family Papers, LOC Collection, Manuscript Division, LOC, Washington, DC; Stoddert to William Bainbridge, September 7, 1798, *NDQW*, I:379–80.
32. For the composition of the Navy Department staff in this era, see McKee, *Gentlemanly and Honorable Profession*, 4–27.
33. Stoddert to Stephen Decatur Sr., June 21, 1798, *NDQW*, I:127. See also Stoddert to Sever, July 6, 1798, *NDQW*, I:172–73.
34. The best source for Stoddert's strategic thinking in the Quasi War is Palmer, *Stoddert's War*. See also Robert Jones, "The Naval Thought and Policy of Benjamin Stoddert," *American Neptune* 24 (January 1964): 61–69.
35. Stoddert to Hugh Campbell, October 13, 1798, *NDQW*, I:528–29; Stoddert to Barry, July 11, 1798, *NDQW*, I:189–91; Stoddert to Nicholson, December 5, 1798, *NDQW*, II:65.
36. Murray to Stoddert, August 5, and August 11, 1799, *NDQW*, IV:30–31; 60–61.

37. Stoddert to Truxtun, *NDQW*, II:5.
38. Stoddert to Campbell, September 21, 1798, *NDQW*, I:434; Stoddert to Barry, November 29, 1798, *NDQW*, II:55–56.
39. Stoddert, "Circular Instructions to the Captains and Commanders of Vessels in the Service of the United States," March 12, 1799, *NDQW*, II:447.
40. Stoddert to Talbot, January 23, 1800, *NDQW*, V:120–21. Although addressed to Talbot, Stoddert urged him to spread the word to his peers that both practices met with Adams' disapproval, and the tone and structure of the missive indicates it was a form letter sent to various commanders, with only Talbot's copy making it into the *NDQW* collection.
41. On the practice of writing newspapers ending after this letter, see William Gary Anderson, "John Adams and the Creation of the American Navy" (PhD diss., State University of New York at Stony Brook, 1975), 128. For examples of unsolicited advice, see Truxtun to Stoddert, *NDQW*, II:516–17; Murray to Stoddert, *NDQW*, IV:229–30.
42. Stoddert to Tingey, June 22, 1799, *NDQW*, III:384. See also Tingey to Stoddert, February 18, 1799, *NDQW*, II:366–68.
43. Stoddert to Adams, April 6, 1799, *NDQW*, III:24–25; Stoddert to Barry, June 17, 1799, *NDQW*, III:349; Stoddert to Barry, September 20, 1799, *NDQW*, IV:211; Stoddert to Barry, October 1, 1799, *NDQW*, IV:241–42.
44. Palmer, *Stoddert's War*, 35–44.
45. Stoddert to Talbot, May 2, 1799, *NDQW*, III:120–21; Stoddert to Alexander Hamilton, February 7, 1799, *Alexander Hamilton Papers*, XXII:468–69; Stoddert to Hamilton, May 3, 1799, *Alexander Hamilton Papers*, XXIII:96–98.
46. Truxtun to Charles Biddle, October 24, 1801, Truxtun-Biddle Letters, HSP.
47. Palmer, *Stoddert's War*, 44–46.
48. Stoddert to Stephen Higginson, March 26, 1799, *NDQW*, II:519–20.
49. Stoddert to Nicholson, October 5, 1798, *NDQW*, I:493; Stoddert initially wrote this very harsh letter but then crossed it out, presumably meaning he never sent it. He did, however, send Adams a letter expressing his disgust with Nicholson's conduct: Stoddert to Adams, October 5, 1798, *NDQW*, I:495. A few days later, he finally sent Nicholson a sharp letter ordering him to return to sea immediately: Stoddert to Nicholson, October 8, 1798, *NDQW*, I:504.
50. Palmer, *Stoddert's War*, 60.
51. Stoddert to Higginson, March 26, 1799, *NDQW*, II:519–20; Stoddert to Decatur, May 31, 1799, *NDQW*, III:285–86; Stoddert to Adams, May 15 & 28, 1799, *NDQW*, III:185 & 264–65; Stoddert to Nicholson, May 15, 1799, *NDQW*, III:186.
52. Palmer, *Stoddert's War*, 60–63; U.S. Secretary of State to British Minster and Envoy Extraordinary to the United States, December 31, 1798, in *NDQW*, II:29–30; Isaac Phillips to Stoddert, February, 11, 1799, in *NDQW*, II:30–32.

53. Stoddert to Phillips, January 10, 1799, in *NDQW*, II:30.
54. Stoddert to Richard Caton, January 24, 1799, in *NDQW*, II:276–77.
55. Stoddert to Phillips, February 20, 1799, in *NDQW*, II:32–34.
56. Stoddert to Truxtun, February 6, 1799, in *NDQW*, II:314–15.
57. Tingey to the *Norfolk Herald*, February 28, 1799, in *NDQW*, II:412–13; Stoddert to Tingey, March 7, 1799, in *NDQW*, II:429–30.
58. Truxtun to Dale, August 3, 1805, quoted in Ferguson, *Truxtun of the* Constellation, 103, original can be found at the New York Public Library.
59. Ferguson, *Truxtun of the* Constellation, 127.
60. "Captain Truxtun concerning mutinous assemblies on board U.S. Frigate *Constellation*," July 2, 1798, *NDQW*, I:156–58.
61. Stoddert to Truxtun, July 2, 1798, *NDQW*, I:158.
62. For the life of ordinary seamen in this era, see Gilje, *Liberty on the Waterfront*; James Valle, *Rocks and Shoals: Order and Discipline in the Old Navy, 1800–1861* (Annapolis, MD: Naval Institute Press, 1980). On the unofficial contract between seamen and officers, see McKee, *A Gentlemanly and Honorable Profession*, 258–61.
63. Truxtun to Stoddert, March 7, 1799, *NDQW*, II:426–27.
64. Truxtun to Robert Rosseter, January 20, 1801, Thomas Truxtun Records, Vol. 4, Letterbook, Historical Society of Pennsylvania, Philadelphia, PA.
65. Truxtun to Lieutenant Cowper, August 15, 1798, Thomas Truxtun Records, Vol. 2, Letterbook, Historical Society of Pennsylvania (HSP), Philadelphia, PA.
66. Truxtun to officers, September, 1798, Letterbook, HSP.
67. Truxtun to Cowper, October 30, 1798, *NDQW*, I:572–73
68. David Dixon Porter, *Memoirs of Commodore David Porter*, 18–19; Long, *Nothing Too Daring*, 8–9.
69. Truxtun to Midshipman Enoch Brown, February 23, 1799, *NDQW*, II:392.
70. Truxtun to Barry, March 20, 1799, *NDQW*, II:491–92.
71. Truxtun to Stoddert, July 2, 1799, *NDQW*, III:455, though it should be noted that the vessel in question was a fairly small one, and Truxtun's lieutenants may have felt that the chance for fame and glory was greater as a subordinate on a frigate than in command of a ship that size. Still, they obviously found Truxtun's command tolerable enough to turn down a chance at leaving, despite his sharp reproofs and harsh discipline.
72. Truxtun to Stoddert, February 10, 1799, in *NDQW*, II:326–27.
73. Andrew Sterrett to his brother, February 9, 1799, in *NDQW*, II:334–35. See also Ferguson, *Truxtun of the* Constellation, 172–73 for this episode.
74. George C. Daughan, *The Shining Sea: David Porter and the Epic Voyage of the U.S.S.* Essex *during the War of 1812* (New York: Basic Books, 2013), 231.
75. Truxtun to Stoddert, February 10, 1799 in *NDQW*, II:326–27.

76. For Hamilton's political machinations behind Adams' back, see Chernow, *Alexander Hamilton*, 510–29, 566–73; Kohn, *Eagle and Sword*, 230–73; and Ferling, *John Adams*, 343–63, 382–96.
77. For Stoddert's response to news of the victory, see Stoddert to Truxtun, March 13, 1799, *NDQW*, II:450–51.
78. Ferguson, *Truxtun of the* Constellation, 123–24.
79. For the discussion of relative rank, see also Sheppard, "There Will Still Remain Heroes and Patriots," 377–81.
80. Stoddert to Murray, September 15, 1798; Stoddert to Tingey, September 15, 1798, *NDQW*, I:407–8.
81. Stoddert to Murray, March 13, 1799, *NDQW*, II:451.
82. Stoddert to William Bainbridge, August 28, 1799, *NDQW*, IV:128–29.
83. For the impact of relative rank on operations, see Palmer, *Stoddert's War*, 81–83.
84. Stoddert to Adams, October 17, 1798, *NDQW*, I:542–43.
85. Adams to Talbot, July 8, 1799, *NDQW*, III:474–75.
86. Stoddert to Truxtun, July 3, 1799, *NDQW*, III:463.
87. Stoddert to Richard Dale, August 30, 1798; October 9, 1798, *NDQW*, I:357, 510; Stoddert to Alexander Hamilton, February 6, 1799, *NDQW*, 313.
88. Stoddert to Talbot, May 2, May 8, May 15, May 28, May 29, 1799, *NDQW*, III:120–21, 157–158, 186, 265–66.
89. Stoddert to Truxtun, July 3, 1799, *NDQW*, III:463.
90. Stoddert to Truxtun, February 6, 1799, *NDQW*, II:314–15.
91. Truxtun to Stoddert, March 26, 1799, *NDQW*, II:516–17.
92. Talbot to Knox, January 31, 1790; Talbot to Knox, July 6, 1799; Stoddert to Knox, August 6, 1799, Henry Knox Papers, David Library of the American Revolution, Washington's Crossing, PA.
93. Talbot to Hamilton, January 15, 1799, *Alexander Hamilton Papers*, XXII:418–20.
94. Chernow, *Alexander Hamilton*, 592–94.
95. Stoddert to Talbot, June 25, 1799, *NDQW* III:401.
96. Adams to Talbot, July 8, 1799, *NDQW*, III:474–75.
97. Talbot to Adams, July 9, 1799, *NDQW*, III:479.
98. Ferguson, *Truxtun of the* Constellation, 180–81.
99. Adams to Stoddert, July 23, 1799, NDQW, III:528–32.
100. Adams to Stoddert, July 20, 1799; Adams to Stoddert, July 23, 1799, NDQW, III:528–32.
101. Stoddert to Truxtun, July 30 1799, *NDQW*, III:567–68.
102. Truxtun to his officers, August 9, 1799, Correspondence, Box 1, HSP.
103. Captain Daniel Carmich, US Marine Corps, to Major Commandant W. W. Burrows, US Marine Corps, May 21, 1799, in *NDQW*, III:227.

104. Ferguson, *Truxtun*, 182–184, quote on page 182.
105. Stoddert to Hamilton, July 19, 1799, *NDQW*, III:516.
106. Stoddert to Truxtun, October 23, 28, and November 6, 1799, *NDQW*, IV:311–12, 333, 361–62.
107. Stoddert to Stephen Decatur, October 24, 1799, *NDQW*, IV:314–15.
108. Stoddert to House of Representatives, February 9, 1799, April 9, 1799, December 29, 1799, *American State Papers: Naval Affairs*, I:34, 56, 65–66, 70–71, 75.
109. Stoddert to Adams, *NDQW*, VI:174–75.
110. Stoddert to Sever, March 18, 1800, *NDQW*, V:322.
111. Stoddert to Talbot, November 18, 1800, *NDQW*, VI:536–37.
112. Stoddert to Truxtun, April 15, 1800, *NDQW*, V:418.
113. Stoddert to Truxtun, April 16, 1800, *NDQW*, V:421.
114. Sentence of Court in Case of Patrick Brown, April 13, 1800, *NDQW*, V:400.
115. Toll, *Six Frigates*, 138.
116. Stoddert to Samuel Barron, May 17, 1800, *NDQW*, V:526–527; Stoddert to Truxtun, May 22, 1800, *NDQW*, V:545–46; Stoddert to Truxtun, May 24, 1800, *NDQW*, V:555.
117. Stoddert to Truxtun, May 24, 1800, *NDQW*, V:555.
118. Stoddert to Truxtun, May 29, 1800, *NDQW*, V:573.
119. DeConde, *Politics and Diplomacy*, 259–293; Allen, *Our Naval War with France*, 245–51.
120. Ferling, *John Adams*, 384–405.
121. Stoddert to Murray, March 27, 1801, *NDQW*, VII:158.
122. Stoddert to Chairman of the Committee on Naval Affairs, January 12, 1801, *NDQW*, VII:80–84; Jones, "Naval Thought and Policy of Benjamin Stoddert," 84–89.

## Chapter 4. "To Make an Impression of Our National Character"

1. Sterrett to Richard Dale, August 6, 1801; Capture of Ship of War *Tripoli* by U.S. Schooner *Enterprize*, November 18, 1801, *Naval Documents Related to the United States Wars with the Barbary Powers*, 6 vols. (Washington, DC: U.S. Government Printing Office, 1939–44), I:537–38. Hereafter *NDBW*.
2. Fowler, *Jack Tars and Commodores*, 68–69.
3. The election of 1800, among the most famous in American history, is well represented in historical literature. See John Ferling, *Adams vs. Jefferson: The Tumultuous Election of 1800* (New York: Oxford University Press, 2004); and Edward Larson, *A Magnificent Catastrophe: The Tumultuous Election of 1800, America's First Presidential Campaign* (New York: Free Press, 2007) for narratives of the contest.

4. Thomas Jefferson, *The Writings of Thomas Jefferson*, 10 vols., ed. Paul Leicester Ford (New York: G.P. Putnam's Sons, 1892–99), I:189; Sean Wilentz, *The Rise of American Democracy: Jefferson to Lincoln* (New York: W. W. Norton, 2005), 94; Ferling, *Adams vs. Jefferson*, 181–91.
5. Ferling, *Adams vs. Jefferson*, 190–91; Jefferson, *The Writings of Thomas Jefferson*, I:189.
6. Christopher McKee, *Edward Preble: A Naval Biography, 1761–1807* (Annapolis, MD: Naval Institute Press, 1972), 101–2; Paullin, *History of Naval Administration*, 119–20; Ian Toll, *Six Frigates: The Epic History of the Founding of the U.S. Navy* (New York: W. W. Norton, 2006), 80–81, 91–92, 174.
7. Jefferson to Gouverneur Morris, May 8, 1801; Jefferson to William Jones, May 16, 1801; Jefferson to Robert Smith, July 9, 1801; Jefferson to Samuel Smith, July 9, 1801, in Julian Boyd, et al., eds., *The Papers of Thomas Jefferson*, 42 vols. (Princeton, NJ: Princeton University Press, 1950–), XXXIV:123–24, 534–35. Hereafter *Jefferson Papers*.
8. McKee, *A Gentlemanly and Honorable Profession*, 7.
9. Parker, *Uncle Sam in Barbary*, 134–35; Lambert, *The Barbary Wars*, 124; Toll, *Six Frigates*, 164–68.
10. Samuel Smith to Richard Dale, "or Officer Commanding the American Squadron in the Mediterranean," May 20, 1801, *NDBW*, I:465–69.
11. Theodore Crackel, *Mr. Jefferson's Army: Political and Social Reform of the Military Establishment, 1801–1809* (New York: New York University Press, 1987), 13.
12. Truxtun to Jefferson, May 18, 1801; Jefferson to Truxtun, May 28, 1801, *Jefferson Papers*, XXXIV:138–40, 201.
13. William M. Fowler Jr., *Silas Talbot: Captain of Old Ironsides* (Mystic, CT: Mystic Seaport Museum, 1995), 182.
14. Samuel Smith to Truxtun, April 2, 1801, *NDBW*, I:426–27; Smith to Truxtun, April 10, 1801, *Naval NDBW*, I:428–29; Truxtun to Smith, April 13, 1801, *NDBW*, I:432; Smith to Truxtun, April 28, 1801, *NDBW*, I:438–40.
15. N. A. M. Rodger, *The Command of the Ocean: A Naval History of Britain, 1649–1815* (London: W. W. Norton, 2004), 390–91; Rodger, "Honour and Duty at Sea, 1660–1815," *Historical Research* 75, no. 190 (2002): 425–47, see page 438 for the question of refusing certain orders.
16. Lambert, *The Barbary Wars*, 125.
17. McKee, *Edward Preble*, 91; London, *Victory in Tripoli*, 94–96, 100–101.
18. Dale to Secretary of the Navy, August 18, 1801, *NDBW*, I:552–54.
19. Alexander Hamilton, "The Examination No. 1," *New York Evening Post*, December 17, 1801; Alexander Hamilton, *The Papers of Alexander Hamilton*, 27 vols., ed. Harold Syrett (New York: Columbia University Press, 1961–87), XXV:444–57.

20. Lambert, *The Barbary Wars*, 130–33.
21. Frank Owsley, "Robert Smith, 27 July, 1801–7 March, 1809," in Paulo Coletta, *American Secretaries of the Navy*, vol. 1: 1775–1913 (Annapolis, MD: Naval Institute Press, 1980), 77–92.
22. Robert Smith to Jefferson, July 13, 1801, *Jefferson Papers*, XXXIV:562.
23. Paullin, *History of Naval Administration*, 121.
24. Frank Owsley, "Robert Smith, 27 July, 1801–7 March, 1809," in *American Secretaries of the Navy*, 2 vols., ed. Paolo E. Coletta (Annapolis, MD: Naval Institute Press, 1980), I:77–90.
25. McKee, *Gentlemanly and Honorable Profession*, 7–9.
26. Seiken, "American Naval Policy," 113–15, 203.
27. Secretary of the Navy Robert Smith to Richard Dale, November 28, 1802, *NDBW*, II:326.
28. Smith to Dale, December 10, 1802, *NDBW*, II:330.
29. Smith to Dale, December 20, 1802, *NDBW*, II:336. Both the letters from Dale that Smith was responding to have apparently been lost. We have no way of knowing exactly what Dale said in his letter of resignation.
30. Truxtun to Smith, March 3, 1802, Truxtun Papers, HSP.
31. Smith to Truxtun, March 13, 1802, *NDBW*, II:83.
32. Decatur to Smith, January 14, 1805, M149, Letters Sent by the Secretary of the Navy to Naval Officers, NARA, Washington, DC (Hereafter "Letters Sent").
33. Smith to Samuel Barron, October 18, 1805, Samuel Barron Papers, Box III, Early Gregg Swemm Library, William and Mary University. Preble to Smith, November 3, 1805; Preble to Bainbridge, November 3, 1805; Bainbridge to Smith, November 15, 1805; James Barron to Smith, November 23, 1805, Letters Received by the Secretary of the Navy from Captains (hereafter "Captains' Letters"), M125, NARA, Washington, DC.
34. Sheppard, "There Will Still Remain Heroes and Patriots," 385–86.
35. For Morris' tenure in the Mediterranean, I have relied heavily on McKee, *Edward Preble*, 109–22; Lambert, *The Barbary Wars*, 136–39; and London, *Victory in Tripoli*, 108–13.
36. Robert Smith to Rodgers, June 21, 1803; Smith to Morris, June 21, 1803, *NDBW*, II:457–58.
37. Jefferson to Gallatin, March 28, 1803, *Jefferson Papers*, *Founder Online*, NARA.
38. Smith to Rodgers, June 21, 1803. This letter was in private hands at the time of publication for McKee, *Edward Preble*, 114, and the owner allowed McKee access to it. The present whereabouts of the letter are unknown.
39. "Concerning Commodore Morris' Squadron in the Mediterranean," August 31, 1803, *NDBW*, II:526–31.

40. "Concerning Commodore Morris' Squadron in the Mediterranean," August 31, 1803, *NDBW*, II:526–31.
41. McKee, *Edward Preble*, 88–89.
42. Smith to Preble, July 13, 1803, *NDBW*, II:476.
43. Charles Morris, *The Autobiography of Charles Morris, U.S. Navy* (Annapolis, MD: Naval Institute Press, 2002), 18–19; McKee, *Edward Preble*, 140–41.
44. Morris, *Autobiography*, 19.
45. McKee, *Edward Preble*, 141; Morris, *Autobiography*, 19.
46. Glenn Tucker, *Dawn Like Thunder: The Barbary Wars and the Birth of the U.S. Navy* (New York: Bobbs-Merrill, 1963), 195, 205.
47. Smith to Preble, July 13, 1803, *NDBW*, II:476–77.
48. Smith to Morris, April 20, 1802, *NDBW*, II:130.
49. Smith to Preble, July 13, 1803, *NDBW*, II:476–77.
50. McKee, *Edward Preble*, 147.
51. Lear to Smith, September 26, 1803, *NDBW*, III:78–80; Paullin, *Commodore John Rodgers*, 112–13.
52. Preble to Rodgers, September 15, 1803, *NDBW*: III, 46–47.
53. Rodgers to Preble, September 15, 1803, *NDBW*: III, 47.
54. Preble to Smith, September 18, 1803, *NDBW*, III:56–59.
55. Parker, *Uncle Sam in Barbary*, 155–57.
56. Preble to Smith, September 18, 1803, *NDBW*, III:56–59.
57. Parker, *Uncle Sam in Barbary*, 156–57; Paullin, *Commodore John Rodgers*, 112–13; McKee, *Edward Preble*, 162–72, 297; John H. Schroeder, *Commodore John Rodgers: Paragon of the Early American Navy* (Gainesville: University Press of Florida, 2006), 35–36.
58. McKee, *Edward Preble*, 224–27.
59. Unknown correspondent to Edward Preble, December 4, 1803, Edward Preble Papers, Box 8, LOC, Manuscript Division, Washington, DC. The signature on this document has become illegible. It is unclear from the text if the sender was with Lieutenant Thorn, who is referred to in the third person, another of the officers present at the time, or another party to whom the events were reported for transmission to Preble.
60. Walter Boyd to Edward Preble, December 5, 1803, Preble Papers, Box 8.
61. McKee, *A Gentlemanly and Honorable Profession*, 403. For dueling in the "Old Navy," my principal sources have been McKee, *A Gentlemanly and Honorable Profession*, 403–406; Toll, *Six Frigates*, 218–21; and Charles Oscar Paullin, "Dueling in the Old Navy," U.S. Naval Institute *Proceedings* (1909): 1155–97. For ideas about honor, reputation, and dueling in the era, see Armstrong Starkey, *War in the Age of Enlightenment, 1700–1789* (Westport, CT: Praeger Press, 2003),

69–78; Joanne Freeman, *Affairs of Honor: National Politics in the New Republic* (New Haven, CT: Yale University Press, 2001); and Douglas Adair, "Fame and the Founding Fathers," in *Fame and the Founding Fathers*, ed. Trevor Colbourn (New York: Norton, 1974), 5–31.

62. Robert J. Allison, *Stephen Decatur: American Naval Hero, 1779–1820* (Amherst, MA: University of Massachusetts Press, 2005), 25–26.
63. Donald Sultana, "Coleridge, Stephen Decatur and the Mysterious Duelist at Malta," *Modern Language Review* 89, no. 2 (April 1994): 282–88.
64. Murray to Smith, November 7, 1802, *NDBW*, II:310–11
65. Allison, *Stephen Decatur*, 32.
66. Bainbridge to Preble, November 25, 1803, in *NDBW*, III:175. For an account of Bainbridge's loss of the *Philadelphia*, see David Long, *Ready to Hazard: A Biography of Commodore William Bainbridge, 1774–1833* (Hanover, NH: University Press of New England, 1981), 71–77.
67. Preble to Secretary of the Navy, December 10, 1803, in *NDBW*, III:256–58.
68. Long, *Ready to Hazard*.
69. Allison, *Stephen Decatur*, 47–54.
70. Preble to Smith, February 19, 1804, *NDBW*, III:441.
71. Sterrett to Smith, June 15, 1805; Smith to Sterrett, June 19, 1805, *NDBW*, VI:120–21, 126.
72. Goldsborough to Preble, June 6, 1804, Preble Papers, Box 11.
73. Sterrett to Smith, June 29, 1805, Officer Resignations, microfilm reel, Naval History and Heritage Command, Navy Yard, Washington, DC (hereafter "Resignations Reel").
74. Smith to Sterrett, July 5, 1805, Letters Sent.
75. Smith to Sterrett, July 13, 1805, Letters Sent.
76. McKee, *Edward Preble*, 199–201.
77. Preble to Smith, March 14, 1804, *NDBW*, III:491. See also Preble to Smith, March 11, 1804, *NDBW*, III:485–88; and Preble to Cathcart, May 28, 1804, *NDBW*, IV:126.
78. McKee, *Edward Preble*, 208.
79. Preble to Bey of Tunis, April 5, 1804; George Davis, U.S. Chargé d'Affaires, Tunis, to Preble, April 6, 1804; Preble to Davis, April 6, 1804; Davis to Preble, April 9, 1804, *NDBW*, IV:10, 13, 17.
80. Allison, *Stephen Decatur*, 63–64, 67–68.
81. McKee, *Edward Preble*, 201–7.
82. Preble to Cathcart, June 1, 1804, *NDBW*, IV:141.
83. McKee, *Edward Preble*, 241–44, 294–96.
84. Smith to Preble, May 7, 1804; Smith to Preble, May 22, 1804, *NDBW*, IV:88, 114–15.

85. Preble to Smith, September 18, 1804, *NDBW*, IV:293–308.
86. Paullin, *Commodore John Rodgers*, 134; Schroeder, *Commodore John Rodgers*, 41–42; Toll, *Six Frigates*, 259–60.
87. Schroeder, *Commodore John Rodgers*, 44.
88. Lambert, *Barbary Wars*, 150.
89. Eaton to Secretary of State, June 8, 1802, *NDBW*, II:166–70.
90. Murray to Eaton, August 18, 1802, *NDBW*, II:238–39.
91. Lambert, *Barbary Wars*, 150–55.
92. Eaton to Rodgers, June 13, 1805, *NDBW*, VI:116–17.
93. The text of the treaty can be found via Yale University's *The Avalon* Project, http://avalon.law.yale.edu/19th_century/bar1805t.asp. On the controversy surrounding the treaty, see Lambert, *The Barbary Wars*, 158–60; and McKee, *Edward Preble*, 334–37.
94. Eaton to Rodgers, July 10, 1805; Bashaw to Eaton, November 29, 1808, Eaton Papers, LOC.
95. Preble to Eaton, February 8, 1806, *NDBW*, VI:364.
96. McKee, *Edward Preble*, 335–36.
97. Rodgers to Bey of Tunis, July 1, 1805, *NDBW*, VI:146–147.
98. Rodgers to George Davis, June 11, 1805, *NDBW*, VI:109.
99. Schroeder, *Commodore John Rodgers*, 47–48.
100. Schroeder, *Commodore John Rodgers*, 47–49; Parker, *Uncle Sam in Barbary*, 152–54.
101. Parker, *Uncle Sam in Barbary*, 154. The letter is included in an appendix on pages 239–41, courtesy of the Tunisian National Archives.
102. B. Cocke to James Barron, July 29, 1806, James Barron Papers, Box I, Earl Gregg Swem Library, College of William and Mary.
103. Rodgers to Barron, July 23, 1806, James Barron Papers, Box I.
104. Thomas Tingey to Franklin Wharton, undated, though it had to have been written in July or August of 1806, James Barron Papers, Box I.
105. Paullin, *Commodore John Rodgers*, 177–78.
106. Barron to Rodgers, January 20, 1807, James Barron Papers, Box I.
107. Smith to Barron, December 17, 1806, Rodgers Family Papers, Part III:Box 1, LOC.
108. Wharton to Tingey, January 10, 1807, Rodgers Family Papers, Part III:Box 1, LOC.
109. Barron to Rodgers, January 20, 1807, James Barron Papers, Box I.
110. Tingey to Wharton, February 1, 1807, James Barron Papers, Box I.
111. Tingey to Wharton, January 20, 1807, James Barron Papers, Box I.
112. Copy of a Certificate for Publication with the Signatures of Franklin Wharton and Thomas Tingey together with a letter from Colonel Stricker to Com.

Rodgers, Box 2, Rodgers Family Papers, Naval Historical Foundation Collection, Manuscript Division, LOC. Stricker, Tingey, and Wharton to Rodgers, March 9, 1807, Rodgers Family Papers, Part II:General Correspondence, Box I, LOC.

### Chapter 5. "A Government Rigorously Frugal and Simple"

1. Goldsborough was briefly removed from the department during the War of 1812, but soon returned. More on that in the following chapter.
2. McKee, *Gentlemanly and Honorable Profession*, 13–15; Paullin, *History of Naval Administration*, 123–24; Owsley, "Robert Smith," I:70.
3. Goldsburough to Preble, February 20, 1801, Edward Preble Papers, Box 3, LOC, Washington, DC.
4. James Fenimore Cooper, for example, dismissed the gunboats as "a species of force that, in its nature, is merely auxiliary to more powerful means, and which is entirely unfitted to the moral character of the people, as it is to the natural formation of the coast." Cooper, *The History of the Navy of the United States of America* (Annapolis, MD: Naval Institute Press, 2001, originally published 1846), 232. Forrest McDonald likewise took a harsh view of the gunboat program, alleging that Jefferson intended to "let the nation's magnificent Humphreys frigates rot in the wharves, and in 1805 [he] began to build a 'mosquito fleet' of gunboats in their place." McDonald, *The Presidency of Thomas Jefferson* (Lawrence, KS: University of Kansas Press, 1976), 44. Finally, Frank Owsley asserts that if "Jefferson had had his way, he would have placed nearly the entire peacetime naval force in the dry dock and discharged most of the officers and seamen." Owsley, "Robert Smith," in *American Secretaries of the Navy*, 83.
5. Jefferson to Gerry, January 26, 1799, Thomas Jefferson, *The Papers of Thomas Jefferson*, 42 vols., ed. by Julian Boyd, et al. (Princeton, NJ: Princeton University Press, 1950–), XXX:46.
6. Crackel, *Mr. Jefferson's Army*, 12–15.
7. Jon Meacham, *Thomas Jefferson: The Art of Power* (New York: Random House, 2012), 260–62, 312–20; Crackel, *Mr. Jefferson's Army*, 18–21.
8. Smelser, *Congress Founds the Navy*, 178–79; Skelton, *American Profession of Arms*, 72–73.
9. Crackel, *Mr. Jefferson's Army*, 36–73. Whether Jefferson wanted officers who were republican (i.e., shared his basic political philosophy on the role of government and the evils of monarchy and excessive central power) or Republican (members of his political party) is open to debate. See Crackel, *Mr. Jefferson's Army*, 65–71; and Skelton, *American Profession of Arms*, 25, 98–99.
10. Smith to Amaziah Jocelin, January 3, 1802, *NDBW*, II:12–13.
11. Samuel Smith to Moses Brown, April 3, 1801, *NDQW*, VII:176. For Brown's Quasi War career, see Frederick Leiner, *Millions for Defense*, 30–52.

12. Smith to Daniel McNeill, October 27, 1802, M149, Letters Sent by the Secretary of the Navy to Officers. Hereafter, Letters Sent.
13. There are numerous letters in the Records of the Secretary of the Navy granting furloughs for service in the merchant marine. A few examples include Smith to Lieutenants, November 6, 1802; Smith to Midshipman Clark, November 13, 1802; Smith to Midshipman Wood, December 13, 1802; Smith to Midshipman Masury, January 24, 1803; Smith to Midshipman Keene, March 14, 1803, Letters Sent.
14. McKee, *Gentlemanly and Honorable Profession*, 412–16, quote on page 414.
15. Samuel Smith to John Rutledge Jr., May 12, 1801, Rutledge Papers, Southern Historical Collection, University of North Carolina, Chapel Hill, NC.
16. Jefferson to Smith, August 28, 1804, *Jefferson Papers, Founders Online*, NARA.
17. McKee, *Gentlemanly and Honorable Profession*, 416–18.
18. Smith to John Darby, November 9, 1805, Letters Sent.
19. "U.S. Navy Regulations Issued by Command of President Thomas Jefferson, 25 January 1802," *NDBW*, II:29–39. McKee, *Gentlemanly and Honorable Profession*, 544n, makes a compelling case for Tingey's having written, or at least significantly influenced, the new regulations, based on his copy of the British *Regulations and Instructions*.
20. McKee, *Edward Preble*, 325.
21. Smith to Barry, August 19, 1802, *NDBW*, II:239–40; Smith to J. Decatur, February 4, 1803, Letters Sent; Smith to Abner Woodruff, February 4, 1803, RG 45, Letters Sent.
22. McKee, *Edward Preble*, 312–15; Allison, *Stephen Decatur*, 78–81.
23. Smith to Jefferson, September 14, 1808, *Jefferson Papers, Founders Online*, NARA.
24. Paullin, *Commodore John Rodgers*, 190–91.
25. Craig Symonds, *Navalists and Antinavalists: The Naval Policy Debate in the United States, 1785–1827* (Newark, DE: University of Delaware Press, 1980), 88–89. For Copenhagen, see N. A. M. Roger, *The Command of the Ocean: A Naval History of Britain, 1649–1815* (London: W. W. Norton, 2004), 469–71.
26. Two recent works are absolutely essential for understanding Jefferson's gunboat program: Gene Smith, *For the Purposes of Defense: The Politics of the Jeffersonian Gunboat Program* (Newark, NJ: University of Delaware Press, 1995); and Spencer Tucker, *The Jeffersonian Gunboat Navy* (Columbia, SC: University of South Carolina Press, 1993).
27. Fowler, *Jack Tars and Commodores*, 144–45; Tucker, *Jeffersonian Gunboat Navy*, 36. For an extended discussion of gunboat design and construction, see Tucker, *Jeffersonian Gunboat Navy*, 36–64.
28. Even John Adams acknowledged Jefferson's pro-Navy credentials, once the bitterness over the 1800 election passed. See Adams to Jefferson, October 15, 1822,

Lester Cappon, ed., *The Adams-Jefferson Letters: The Complete Correspondence between Thomas Jefferson and Abigail and John Adams*, 2 vols. (Chapel Hill, NC: University of North Carolina Press, 1959), II:582–84. See also, Jefferson to Adams, November 1, 1822, Cappon, *Adams-Jefferson Letters*, II:584–85, for a concise summary of Jefferson's largely unchanged views on navies late in life.

29. Gallatin to Jefferson, October 29, 1804, *Jefferson Papers, Founders Online*, NARA.
30. Smith, *Purposes of Defense*, 34.
31. Toll, *Six Frigates*, 286.
32. Tucker, *Jeffersonian Gunboat Navy*, 7.
33. Smith, *Purposes of Defense*, 23–26, 73–93; Tucker, *Jeffersonian Gunboat Navy*, 17.
34. George Davies, "Robert Smith and the Navy," *Maryland Historical Magazine* XIV, no. 4 (December 1919): 305–22; Owsley, "Robert Smith," in *American Secretaries of the Navy*, 85; Seiken, "American Naval Policy," 203.
35. Smith, *Purposes of Defense*, 34.
36. McKee, *Gentlemanly and Honorable Profession*, 156–58.
37. Allison, *Stephen Decatur*, 81; Tucker, *Stephen Decatur*, 86–88.
38. Barron to Jefferson, February 8, 1807; Tingey to Jefferson, February 9, 1807, *American State Papers: Naval Affairs*, I:164.
39. Long, *Ready to Hazard*, 104–5, 112–15.
40. Boxes 18 and 19 of the Edward Preble Papers at the Library of Congress contain Preble's voluminous correspondence on the design, construction, and manning of gunboats. That Preble performed the task to the best of his abilities with his usual keen attention to detail is obvious. This is not the correspondence of a man half-heartedly performing a distasteful job.
41. Maloney, *Captain from Connecticut*, 122–24.
42. Smith, Circular, October 26, 1808, David D. Porter Family Papers, Box 15, LOC, Washington, DC. Hereafter Porter Papers.
43. Gordon S. Brown, *The Captain Who Burned His Ships: Captain Thomas Tingey, USN, 1750–1829* (Annapolis, MD: Naval Institute Press, 2011), 52–53.
44. Robert Smith to Jefferson, March 12, 1803, Barbara B. Oberg, ed., *The Papers of Thomas Jefferson*, 45 vols. (Princeton, NJ: Princeton University Press), IV:56.
45. Jefferson to Smith, March 19, 1803, Oberg, *Jefferson Papers*, IV:88.
46. Tingey to Robert Smith, January 16, 1805, Captains' Letters.
47. Brown, *Captain Who Burned His Ships*, 54.
48. Smith to Tingey, June 26, 1806, Smith to Tingey, July 11, 1806, Letters Sent; Brown, *Captain Who Burned His Ships*, 52–53, 60. See also Sheppard, "There Will Still Remain Heroes and Patriots," 390.
49. Smith to Porter, August 13, 1807, Porter Papers, Box 16.
50. Long, *Nothing Too Daring*, 39–43.

51. Smith to Porter, June 10, July 5, and August 13, 1808, Letters Sent.
52. Porter to Smith, September 7, 1808, M147, Letters Received by the Secretary of the Navy from Commanders.
53. Porter, *Memoir of Commodore David Porter*, 81.
54. Porter to Hambleton, December 19, 1808, Porter Papers, Box 1, LOC.
55. Smith circular to officers, July 26, 1808, Porter Papers, Box 15, LOC; Smith circular to officers, July 27, 1809, Porter Papers, Box 1, LOC.
56. McKee, *Edward Preble*, 323.
57. McKee, *Edward Preble*, 337–42; Symonds, *Navalists and Antinavalists*, 110–15.
58. "Petitions of the officer of the Navy of the United States," January 16, 1810, HR11A-F6.1, Petitions and Memorials, U.S. House of Representatives, 11th Congress, RG 233, Box 16.
59. Hull to Senator David Daggett, November 19, 1814, Isaac Hull Papers, vol. 7, Naval Historical Society Collection, New York Historical Society.
60. For the events of the *Chesapeake–Leopard* encounter, see Spencer C. Tucker and Frank T. Reuter, *Injured Honor: The* Chesapeake-Leopard *Affair, June 22, 1807* (Annapolis, MD: Naval Institute Press, 1996); and K. Michael Latshaw, "Flawed Judgment: The Court-Martial of Commodore James Barron," *Virginia Magazine of History and Biography* 105, no. 4 (Autumn 1997): 377–408.
61. The circular is reprinted in its entirety in William Oliver Stevens, *An Affair of Honor: The Biography of Commodore James Barron, USN* (Norfolk, VA: Norfolk County Historical Society, 1969), 60–61.
62. A copy of Humphry's letter is contained in Barron to Smith, July 22, 1807, M125, Letters Received by the Secretary of the Navy from Captains, NARA, Washington, DC (hereafter "Captains' Letters").
63. Barron to Humphreys, June 22, 1807, *NDBW*, VI:536; Tucker and Reuter, *Injured Honor*, 5–6.
64. Humphreys made these comments in a newspaper clipping, but the title of the paper was torn off. James Barron Papers, Box I, Earl Gregg Swem Library, College of William and Mary.
65. Tucker and Reuter, *Injured Honor*, 9.
66. Toll, *Six Frigates*, 296.
67. Tucker and Reuter, *Injured Honor*, 11–13.
68. Log of the US Frigate *Chesapeake*, June 22, 1807, Dudley, *Naval War of 1812*, 27–28; William Oliver Stevens, *An Affair of Honor: The Biography of Commodore James Barron, USN* (Norfolk, VA: Norfolk County Historical Society, 1969), 72–73. The British did eventually return two of the men who were seized. Bainbridge to Secretary of the Navy Paul Hamilton, July 11, 1812, Dudley, *Naval War of 1812*, I:190–91.

69. Barron to William Jones, July 22, 1813, James Barron Papers, Box II, Earl Gregg Swem Library, College of William and Mary.
70. Officers of the *Chesapeake* to Smith, June 23, 1807, Captains' Letters.
71. Latshaw, "Flawed Judgment," 381–82.
72. Latshaw, "Flawed Judgment," 384. Latshaw argues that the court was prejudiced against Barron, that the hearing was not conducted properly, and that Barron deserves to be vindicated.
73. Decatur to Smith, December 17, 1807, Letters Received by the Secretary of the Navy from Captains ("Captains' Letters"), M125, NARA, Washington, DC.
74. Tucker and Reuter, *Injured Honor*, 164.
75. Malone, *Jefferson the President: Second Term*, 469–84; Toll, *Six Frigates*, 309–12.
76. Hickey, *Forgotten Conflict*, 18–20; Allison, *Decatur*, 99–100; Paullin, *Commodore John Rodgers*, 98.
77. J. C. A. Stagg, *The War of 1812: Conflict for a Continent* (New York: Cambridge University Press, 2012), 34–35; Gordon Wood, *Empire of Liberty: A History of the Early Republic, 1789–1815* (New York: Oxford University Press, 2009), 663.
78. Irving Brant, *The Fourth President: A Life of James Madison* (New York: Bobbs-Merrill, 1970), 406; Frank Owsley, "Paul Hamilton," Coletta, *American Secretaries of the Navy*, 93–100.
79. Tingey to Rodgers, November 21, 1809, Rodgers' Family Papers, Part III:Box 1, LOC.
80. Paullin, *History of Naval Administration*, 137.
81. Paullin, *History of Naval Administration*, 136.
82. Maloney, *Captain from Connecticut*, 136–37.
83. Hull to Hamilton, April 11, 1810, Hull Papers, NYHS.
84. John Eppes to George Pearce, March 4, 1809, Rodgers Family Papers, Naval Historical Foundation Collection, Box 1, LOC.
85. Hull to Hamilton, April 1, 1810, and July 12, 1810, Hull Papers, NYHS.
86. Porter to Hambleton, October 12, 1812, Porter Papers, Box 2.
87. McKee, *Gentlemanly and Honorable Profession*, 10.
88. Hamilton to Porter, June 1, 1810, Porter Papers, Box 15, LOC; Rodgers to Hull, June 19, 1810, William S. Dudley, et al., eds., *The Naval War of 1812: A Documentary History* (Washington, DC: Naval Historical Center, Department of the Navy, 1985–2021), I:39–40 (hereafter *NW*). See also Hamilton to Porter, June 5, 1810, Porter Papers, Box 15, LOC, where he elaborates on this view and orders Porter to protect American merchant ships from British or French molestation.
89. Hamilton to Madison, July 23, 1810, *Papers of James Madison: Presidential Series*, ed. J. C. A. Stagg, et al. (Charlottesville, VA: University of Virginia Press, 1992–), II:432.

90. Trippe to Hamilton, May 29, 1810, M148, Letters Received by the Secretary of the Navy from Commissioned Officers below the Rank of Commander and from Warrant Officers; David F. Long, *Gold Braid and Foreign Relations: Diplomatic Activities of US Naval Officers, 1798–1883* (Annapolis, MD: Naval Institute Press, 1988), 42.
91. Hamilton to Madison, July 23, 1810; Madison to Hamilton, July 26, 1810, *Madison Papers: Presidential Series*, II:432, 438–39.
92. Hamilton to Trippe, July 20, 1810, Letters Sent.
93. Long, *Gold Braid and Foreign Relations*, 41–42.
94. Commander Arthur Bingham, RN to Vice Admiral Herbert Sawyer, RN, May 21, 1811; Commodore John Rodgers to Secretary of the Navy Paul Hamilton, May 23, 1811, Dudley, *NW*, I:44–49.
95. Hamilton to Rodgers, May 28, 1811, Dudley, *NW*, I:44–49.
96. Hamilton to Rodgers, May 28, 1811, Dudley, *NW*, I:44–49.

## CHAPTER 6. "The Precious Germ of Our National Glory"

1. Samuel Leech, *A Voice from the Main Deck: Being a Record of the Thirty Years Adventures of Samuel Leech* (1857. Reprint, London: Chatham Publishing, 1999), 72–77.
2. Leech, *A Voice from the Main Deck*, 90–91.
3. Wood, *Empire of Liberty*, 671–72; Samuel Watson, "Trusting to 'the Chapter of Accidents': Contingency, Necessity, and Self-Constraint in Jeffersonian National Security Policy," *The Journal of Military History* 76, no. 4 (October 2012): 978–1,000.
4. Sailing Master Thomas Gautier to Captain John Dent, April 22, 1812; Dent to Hamilton, April 27, 1812; Lieutenant Colonel Commandant Franklin Wharton to Captain John Hall, May 4, 1812; Hamilton to Selected Officers, May 6, 1812; Master Commandant Samuel Evans to Hamilton, May 7, 1812; Dent to Hamilton, June 4, 1812; Bainbridge to Hamilton, June 5, 1812; Tingey to Hamilton, June 9, 1812; Tingey to Hamilton, June 15, 1812, *NW*, I:98–107, 128–30, 186–89.
5. Hamilton to Langdon Cheves, Chairman of the Congressional Naval Committee, June 30, 1812, *NW*, I:176–79.
6. Troy Bickham, *The Weight of Vengeance: The United States, the British Empire, and the War of 1812* (New York: Oxford University Press, 2012), 103–20. Bickham, it should be noted, goes on to argue that after the initial frustrations in the opening months of the war, and especially what were seen as brutal actions by Native American allies of the British, American attitudes shifted toward conquering and keeping Canada rather than using it as a bargaining chip. Wayne Lee notes that the repeated setbacks of the Canadian invasion, plus the arrival of seasoned veterans for the British after Napoleon's abdication, pushed American diplomats

back toward using any territorial gains as bargaining chips. Matthew Moten, ed., *Between War and Peace: How America Ends Its Wars* (New York: Free Press, 2011), 43–63.

7. Lieutenant Sidney Smith to Hamilton, June 16, 1812, *NW*, I:275.
8. Woolsey to Hamilton, August 3, 1812; Woolsey to Hamilton, August 8, 1812; Hamilton to Woolsey, August 21, 1812, *NW*, I:286, 289, 294.
9. For Madison and the U.S. Navy in the war, see Daughan, *1812*, 31–41, 55; and Symonds, *Navalists and Antinavalists*, 148–49. For Madison as a wartime leader, see Daughan, *1812*, 416; Hickey, *War of 1812*, 69–70, 304–305; and Stagg, *Mr. Madison's War*, 502–505.
10. Charles Stewart, "Biographical Sketch of Commodore Charles Stewart of the Navy of the United States," Philadelphia, 1852, 13–14, recounts this episode, but places it in June, after the outbreak of hostilities. Long, *Ready to Hazard*, 129–32, makes a compelling case that it actually occurred in February, when Madison realized that war with Britain was almost certain, but before he presented his war message to Congress. See also Charles Stewart to Charles Jared Ingersoll, September 23, 1845, and Ingersoll to Stewart, September 28, 1845, Charles Jared Ingersoll Papers, Historical Society of Pennsylvania, Philadelphia, PA, wherein Stewart discusses the episode with Ingersoll and defends his and Bainbridge's motives for acting. For another secondary account of the episode, this time from Stewart's perspective, see Claude Berube and John Rodgaard, *A Call to the Sea: Captain Charles Stewart of the* USS Constitution (Washington, DC: Potomac Books, 2005), 60–63. There is, however, considerable historical debate as to what exactly happened, and some have argued that Stewart made the whole thing up. Both Stewart's and Bainbridge's biographers accept the story as having happened, and George Daughan also agrees that Madison at least "toyed with" the idea of confining the Navy to port. Daughan, *1812*, 40. Christopher McKee, however, views the account as a likely fabrication, and he calls into question a great deal that Stewart took credit for in his later life. McKee, *Edward Preble*, 368, n1. Likewise, Linda Maloney asserts that there was no "real truth to the story, fabricated in 1845 by Commodore Charles Stewart" that Madison planned to bottle up the Navy. Maloney, "The War of 1812: What Role for Sea Power?" Keneth Hagan, ed., *In Peace and War: Interpretations of American Naval History, 1775–1978* (Westport, CT: Praeger, 1978), 46–47.
11. Hamilton to Rodgers, May 21, 1812, Rodgers to Hamilton, June 3, 1812, Decatur to Hamilton, June 8, 1812, *NW*, I:117–24. Hamilton's letter to Decatur is not included, but Decatur mentions being delayed in seeing Hamilton's letter to him in his response, making it clear he was consulted as well, and not volunteering his thoughts.

12. Decatur to Hamilton, *NW*, I:123.
13. Rodgers to Hamilton, *NW*, I:118–22.
14. Reginald Hitsman, *The Incredible War of 1812: A Military History*, updated by Donald E. Graves (Toronto: Robin Brass Studio, 1999, originally published 1965), 269–70; Daughan, *If By Sea*, 430.
15. Maloney, "War of 1812," 2.
16. Rodgers to Hamilton, *NW*, I:120.
17. Decatur to Hamilton, *NW*, I:122–24.
18. McCranie, *Utmost Gallantry*, 26–27.
19. Hamilton to Hull, June 18, 1812, *NW* I:135–36. Schroeder, *Commodore John Rodgers*, 113, notes that Rodgers received identical orders.
20. Hamilton to Rodgers, June 22, 1812, *NW*, I:148–49. See also, Brant, *James Madison*, VI:35–37.
21. McCranie, *Utmost Gallantry*, 27; Daughan, *If By Sea*, 412–13; Schroeder, *Commodore John Rodgers*, 113–14.
22. Rodgers to Hamilton, September 1, 1812, *NW*, I:262–64. See also, Daughan, *1812*, 80–82.
23. All quotations taken from McCranie, *Utmost Gallantry*, 84, 91. For the British reaction to defeat, see, in addition to McCranie, Toll, *Six* Frigates, 370–72. Daughan, *1812*, 149, notes that the victories might not have had a significant impact in the final outcome of the war, but they did serve the United States well in the aftermath of the conflict. The war, he argues, was waged "in part because Britain refused to accord America the respect she demanded. The naval victories were changing attitudes in London, laying the groundwork for a more equitable and peaceful relationship in the future."
24. Quoted in Toll, *Six* Frigates, 381.
25. Hamilton to Hull, September 9, 1812, *NW*, I:472–73. See also, Hamilton to Decatur, December 29, 1812, *NW*, I:638–39.
26. Allison, *Stephen Decatur*, 127.
27. Maloney, "The War of 1812," 47–48.
28. Hamilton to Rodgers, September 9, 1812, *NW*, I:471–72.
29. Fowler, *Jack Tars and Commodores*, 185.
30. Skaggs and Atloff, *A Signal Victory*, 41–42.
31. Porter to Hamilton, June 28, 1812, *NW*, I:171.
32. Hamilton to Porter, June 30, 1812, *NW*, I:176.
33. Tingey to Hamilton, October 7, 1812, *NW*, I:524.
34. McKee, *Gentlemanly and Honorable Profession*, 299.
35. Hamilton to Charles Morris, October 5, 1812; Arthur Sinclair to Hamilton, October 7, 1812; Bainbridge to Hamilton, October 8, 1812; Lawrence to Hamilton, October 10, 1812, *NW*, I:516–20.

36. Hamilton to Lawrence, October 17, 1812; Lawrence to Hamilton, October 22, 1812, *NW*, I:520–23.
37. Allison, *Stephen Decatur*, 119.
38. Sheppard, "There Will Still Remain Heroes and Patriots," 392–94.
39. McKee, *Gentlemanly and Honorable Profession*, 299–301.
40. Daughan, *1812*, 156; Stagg, Mr. *Madison's War*, 290; McCranie, *Utmost Gallantry*, 111–13.
41. McCranie, *Utmost Gallantry*, 92–96.
42. George Cross to Jones, August 23, 1798, Jones and Clark Papers, Box 2, HSP.
43. Congressman Jonathon Roberts to Jones, December 28, 1812, *NW*, I:635–37.
44. Fowler, *Jack Tars and Commodores*, 186.
45. Jones to Madison, April 25, 1814, *JMP: Presidential Series*, VII:437–39. For more on Jones' personal views of the war, see: Jones to W. B. Giles, February 4, 1809; Jones to Eleanor Jones, July 12, 1812; and Jones to William Young, 1813, Box 1, Uslema Clarke Smith Collection D, HSP.
46. William Jones to Eleanor Jones, March 8, 1813, Box 1, Uslema Clarke Smith Collection D, HSP.
47. William Jones to Eleanor Jones, January 23, 1813, *NW*, II:34–35.
48. "Notes Made by Secretary of the Navy William Jones Regarding a Visit by Chief Clerk Charles W. Goldsburough," undated, *NW*, II:54–55. The editors conclude that this meeting almost certainly occurred on February 28, 1813. William Jones to Eleanor Jones, January 13, 1813, Box 1, Uslema Clarke Smith Collection D, HSP. Jones' firing of all employees but one is taken from McKee, *Gentlemanly and Honorable Profession*, 11–12.
49. McKee, *Gentlemanly and Honorable Profession*, 17.
50. "Notes Made by Secretary Jones," *NW*, II:54–55.
51. Homans to Jones, n.d., *NW*, II:55–56.
52. Decatur to Jones, January 26, 1813, Uselma Clark Smith Collection, Box 1, HSP.
53. Bainbridge to Jones, March 1, 1813, Uselma Clarke Smith Collection, Box 1, HSP.
54. Jones to John Dent, April 9, 1813, *NW*, II:95.
55. Jones to Captain John Smith, February 5, 1813, *NW*, II:638–39.
56. Jones to Dent, April 9, 1813, *NW*, II:96.
57. Gordon to Jones, December 13, 1813, *NW*, II:397–98; Tarbell to Jones, February 15, and February 24, 1814; Gordon to Jones, February 26, 1814, *NW*, III:8–12.
58. Jones to Gordon, March 4 and April 15, 1814, *NW*, III:12–13.
59. Bainbridge to Jones, January 12, 1814; Jones to Bainbridge, January 12, 1814, *NW*, IV:5–6.
60. Jones to Arthur Sinclair, May 25, 1814, Uselma Clarke Smith Collection, Box 1, HSP.

61. Master Commandant Lewis Warrington to Jones, October 2, 1813; Jones to Warrington, October 7, 1813, *NW*, II:259–60. Despite his clear annoyance with Warrington and complete confidence in the lieutenant in question, Jones still granted Warrington's request.
62. Jones to Perry, July 3, 1813, *NW*, II:487. For the Perry-Chauncey feud, see, Skaggs and Atloff, *A Signal Victory*, 76–78, 97.
63. Perry to Jones, August 10, 1813; Jones to Perry, August 18, 1813, *NW*, I:98–107, 128–30, 186–89; II:532–33.
64. Skaggs and Atloff, *A Signal Victory*, 118–48; John H. Schroeder, *The Battle of Lake Champlain: A Brilliant and Extraordinary Victory* (Norman, OK: University of Oklahoma Press, 2015), 71–109.
65. Jones to Robert Spence, July 26, 1813, M149: Letters Sent by the Secretary of the Navy to Officers, NARA, Washington, DC.
66. Jones to Isaac Chauncey, July 14, 1813, *NW*, II:500–501.
67. Jones to Madison, October 13, 1813, *Madison Papers: Presidential Series*, VI:693–94.
68. Eckart, *Navy Department*, 21; McCranie, *Utmost Gallantry*, 116–17.
69. Jones Circular to Officers, February 22, 1813, *NW*, II:48.
70. Hamilton to Porter, June 1, 1810, Porter Papers, Box 15, LOC; Jones to Master Commandant George Parker, December 8, 1813, *NW*, II:294–96.
71. Jones Circular to Officers, February 22, 1813, *NW*, II:48.
72. Madison to Jones, October 15, 1813, *Madison Papers: Presidential Series*, VI:697–98.
73. Lambert, *The Challenge*, 228–30.
74. Rodgers to Jones, September 27, 1813, *NW*, II:251–53.
75. Jones to Rodgers, October 4, 1813, *NW*, II:253–54.
76. London *Morning Chronicle*, November 3, 1813, quoted in McCranie, *Utmost Gallantry*, 127.
77. McCranie, *Utmost Gallantry*, 116–17.
78. Lambert, *The Challenge*, 177. McCranie, *Utmost Gallantry*, 152, further contends that Lawrence urged his men to continue fighting until the ship sank.
79. Leech, *Voice from the Main Deck*, 77.
80. Lambert, *The Challenge*, 192.
81. Lambert, *The Challenge*, 191–94; Daughan, *1812*, 195.
82. Jones to Charles Stewart, September 19, 1813, K. Jack Bauer, ed., *The New American State Papers: Naval Affairs*, 10 vols. (Wilmington, DE: Scolarly Resources Inc, 1981), 182. See also Jones to Decatur, March 12, 1814, *NW*, IV:87.
83. Frederick Leiner, "The Squadron Commander's Share: *Decatur v. Chew* and the Prize Money for the *Chesapeake*'s First Cruise of the War of 1812," *Journal of Military History* 73, no. 1 (January 2009): 69–82. Evans did not suffer too much from his losses. Despite making only one cruise, the incredibly lucrative cargo

on the *Volunteer* meant that he still emerged from the war with the eighth most prize money of any American officer.

84. Decatur to Hamilton, December 28, 1812; John Shaw to Hamilton, January 18, 1813; Bainbridge to Jones, December 31, 1813; Barney to Jones, April 4, 1814, I:638, II:273–74, 632–33, III:53–54. For Americans trading with and aiding the enemy, see Hickey, *Forgotten Conflict*, 113–14, 169–75, 258–59.
85. Macdonough to Jones, August 20, 1814; Macdonough to Drury, November 12, 1814, *NW*, III:592–93. Skaggs, *Thomas Macdonough*, 107.
86. Hull to Jones, February 24, 1814; Jones to Hull, March 5, 1814; Hull to Jones, March 27, 1814; News Report of Marine Aaron Smith's Trial for Murder, May 21, 1814, *NW*, IV:209–13.
87. Daughan, *1812*, 416; Stagg, Mr. *Madison's War*, 501–509; Hickey, *War of 1812*, 304–5.
88. Joshua Barney's Defense Proposal; Jones to Barney, August 20, 1813; Barney to Jones, December 15, 1813 *NW*, II:373–79, 398–400.
89. Norton, *Joshua Barney*, 175–76.
90. Newspaper clipping, September 1813, Uselma Smith Clarke Collection D, Box 1, HSP.
91. Norton, *Joshua Barney*, 170–71.
92. Reginald Stuart, *Civil-Military Relations in the War of 1812* (Santa Barbara, CA: ABC-Clio, 2009), 101. For a broader discussion of martial law during the war, see pages 101–20.
93. Barney to Jones, April 4, 1814, *NW*, III:53–54.
94. Norton, *Joshua Barney*, 180–82; Footner, *Sailor of Fortune*, 267–78.
95. Barney to Acting Secretary of the Navy, Benjamin Homans, January 3, 1815, *NW*, III:353–54; Norton, *Joshua Barney*, 192–95.
96. Barney to Crowninshield, February 18, 1815, *NW*, III:355.
97. News Report of Nantucket's Declaration of Neutrality, December 30, 1814, *NW*, IV:467–68.
98. Long, *William Bainbridge*, 178–83.
99. Bainbridge to Jones, July 7, 1814; Jones to Bainbridge, July 16, 1814, *NW*, IV:430–33.
100. Bainbridge to Jones, September 13, 1814; Jones to Bainbridge, September 20, 1814, *NW*, IV:436–37.
101. Hull to Jones, June 5, 1813, Letters Received.
102. Maloney, *Captain from Connecticut*, 244.
103. See Stuart, *Civil-Military Relations in the War of 1812*, 109, for discussion of state vs. federal control of militia and resources. The Supreme Court ultimately ruled

in favor of the President on such issues, but not until 1827. During the War of 1812, such debates were hashed out in an ad hoc fashion, with the overwhelmed federal government limited in its ability to enforce its will on the states.

104. Maloney, *Captain from Connecticut*, 247–58.

105. "The Republican Citizens to Newburyport" to Vice President Elbridge Gerry, September 8, 1813, reported rampant trade with the enemy. Gerry to "Republican Citizens," September 19, 1813, the vice president promised to forward their concerns to Madison and the rest of the cabinet. The report certainly ended up in Jones' hands, since it is filed among his personal papers. Box 1, Uselma Clarke Smith Collection D, HSP.

106. Stuart, *Civil-Military Relations in the War of 1812*, 106.

107. Lambert, *The Challenge*, 309.

108. Jones to Madison, April 25, 1814, *JMP: Presidential Series*, VII:437–39.

## Chapter 7. "A Radical Change of System"

1. Rodgers to Madison, November 29, 1814, Rodgers Family Papers, Box 2, LOC.
2. Paullin, *Commodore John* Rodgers, 190–91.
3. Certificate of the Bunker Hill Monument Association, undated, but in or close to the year 1823, Folder 11, Crowninshield Papers, Series 1: Benjamin Crowninshield Sr. Papers, Peabody-Essex Museum, Salem, MA.
4. Crowninshield Sr.'s career in merchant shipping is documented in Box 1: Folder 1: *Prudent* (Ship) papers, 1800–1801; Folder 2: *Prudent* (Ship), ledger, 1800–1805, 1885; Folder 3: *Prudent* (Ship), day book, 1799–1821; and Folder 4: Various ships papers, *Alexander* (Ship); *Belisarius* (Ship); *Commerce* (Sloop); *Eunice* (Brig); *Peggy* (Schooner), 1788, 1798, 1813, 1819, Crowninshield Papers, Series 1; Hall, "Benjamin Crowninshield," 113.
5. Hall, "Benjamin Crowninshield," 113; "Crowninshield, Benjamin Williams (1772–1851)," Biographical Directory of the United States Congress, bioguide .congress.gov; "Rules and Orders to be Observed in the Massachusetts House of Representatives for the year 1827–1828" (Boston: Printed by True and Greene, 1827), lists Crowninshield among the representatives from Salem County, although he is listed as being on leave of absence, Crowninshield Papers, Box 2, Folder 1.
6. The only voyages Crowninshield took that are recorded in his personal papers he sailed as a passenger. "Journal on board *Cleopatra's Barge*, on a voyage of Amusement and travels to the Western Islands and the Mediterranean in the year 1817," typed transcript, Box 2, Folder 8; "Three Specimens of Poetry, written on board US Ship *Columbus*," June 15, 1821, May 1821, and January 1821, Box 3, Folder 1, Crowninshield Papers.

7. Crowninshield, "Journal on board *Cleopatra's Barge*."
8. For his scientific pursuits, see Crowninshield to Dr. B. L. Oliver, May 30, 1804: noteworthy because Crowninshield talks about "Newton's theory of Light" and describes his efforts to learn more on the subject and perform his own experiments, Box 1, Folder 13; Crowninshield, untitled, incomplete (it begins on page 105), notebook with an essay on various scientific experiments, Box 2, Folder 1; Crowninshield, "View of the Science of Life," Box 3, Folder 3, Crowninshield Papers. For Crowninshield's philosophical bent, see unaddressed letter dated from Williamsburg (where Crowninshield was studying at William and Mary), May 13, 1804, regarding a lengthy conversation he had with Thomas Jefferson, apparently a friend of the family, Box 1, Folder 13; "Journal on board *Cleopatra's Barge*" contains a host of personal observation on slavery, religion, and government, Box 2, Folder 8; Crowninshield, "Observations on Mr. King's remarks, etc. which looks philosophically at god's purposes in creating the world," Box 2, Folder 9, Crowninshield Papers.
9. Hall, "Crowninshield," 114.
10. Crowninshield, booklet entitled "A General History of Mankind from the beginning of the world to the present time," that includes chapters on "The State of the World before the Flood," and "From the blockading of Boston port to the capture of General Burgoyne in 1777," Box 2, Folder 10; Box 3, Folder 1 also contains a map and narrative of the Battle of Quebec in the French and Indian War. Box 3, Folder 3 contains an extended essay on the Black Death in Europe, and an essay on "Definition of the Continent of America in General, more particularly of the United States," Crowninshield Papers.
11. Bemis, *John Quincy Adams and the Foundations of American Foreign Policy* (New York: Alfred Knopf, 1949), 252; Hall, "Benjamin Crowninshield," 113.
12. Lambert, *Barbary Wars*, 182–95.
13. Opinion of the Court of Inquiry into the Loss of *President*, *NW*, IV:709–10.
14. Allison, *Stephen Decatur*, 164–71; Long, *Ready to Hazard*, has a detailed and very well researched analysis of the entire episode, emphasizing the Decatur–Bainbridge rivalry, on pages 188–206. Long is openly hostile to Decatur and portrays Bainbridge, with some justification, as a grievously wronged victim in the affair.
15. Secretary of the Navy William Jones, "Reorganization and Extension of the Navy, the Establishment of a Board of Inspectors, and a Naval Academy," communicated to the Senate, November 15, 1814, *American State Papers, Naval Affairs*, 4 vols. (Washington, DC: Gales and Seaton, 1832), I:320–24.
16. Stoddert to Chairman of the Committee on Naval Affairs, January 12, 1801, *NDQW*, VII:80–84.
17. McKee, *Edward Preble*, 338.

18. Opinions of eleven commodores—Bainbridge, Stewart, Hull, Decatur, Perry, Porter, Warrington, Evans, Morris, Shaw, and Tingey—on the establishment of a Board of Naval Inspectors. *American State Papers, Naval Affairs*, I:354–58.
19. Jones, "Reorganization and Extension of the Navy," 323.
20. "An act to alter and amend the several acts for establishing a Navy Department, by adding thereto a board of commissioners," Richard Peters, ed., *By Authority of Congress: The Public Statutes at Large of the United States of America from the organization of the government in 1789, to March 3, 1845*, 8 vols. (Boston: Little, Brown, 1855–62), III:202–3.
21. See Paullin, *History of Naval Administration*, 171–72; Long, *Nothing Too Daring*, 176; and Maloney, *Captain from Connecticut*, 262.
22. Peters, ed., "An act to alter and amend the several acts for establishing a Navy Department."
23. Rodgers to Crowninshield, February 11, 1815, *NW*, IV:753–54.
24. *National Intelligencer*, April 25, 1815.
25. BNC, "Journal of Meetings," April 25–27, 1815.
26. BNC to Crowninshield, April 26, 1815 Miscellaneous Letters Received by the Secretary of the Navy (hereafter Miscellaneous Letters), M124, NARA, Washington, DC; Crowninshield to BNC, April 27, 1815, Letters Sent by the Secretary of the Navy to the Board of Navy Commissioners (hereafter Letters Sent—Secretary), NARA.
27. Crowninshield to BNC, April 27 and April 29, 1815, Letters Sent—Secretary.
28. Crowninshield to BNC, April 29, 1815, Letters Sent—Secretary; BNC, "Circular to Navy Commanding Officers," April 29, 1815, "Letters Sent to Officers."
29. BNC, May 11, 1815, Letters Sent—Secretary.
30. BNC to Crowninshield, May 16, 1815, Miscellaneous Letters; Crowninshield to BNC, May 18, 1815, Letters Sent—Secretary.
31. Crowninshield to BNC, May 23, 1815, Miscellaneous Letters; BNC, "Journal of Meetings," May 20, 22, and 23.
32. BNC, "Journal of Meetings," May 24–June 14.
33. Bainbridge to David Porter, June 5, 1815, quoted in Long, *Nothing Too Daring*, 176.
34. Madison to Benjamin Crowinshield, June 12, 1815 in *Letters and Other Writings of James Madison, Fourth President of the United States*, 4 vols. (Philadelphia: J. B. Lippincott, 1865): II:603–6.
35. Maloney, *Captain from Connecticut*, 270–71. Maloney also indicates that Hull found life in the nation's capital unappealing and was eager for a chance to leave apart from the clash between Crowninshield and the Navy Board.
36. BNC, "Journal of Meetings," June 15.
37. BNC to Joseph Bainbridge, March 19, 1816, "Letters Sent to Naval Officers," (hereafter BNC Letters Sent), Vol. 1: April 21, 1815–July 22, 1833, NARA.

38. BNC to Lieutenant Edgar Freeman, February 22, 1820, BNC Letters Sent.
39. BNC to [illeg.], November 17, 1817; BNC to Captain Wadsworth, July 8, 1819, BNC Letters Sent.
40. "Report of the Board of Navy Commissioners," November 25, 1815, Rodgers Family Papers, Box 4, LOC. The report in the Rodgers Papers is a typed transcript. An original report is also available in "Letters Sent by BNC to the Secretary of the Navy" (hereafter BNC Letters Sent—Secretary), vol. 1, NARA.
41. Crowninshield to BNC, Letters Sent—Secretary.
42. "Report of the Board of Navy Commissioners," November 25, 1815.
43. Mackenzie, *Decatur*, 297–98; Tucker, *Stephen Decatur*, 173.
44. A sense of the where the Board's attention was focused can be seen in its outgoing correspondence. It kept a register of every letter it sent, listing only the name of the recipient and date. The list of letters sent to Thomas Tingey, the longtime commandant of the Washington Navy Yard, extends for twenty-six pages. Isaac Hull, for many years the commandant of the Charleston Navy Yard, takes up eleven pages, while the various Secretaries of the Navy are allocated ten. No other correspondents fill up a page. "Register of Letters Sent, July 1817–August 1842," NARA.
45. "Journal of Meetings," Thursday, September 14, 1815; February 12, 1816; July 22, 1816; January 12, 1817; Tuesday, August 26, 1817.
46. BNC Circular to the Surgeons of Hospitals, April 28, 1815, Letters Sent; BNC, March 19, 1822, Letters Sent—Secretary.
47. "Rules, Regulations, and Instructions, for the Naval Service of the United States: Prepared by the Board of Naval Commissioners of the United States, with the Consent of the Secretary of the Navy," Historical Society of Pennsylvania, Philadelphia, PA.
48. Schroeder, *Commodore John Rodgers*, 149.
49. Paullin, *History of Naval Administration*, 161.
50. Edwin Hall, "Smith Thompson," 123–30.
51. John Quincy Adams, *Memoirs*, IV:310–11.
52. BNC, "Letters Sent—Secretary," February 6, 1816, and March 22, 1816.
53. BNC, "Letters Sent—Secretary," February 11, 1817.
54. BNC "Letters Sent—Secretary," December 4, 1815.
55. BNC, "Letters Sent—Secretary," September 14, 1815.
56. Skaggs, *Thomas Macdonough*, 181–82, sees the episode as largely ending in vindication for Macdonough, while Stewart biographers Berube and Rodgaard, 131–32, praise their subject's wise handling of the situation and imply that Macdonough eventually conceded that he was in the wrong. Berube and Rodgaard also do not mention the board's influence in the affair; that is taken from Skaggs.
57. James Barron to Jane Barron, March 15, 1815, James Barron Papers, Box II, Earl Gregg Swem Library, College of William and Mary, Williamsburg, VA.

58. James Barron to Jane Barron, July 16, 1816, James Barron Papers, Box II.
59. Barron was a prolific inventor throughout his life, though he never enjoyed much success. See William Oliver Stevens, *An Affair of Honor: The Biography of Commodore James Barron, USN* (Norfolk, VA: Norfolk County Historical Society, 1969), especially the chapter entitled, "James Barron, the Inventor," 173–82, for a discussion of this aspect of his life.
60. Allison, *Decatur*, 200–205.
61. Barron to Decatur, October 23, 1819, Don C. Seitz, ed., *Famous American Duels, with some Account of the Causes that led to them and the Men Involved* (New York: Books for Libraries Press, 1966): 193–95
62. Decatur to Barron, December 29, 1819; Barron to Decatur, January 16, 1820, Seitz, *Famous American Duels*, 216–21.
63. David F. Long, "William Bainbridge and the Decatur-Barron Duel: Mere Participant or Active Plotter?," *Pennsylvania Magazine of History and Biography* 103, no. 1 (January 1979): 34–52; and Long, *Ready to Hazard*, 227–46.
64. Allison, *Decatur*, 216; Paul Barron Watson, *The Tragic Career of Commodore James Barron, U.S. Navy (1769–1851)* (New York: Cowan-McCann, 1942), 79–84.
65. Watson, *Tragic Career*, 83.
66. Symonds, *Navalists and Antinavalists*, 225–27.
67. Symonds, *Navalists and Antinavalists*, 225–26.
68. Thompson to Babour, December 18, 1820; BNC to Thompson, December 9, 1820, *ASP: Naval Affairs*, I:675–80.
69. Symonds, *Navalists and Antinavalists*, 229–31.
70. Paullin, *History of Naval Administration*, 173.

## Conclusion

1. The discussion of Porter's sojourn into the West Indies and the fallout in the United States is taken primarily from Long, *Nothing Too Daring*, 203–55. Porter's account can be found in Porter, *Memoir of Commodore David Porter*, 278–308.
2. Long, *Nothing Too Daring*, 206.
3. George Herring, *From Colony to Superpower: U.S. Foreign Relations since 1776* (New York: Oxford University Press, 2008), 144–49, 153–60.
4. Long, *Nothing Too Daring*, 209; Edwin Hall, "Samuel Lewis Southard," in *American Secretaries of the Navy*, vol. 1: 1775–1913, ed. Paolo Coletta (Annapolis, MD: Naval Institute Press, 1980), 131–42.
5. Porter, *Memoir of Commodore David Porter*, 298–99.
6. Long, *Nothing Too Daring*, 229.
7. Stoddert circular to captains, June 27, 1799, in *NDQW*, III:420–21.
8. Long, *Nothing Too Daring*, 233.
9. Hall, "Southard," 137; Long, *Nothing Too Daring*, 234–35.
10. Long, *Nothing Too Daring*, 236–40.

11. David Porter, *Constantinople and its Environs*, 10–11.
12. Paullin, *History of Naval Administration*, 163, 173.
13. Sheppard, "There Will Still Remain Heroes and Patriots, 369–94.
14. Charles Oscar Paullin, "Dueling in the Old Navy," U.S. Naval Institute *Proceedings* 35, no. 4 (1909): 1,155–97.
15. *Proceedings of the Court of Inquiry Appointed to Inquire into the Intended Mutiny on Board the United States Brig of War Somers, on the High Seas* (New York: Greeley & McElrath, 1843), 8. See also Buckner Melton, *A Hanging Offense: The Strange Affair of the Warship Somers* (New York: Free Press, 2003).
16. Buckner, *A Hanging Offense*, 242–44.
17. A total of fourteen ships in the U.S. Navy have been named after these three, *Dictionary of American Naval Fighting Ships*, history.navy.mil.

# Bibliography


### National Archives and Records Administration, Washington, DC

Board of Navy Commissioners–Journal of Meetings
Board of Navy Commissioners–Letters Sent to the Secretary of the Navy
Board of Navy Commissioners–Letters Sent to Naval Officers
Board of Navy Commissioners–Letters Sent to Commandants of Naval Yards and Naval Stations
Board of Navy Commissioners–Miscellaneous Letters Sent
Board of Navy Commissioners–Miscellaneous Letters Received
M125: Letters Received by the Secretary of the Navy from Captains
M147: Letters Received by the Secretary of the Navy from Commanders
M149: Letters Sent by the Secretary of the Navy to Officers
M209: Miscellaneous Letters Sent by the Secretary of the Navy

### Library of Congress, Washington, DC

Edward Preble Papers
Isaac Hull Papers
John Paul Jones Papers
Joshua Barney Papers
Porter Family Papers
Rodgers Family Papers

### Earl Gregg Swem Library, College of William and Mary, Williamsburg, VA

James Barron Papers
Samuel Barron Papers

### Historical Society of Pennsylvania, Philadelphia, PA

Jones and Clark Papers
Thomas Truxtun Correspondence, 1797–1946
Thomas Truxtun Records, 1797–1801
Truxtun-Biddle Letters, 1787–1820
William Jones Papers, Uselma Smith Clark Collection

### Peabody-Essex Museum, Salem, MA

Benjamin Crowninshield Papers

### Published Primary Sources

Adams, John. *The Papers of John Adams*. Edited by Robert J. Taylor, et al. Cambridge, MA: Belknap Press of Harvard University Press, 1977–.

Clark, William Bell, ed. *Naval Documents of the American Revolution*. 13 vols. Washington, DC: Naval History Division, Department of the Navy, 1964–.

Dudley, William S., Michael J. Crawford, and Christine Hughes, eds. *The Naval War of 1812: A Documentary History*. 4 vols. Washington: Naval Historical Center, Department of the Navy, 1985–.

Hamilton, Alexander. *The Papers of Alexander Hamilton*. 27 vols. Edited by Harold C. Syrett and Jacob E. Cook. New York: Columbia University Press, 1961–87.

Jefferson, Thomas. *The Papers of Thomas Jefferson*. Edited by Julian P. Boyd, et al. Princeton, NJ: Princeton University Press, 1950–.

Leech, Samuel. *Thirty Years from Home, or, a Voice from the Main Deck, Being the Experiences of Samuel Leech*. 1843. Reprint, London: Chatham Publishing, 1999.

US Congress. *American State Papers, Documents, Legislative and Executive of the Congress of the United States:* Class VI, *Naval Affairs*. 4 vols. Washington, DC: Gales and Seaton, 1832.

———. *Naval Documents Relating to the Quasi-War between the United States and France: Naval Operations from February 1797 to December 1801*. Washington, DC: U.S. Government Printing Office, 1935.

———. *Naval Documents Relating to the United States Wars with the Barbary Powers: Naval Operations Including Diplomatic Background*. Washington, DC: U.S. Government Printing Office, 1939.

### Secondary Sources

Adair, Douglas. "Fame and the Founding Fathers." In *Fame and the Founding Fathers: Essays of Douglas Adair*. Edited by Trevor Coulburn, 5–31. New York: Norton, 1974.

Albion, Robert J. "The First Days of the Navy Department." *Military Affairs* 12, no. 1 (Spring 1948): 1–11.

Allen, Gardner. *A Naval History of the American Revolution*. 2 vols. Williamstown, MA: Corner House Publishers, 1970. First published 1913.

———. *Our Naval War with France*. Hamden, CT: Archon Books, 1967. First published 1910.

Allison, Robert J. *Stephen Decatur: American Naval Hero: 1779–1820*. Amherst: University of Massachusetts Press, 2005.

Anderson, William Gary. "John Adams and the Creation of the American Navy." PhD diss., State University of New York at Stony Brook, 1975.

Atloff, Gerard T. "The Perry-Elliot Controversy." *Northwest Ohio Quarterly* 60 (Autumn 1988): 135–52.

Berube, Claude, and Norman Rodgaard. *A Call to the Sea: Captain Charles Stewart of the USS Constitution*. Washington, DC: Potomac Books, 2006.

Bickham, Troy. *The Weight of Vengeance: The United States, the British Empire, and the War of 1812*. New York: Oxford University Press, 2012.

Bradford, James C., ed. *Command under Sail: Makers of the American Naval Tradition*. Annapolis, MD: Naval Institute Press, 1985.

Brant, Irving. *The Fourth President: A Life of James Madison*. New York: Bobbs-Merrill, 1970.

Brown, Bertram Wyatt. *Honor and Violence in the Old South*. New York: Oxford University Press, 1986.

Brown, Gordon. *The Captain Who Burned His Ships: Captain Thomas Tingey, USN, 1750–1829*. Annapolis, MD: Naval Institute Press, 2011.

Budiansky, Stephen. *Perilous Fight: America's Intrepid War with Britain on the High Seas, 1812–1815*. New York: Alfred A Knopf, 2010.

Chernow, Ron. *Alexander Hamilton*. New York: Penguin Press, 2004.

Clark, William B. *Gallant John Barry: The Story of a Naval Hero of Two Wars*. New York: The Macmillan Company, 1938.

Cohen, Eliot. *Supreme Command: Soldiers, Statesmen, and Leadership in Wartime*. New York: Free Press, 2002.

Coletta, Paolo E., ed. *American Secretaries of the Navy*. Volume 1: *1775–1913*. Annapolis: Naval Institute Press, 1980.

Crackel, Theodore. *Mr. Jefferson's Army: Political and Social Reform of the Military Establishment, 1801–1809*. New York: New York University Press, 1987.

Cunliffe, Marcus. *Soldiers and Civilians: The Martial Spirit in America, 1775–1865*. Boston: Little, Brown, 1968.

Daughan, George C. *1812: The Navy's War* New York: Basic Books, 2011.

———. *If By Sea: The Forging of the American Navy to the War of 1812*. New York: Basic Books, 2008.

———. *The Shining Sea: David Porter and the Epic Voyage of the U.S.S. Essex during the War of 1812*. New York: Basic Books, 2013.

DeConde, Alexander. *The Quasi-War: The Politics and Diplomacy of the Undeclared War with France, 1797–1801*. New York: Charles Scribner's Sons, 1966.

Dull, Jonathan. *American Naval History, 1607–1865: Overcoming the Colonial Legacy*. Lincoln, NE: University of Nebraska Press, 2012.

Eckert, Edward. "Early Reform in the Navy Department." *American Neptune* 33 (1973), 231–45.

———.*The Navy Department in the War of 1812*. Gainesville, FL: University of Florida Press, 1971.

———. "William Jones and the Role of the Secretary of the Navy in the War of 1812." PhD diss., University of Florida, 1969.

———. "William Jones: Mr. Madison's Secretary of the Navy." *Pennsylvania Magazine of History and Biography* 96 (1972): 167–82.

Elting, John R. *Amateurs to Arms!: A Military History of the War of 1812*. Chapel Hill, NC: Algonquin Books, 1991.

Feaver, Peter. *Armed Servants: Agency, Oversight, and Civil-Military Relations*. Cambridge, MA: Harvard University Press, 2003.

Ferguson, Eugene. *Truxtun of the Constellation: The Life of Commodore Thomas Truxtun, US Navy, 1755–1822*. Baltimore: Johns Hopkins University Press, 1956.

Ferling, John. *Adams vs. Jefferson: The Tumultuous Election of 1800*. New York: Oxford University Press, 2004.

———. *Almost A Miracle: The American Victory in the War of Independence*. New York: Oxford University Press, 2007.

———. *John Adams: A Life*. Knoxville: University of Tennessee Press, 1992.

Fowler, William. *Jack Tars and Commodores: The American Navy, 1793–1815*. Boston: Houghton-Mifflin Company, 1984.

———. *Rebels under Sail: The American Navy during the Revolution*. New York: Scribner, 1976.

Freeman, Joanne. *Affairs of Honor: National Politics in the New Republic*. New Haven, CT: Yale University Press, 2001.

Friedman, Lawrence J., and David Curtis Skaggs. "Jesse Duncan Elliott and the Battle of Lake Erie: The Issue of Mental Stability." *Journal of the Early Republic* 10, no. 4 (Winter: 1990): 493–516.

Gilbert, Arthur. "Law and Honour among Eighteenth-Century British Army Officers." *Historical Journal* 19, no. 1 (1976): 75–87.

Gurn, Joseph. *Commodore John Barry: Father of the American Navy*. Cranbury, NJ: Scholar's Bookshelf, 2005. First published 1933.

Hagan, Kenneth J. *In Peace and War: Interpretations of American Naval History, 1775–1978*. Westport, CT: Greenwood, 1978.

Hastings, George Everett. *The Life and Works of Francis Hopkinson*. Chicago: University of Chicago Press, 1926.

Hickey, Donald. *The War of 1812: A Forgotten Conflict*. Urbana: University of Illinois Press, 1989.

Huntington, Samuel. *The Soldier and the State: The Theory and Politics of Civil-Military Relations*. Cambridge, MA: Belknap Press of Harvard University Press, 1957.

Irwin, Ray. *The Diplomatic Relations of the United States with the Barbary Powers, 1776–1816*. Chapel Hill, NC: University of North Carolina Press, 1931.

Janowitz, Morris. *The Professional Soldier: A Social and Political Portrait*. New York: Free Press, 1960.

Jones, Robert F. "The Naval Thought and Policy of Benjamin Stoddert, First Secretary of the Navy, 1798–1801." *American Neptune* 24 (January 1964): 61–69.

Kitzen, Michael. *Tripoli and the United States at War: A History of American Relations with the Barbary States, 1785–1805*. Jefferson, NC: McFarland, 1993.

Kohn, Richard H. *Eagle and Sword: The Federalists and the Creation of the Military Establishment in America, 1783–1802*. New York: Free Press, 1975.

———, ed. *The United States Military under the Constitution of the United States, 1789–1989*. New York: New York University Press, 1991.

Lambert, Andrew. *The Challenge: Britain, the United States, and the War of 1812*. London: Faber and Faber, 2012.

Lambert, Frank. *The Barbary Wars: American Independence in the Atlantic World*. New York: Hill and Wang, 2005.

Latshaw, Michael. "Flawed Judgment: The Court-Martial of James Barron." *Virginia Magazine of History and Biography* 105, no. 4 (August 1997): 377–408.

Leeman, William. *The Long Road to Annapolis: The Founding of the Naval Academy and the Emerging American Republic*. Chapel Hill: University of North Carolina Press, 2010.

Leiner, Frederick C. "Decatur and Naval Leadership." *Naval History* 15, no. 5 (2001): 30–34.

———. *The End of the Barbary Terror: America's 1815 War against the Pirates of North Africa*. New York: Oxford University Press, 2006.

Long, David F. *Gold Braid and Foreign Relations: Diplomatic Activities of US Naval Officers, 1798–1883*. Annapolis, MD: Naval Institute Press, 1988.

———. *Nothing Too Daring: A Biography of Commodore David Porter, 1780–1843*. Annapolis, MD: Naval Institute Press, 1970.

———. *Ready to Hazard: A Biography of Commodore William Bainbridge, 1774–1833*. Ann Arbor, MI: University Press of New England: 1981.

Macleod, Julia H. "Jefferson and the Navy: A Defense." *Huntington Library Quarterly* 8, no. 2 (February 1945): 153–84.

Malone, Dumas. *Jefferson and His Time*. 6 volumes. Boston: Little-Brown and Company, 1948–1981.

Maloney, Linda. *The Captain from Connecticut: The Life and Naval Times of Isaac Hull*. Boston: Northeastern University Press, 1986.

McCranie, Kevin. "Dueling with Warships to Satisfy Honor: The Use of Naval Challenges in the War of 1812." *International Journal of Maritime History* 25, no. 61 (2013): 61–84.

———. *Utmost Gallantry: The US and Royal Navies at Sea in the War of 1812*. Annapolis, MD: Naval Institute Press, 2011.

McKee, Christopher. *Edward Preble: A Naval Biography 1761–1807*. Annapolis, MD: Naval Institute Press, 1972.

———. *A Gentlemanly and Honorable Profession: The Creation of the U.S. Naval Officer Corps, 1794–1815*. Annapolis, MD: Naval Institute Press, 1991.

McGrath, Tim. *Give Me a Fast Ship: The Continental Navy and America's Revolution at Sea*. New York: NAL-Caliber, 2014.

———. *John Barry: An American Hero of the Age of Sail*. Yardley, PA: Westholme Press, 2010.

Meacham, John. *Thomas Jefferson: The Art of Power*. New York: Random House, 2012.

Miller, Charles H. *Admiral Number One: Some Incidents in the Life of Esek Hopkins, 1718–1802, First Admiral of the Continental Navy*. New York: William-Frederick Press, 1962.

Miller, Nathan. *Sea of Glory: A Naval History of the American Revolution*. Annapolis, MD: Naval Institute Press, 1992. First published 1974.

Morison, Samuel Eliot. *John Paul Jones: A Sailor's Biography*. Boston: Little-Brown, 1959.

Nelson, James L. *George Washington's Secret Navy: How the American Revolution Went to Sea*. New York: McGraw-Hill, 2008.

Norton, Louis A. *Captains Contentious: The Dysfunctional Sons of the Brine*. Columbia, SC: University of South Carolina Press, 2009.

———. *Joshua Barney: Hero of the Revolution and 1812*. Annapolis, MD: Naval Institute Press, 2000.

Odintz, Mark. "The British Officer Corps, 1754–1783." PhD diss., University of Michigan, 1988.

Palmer, Michael. *Stoddert's War: Naval Operations During the Quasi-War with France, 1798–1801*. 1987. Reprinted with a new introduction by the author, Annapolis, MD: Naval Institute Press, 2000.

Paullin, Charles Oscar. *Commodore John Rodgers: Captain, Commodore and Senior Officer of the American Navy, 1773–1838*. Annapolis, MD: Naval Institute Press, 1967. First published 1909.

———. *Diplomatic Negotiations of American Naval Officers, 1778–1883*. Glouchester, MA: P. Smith, 1967. First published 1912.

———. *The Navy of the American Revolution: Its Administration, its Policy, and its Achievements*. New York: Haskell House Publishers, 1906.

———. *Paullin's History of Naval Administration, 1775–1911: A Collection of Articles from the US Naval Institute* Proceedings. Annapolis, MD: US Naval Institute, 1968.

Rackove, Jack. *The Beginnings of National Politics: An Interpretive History of the Continental Congress*. New York: Knopf, 1979.

Raffety, Matthew Taylor. *The Republic Afloat: Law, Honor, and Citizenship in Maritime America*. Chicago: University of Chicago Press, 2013.

Rappleye, Charles. *Robert Morris: Financier of the American Revolution*. New York: Simon and Schuster, 2010.

Schroeder, John H. *The Battle of Lake Champlain: A Brilliant and Extraordinary Victory*. Norman, OK: University of Oklahoma Press, 2015.

———. *Commodore John Rodgers: Paragon of the Early American Navy*. Gainesville: University Press of Florida, 2006.

Seitz, Don C. *Famous American Duels, with some Account of the Causes that led to them and the Men Involved*. New York: Books for Libraries Press, 1966. First published 1929.

Skaggs, David Curtis. *Oliver Hazard Perry: Honor Courage and Patriotism in the U.S. Navy*. Annapolis, MD: Naval Institute Press, 2006.

———. *Thomas Macdonough: Master of Command in the Early U.S. Navy*. Annapolis, MD: Naval Institute Press, 2002.

Skaggs, David Curtis, and Gerard Atloff. *A Signal Victory: The Lake Erie Campaign, 1812–1813*. Annapolis, MD: Naval Institute Press, 1997.

Skelton, William. *An American Profession of Arms: The Army Officer Corps, 1784–1861*. Lawrence: University Press of Kansas, 1992.

Smelser, Marshall. *The Congress Founds the Navy, 1787–1798*. Notre Dame, IN: University of Notre Dame Press, 1959.

Smith, Gene. *For the Purposes of Defense: The Politics of the Jeffersonian Gunboat Navy*. Newark, DE: University of Delaware Press, 1995.

Stagg, J. C. A. *Mr. Madison's War: Politics, Diplomacy and Warfare in the Early American Republic, 1783–1815*. Princeton, NJ: Princeton University Press, 1983.

Starkey, Armstrong. *War in the Age of Enlightenment, 1700–1789*. Westport, CT: Praeger, 2003.

Stevens, William Oliver. *An Affair of Honor: The Biography of Commodore James Barron, USN*. Norfolk, VA: Norfolk County Historical Society of Chesapeake Virginia, in cooperation with the Earl Gregg Swem Library of the College of William and Mary, 1969.

Stuart, Reginald C. *Civil-Military Relations during the War of 1812*. Santa Barbara, CA: Praeger Security International, an imprint of ABC-Clio Press, 2009.

Sultana, Donald. "Coleridge, Stephen Decatur and the Mysterious Duelist at Malta." *Modern Language Review* 89, no. 2 (April 1994): 282–88.

Symonds, Craig L. *Navalists and Antinavalists: The Naval Policy Debate in the United States, 1785–1827*. Newark, DE: University of Delaware Press, 1980.

Thomas, Evan. *John Paul Jones: Sailor, Hero, Father of the American Navy*. New York: Simon and Schuster, 2003.

Toll, Ian W. *Six Frigates: The Epic History of the Founding of the U.S. Navy*. New York: Norton, 2004.

Tucker, Spencer. *The Jeffersonian Gunboat Navy*. Columbia: University of South Carolina Press, 1993.

———. *Stephen Decatur: A Life Most Bold and Daring.* Annapolis, MD: Naval Institute Press, 2005.

Tucker, Spencer, and Frank T. Reuter. *Injured Honor: The* Chesapeake-Leopard *Affair, June 22, 1807.* Annapolis, MD: Naval Institute Press, 1996.

Valle, James E. *Rocks & Shoals: Order and Discipline in the Old Navy, 1800–1861.* Annapolis, MD: Naval Institute Press, 1980.

Volo, James M. *Blue Water Patriots: The American Revolution Afloat.* Westport, CT: Praeger Publishers, 2007.

Watson, Paul Barron. *The Tragic Career of Commodore James Barron, U.S. Navy (1769–1851).* New York: Cowan-McCann, 1942.

Watson, Samuel. *Jackson's Sword: The Army Officer Corps on the American Frontier, 1810–1821.* Lawrence, KS: University of Kansas Press, 2012.

———. "Trusting to 'the Chapter of Accidents': Contingency, Necessity, and Self-Constraint in Jeffersonian National Security Policy." *Journal of Military History* 76, no. 4 (October 2012): 973–1,000.

Wood, Gordon. *Empire of Liberty: A History of the Early Republic, 1789–1815.* New York: Oxford University Press, 2009.

———. *The Radicalism of the American Revolution.* New York: Vintage Books, 1993.

# Index

# About the Author

**Thomas Sheppard** is an assistant professor of military history at the Marine Corps University Command and Staff College in Quantico, Virginia. He earned his doctorate in military history from the University of North Carolina at Chapel Hill. His work has appeared in the *Journal of Military History* and *Strategic Studies Quarterly*. He lives in northern Virginia.

**The Naval Institute Press** is the book-publishing arm of the U.S. Naval Institute, a private, nonprofit, membership society for sea service professionals and others who share an interest in naval and maritime affairs. Established in 1873 at the U.S. Naval Academy in Annapolis, Maryland, where its offices remain today, the Naval Institute has members worldwide.

Members of the Naval Institute support the education programs of the society and receive the influential monthly magazine *Proceedings* or the colorful bimonthly magazine *Naval History* and discounts on fine nautical prints and on ship and aircraft photos. They also have access to the transcripts of the Institute's Oral History Program and get discounted admission to any of the Institute-sponsored seminars offered around the country.

The Naval Institute's book-publishing program, begun in 1898 with basic guides to naval practices, has broadened its scope to include books of more general interest. Now the Naval Institute Press publishes about seventy titles each year, ranging from how-to books on boating and navigation to battle histories, biographies, ship and aircraft guides, and novels. Institute members receive significant discounts on the Press' more than eight hundred books in print.

Full-time students are eligible for special half-price membership rates. Life memberships are also available.

For a free catalog describing Naval Institute Press books currently available, and for further information about joining the U.S. Naval Institute, please write to:

Member Services
**U.S. Naval Institute**
291 Wood Road
Annapolis, MD 21402-5034
Telephone: (800) 233-8764
Fax: (410) 571-1703
Web address: www.usni.org